A GUIDE TO THE EU

INSTITUTIONS, POLICIES, PROGRAMMES, FUNDS

and

ENTRY TESTS TO THE EU INSTITUTIONS

by

Maria Dimitropoulou-Hassiotis

Porphyrogenitus 1999

Porphyrogenitus Ltd.,
27/1 Upper Gordon Road,
Camberley, Surrey, GU15 2HJ.

British Library Cataloguing in Publication Data.
A catalogue for this book is available from the British Library.

ISBN   1 871328 13 6

Set by Porphyrogenitus Ltd.

To my Parents

and

Nikos

CONTENTS

CONTENTS v

ACKNOWLEDGEMENTS vii

LIST OF ABBREVIATIONS viii

MAP OF THE EUROPEAN UNION IN 1999 xv

PREFACE xvii

PART I: DICTIONARY 1

PART II: APPENDICES 201
   1. Principal European Community Institutions 201
   2. Other Institutions Constituting an Integral Part
      in the Functioning of the European
      Community. 202
   3. Other EU Institutions and specialized Agencies . . . 203
   4. European Commission Directorates- General 205
   5. Presidents of the European Commission 206
   6. Commissioners and their portfolios, 1995-2000 . . . 207
   7. Political Groups in the European Parliament 209
   8. List of European Parliament Presidents since
      1979 209
   9. Parliamentary Committees 210
  10. Electoral systems used in European Parliament
      elections 211
  11. Representation of Member States in the Main
      Community Institutions 212
  12. European Community Budget 85, 90, 96, 97 213
  13. Member states performance in relation to
      convergence 214
  14. The seven Titles of the Maastricht Treaty 215
  15. Types of Government of the Member States of
      the EU 216
  16. Prime Ministers of the EU Member States 216
  17. Security Organizations — Membership 217
  18. ACP Countries 219
  19. List of OCTs 219
  20. The Size of the European Community in 1996 . . . 220

21. The European Community: GDP, GDP per inhabitant, unemployment (1997) 221
22. Employment by sector, %, 1995 222
23. Gross value added by sector, 1995 222
24. Share of intra-European trade, %, 1996 223
25. Foreign trade, % GDP, 1995 223

PART III: QUESTIONS 225
   1. HISTORY OF THE EUROPEAN COMMUNITY 225
   2. INSTITUTIONS OF THE EU 231
      2.1. European Parliament 231
      2.2. European Commission 234
      2.3. The Council of European Union 237
      2.4. The Court of Justice of the European
          Communities - The Court of First
          Instance 239
      2.5. Court of Auditors 241
      2.6. Economic and Social Committee 242
      2.7. Committee of the Regions 243
      2.8. Other European Institutions 244
   3. POLICIES OF THE EUROPEAN COMMUNITY 245
   4. ECONOMY 254
   5. THE EU AND THE REST OF THE WORLD 261
   6. GENERAL QUESTIONS ON THE EUROPEAN
      COMMUNITY 268
   7. GENERAL KNOWLEDGE 279

ANSWERS 281

BIBLIOGRAPHY 284

SELECT INDEX 289

ACKNOWLEDGEMENTS

This book owes much to those persons who not only encouraged my efforts when they first heard about the idea of this publication, but also left me little time to contemplate the possibility of abandoning it before I had even started. As it is impossible to cite all of them by name, I would like to express my gratitude to my publisher, tutor and friend, J. Chrysostomides, for providing me with constant support and encouragement throughout this project. But above all for believing I could really write this book.

I would like to thank Ann Lewins for her illuminating arguments especially on the entries of democratic deficit, sovereignty and subsidiarity; Inger Buxton for her invaluable comments particularly on the entries related to security issues in Europe as well as on the workings of the EU institutions; Panos Pantelides for his shrewd comments on the need for strengthening certain entries; Doreen Buxton for her warm encouragement and corrections; and Vasilis Tsompanides for his help in communicating electronically with the EU institutions on matters that needed clarification. Most of their comments were directly incorporated into the text and many more triggered a train of thought that resulted in a considerable improvement of this book.

I would like to thank above all Kara Hattersley-Smith for the painstaking and invaluable revision of the book suggesting improvements and amendments which contributed greatly to the lucidity of the text.

Last, but not least, I would like to thank Nikos Hassiotis not only for his support but also for his constructive argument on several issues, as well as sharing with him the initial idea of writing this book.

It is not expected, however, that all shortcomings have been eliminated, and I alone am responsible for those that remain.

ACEA	Association of European Automobile Constructors
ACP	African, Caribbean and Pacific Ocean Countries (signatories to the Lomé Convention)
ACUSE	Action Committee for the United States of Europe
ADAPT	Initiative for the Adaptation of the Workforce to Industrial Change
ALTENER	Promotion of Renewable Energy Sources
AMUE	Association for the Monetary Union of Europe
ANSA	Agenzia Nazionale Stampa Associata
ASEAN	Association of South-East Asian Nations
CAP	Common Agricultural Policy
CCP	Common Commercial Policy
CE	Council of Europe
CEDEFOP	European Centre for the Development of Vocational Training
CEFTA	Central European Free Trade Area
CELAD	European Committee to Combat Drugs
CELENEC	European Committee of Electrotechnical Standardisation
CEN	Committee for European Normalisation
CEPT	European Conference of Postal and Telecommunications Administrations
CERN	European Nuclear Research Organisation
CFI	Court of First Instance
CFP	Common Fisheries Policies
CFSP	Common Foreign and Security Policy
CJTFS	Combined Joint Task Forces Sectoral
COA	Court of Auditors
COMETT	Community Action Programme in Education and Training Technology
COPA	Committee of Professional Agricultural Organisation
COR	Committee of the Regions
CORDIS	Community Research and Development Information Service
COREPER	Committee of Permanent Representatives
COST	European Cooperation on Scientific and Technical Research
CSCE	Conference on Security and Cooperation in Europe

CTP	Common Transport Policy
DG	Directorate-General
DIANE	Direct Information Access Network for Europe
DTEU	Draft Treaty establishing the European Union
EAGGF	European Agricultural Guidance and Guarantee Fund
EBRD	European Bank for Reconstruction and Development
EC	European Community
ECB	European Central Bank
ECHO	European Community Humanitarian Office
ECOFIN	Council of Economic and Finance Ministers
ECSC	European Coal and Steel Community
ECU	European Currency Unit
EDC	European Defence Community
EDF	European Development Fund
EEA	European Economic Area
EEA	European Environment Agency
EEC	European Economic Community
EFTA	European Free Trade Association
EIB	European Investment Bank
EIF	European Investment Fund
ELDO	European Organization for the Development and Construction of Space Vehicles Launchers
EMCDDA	European monitoring Centre for Drugs and Drug Addiction
EMCF	European Monetary Cooperation Fund
EMEA	European Medicine Evaluation Agency
EMI	European Monetary Institute
EMS	European Monetary System
EMU	Economic and Monetary Union
EP	European Parliament
EPC	European Political Cooperation
ERASMUS	European Action Scheme for the Mobility of Students in Europe
ERDF	European Regional Development Fund
ERM	Exchange Rate Mechanism
ESA	European Space Agency
ESC	Economic and Social Committee
ESCB	European System of Central Banks
ESF	European Social Fund
ESRO	European Space Research Organisation

ETSI	European Telecommunications Standard Institute
ETUC	European Trade Union Confederation
EU	European Union
EUCOFIL	European Union of Fruit and Vegetable Wholesalers, Shippers, Importers and Exporters
EUI	European University Institute
EURATOM	European Atomic Energy Community
EUREKA	European Research Coordination Agency
EUROPOL	European Police Office
EUROSTAT	European Community Statistical Office
EURYDICE	Programme to promote information exchanges on education systems
FEEM	Federation of European Explosive Manufacturers
FIFG	Financial Instrument for Fisheries Guidance
FORCE	Action programme for the development of continuing vocational training
FYROM	Former Yugoslav Republic of Macedonia
G8	Group of Eight
G7	Group of Seven
GATT	General Agreement on Tariffs and Trade
GDP	Gross Domestic Product
GNP	Gross National Product
GSP	Generalized System of Preferences
HELIOS	Handicapped People in Europe Living Independently in an Open Society
HORIZON	Initiative concerning handicapped persons and certain other disadvantaged groups
IBRD	International Bank for Reconstruction and Development
IGC	Intergovernmental Conference
IMF	International Monetary Fund
IMP	Integrated Mediterranean Programmes
IMPACT	Information Market Policy Actions
INTERREG	Initiative concerning cross-border cooperation and energy networks
ISDN	Integrated Services Digital Network
JET	Joint European Torus
JHA	Justice and Home Affairs
JOULE	Joint Opportunities for Unconventional or Long Term Energy Supply
JRC	Joint Research Centre

KALEIDOSCOPE	Programme to support artistic and cultural events having a European dimension
KONVER	Programme to assist areas affected by the decline of defence industries and military installations
LEADER	Initiative for Rural Development
LEONARDO	Action programme for the implementation of a European Community vocational training policy
LIFE	Financial Instrument for the Environment
LINGUA	Programme to promote the teaching and learning of foreign languages in the European Community
MAG (IV)	Fourth Multi-annual Programme
MATTHAEUS	Specific common programmes for the vocational training of customs officials
MEDIA	Action programme to promote the development of the European audiovisual industry
MEP	Member of the European Parliament
NACC	North Atlantic Cooperation Council
NAFTA	North American Free Trade Area
NATO	North Atlantic Treaty Organisation
NGO	Non-governmental Organisation
NOW	New Opportunities for Women
NPT	Non-Proliferation of Nuclear Weapons Treaty
OCTs	Overseas Countries and Territories
ODIHR	Office of Democratic Institutions and Human Rights
OECD	Organization for Economic Cooperation and Development
OEEC	Organization for European Economic Cooperation
OSCE	Organization for Security and Cooperation in Europe
OJ	Official Journal of the European Communities
OPEC	Organization of Petroleum Exporting Countries
OSCE	Organization for Security and Cooperation in Europe
PACT	Pilot Actions for Combined Transport Programme
PESCA	Initiative aimed at solving the problems caused by the restructuring of the fisheries sector
PETRA	Action programme for the vocational training of young people and their preparation of adult and working life
PFP	Partnership for Peace

PHARE	Aid for Economic Restructuring of central and eastern European countries
QMV	Qualified Majority Voting
RACE	Research and Development in Advanced Communications Programme for Europe
RAPHAEL	Cultural heritage programme
RICHAR	Initiative concerning the economic conversion of coal mining areas
REGIS	Initiative concerning the most remote regions
RESIDER	Programme to assist the conversion of steel areas
RETEX	Initiative for regions heavily dependent on the textiles and clothing sectors
RTD	Research and Technological Development
SAD	Single Administrative Document
SAVE	Special action programme for vigorous energy efficiency
SEA	Single European Act
SEM	Single European Market
SIGMA	A publication of the statistical office of the EU
SIS	Schengen Information System
SMEs	Small and Medium-sized Enterprises
SOCRATES	Action programme for the development of quality education and training and of a European dimension in studies at all levels
STABEX	System for the stabilization of export earnings
SYSMIN	System for the stabilization of export earnings from mining products
TAC	Total Allowance Catches
TACIS	Technical Assistance to the Commonwealth of Independent States
TARGET	Trans-European Automated Real-time Gross settlement Express Transfer System
TENs	Trans-European Networks
THERMIE	Programme for the promotion of European energy technology
TREVI	Group for terrorism, radicalism, extremism and international violence
UCLAF	Unit for the Coordination of Fraud Prevention
UN	United Nations
UNESCO	United Nations Educational Scientific and Cultural Organisation

UNICE	Union of Industrial and Employers Confederation of Europe
URBAN	Initiative for urban areas
USA	United States of America
USSR	Union of Soviet Socialist Republics
V4	Visegrad Group
VAT	Value Added Tax
WEU	Western European Union
WTO	World Trade Organisation
YOUTHSTART	Programme to assist the integration of young people into the labour market

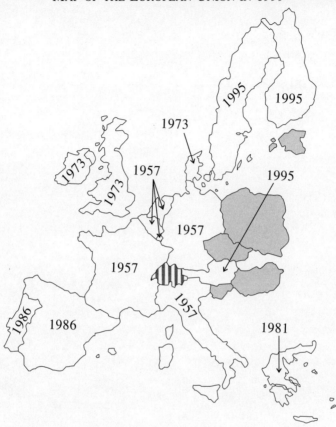

Countries in grey are expected to join in 2002.
Dates show year of accession.

PREFACE

The idea of writing this book occurred to me while preparing for an entry test to the institutions of the EU. The more involved I became in researching and organising the knowledge I acquired, the more I became convinced of the necessity for such a book. For although during my research I came across an extensive bibliography, I found no comprehensive guide to the EU. Some of the studies were, and still are, either largely legalistic in character, or rather business orientated. At the same time, I became aware of the lack of a reference book for either students or, more specifically, for those preparing for competition-tests for administrators A or B of the EU institutions.

This guide, therefore, has a dual purpose: a) to define and clarify EU terminology; and b) to offer some guidance as to the form an entry test might take, the kinds of questions it might include, and the fundamental knowledge required. Bearing these two objectives in mind, the book has been divided into three parts. The first contains a dictionary, the second appendices, and the third a list of multiple-choice questions and answers.

The dictionary consists of about 350 entries, in alphabetical order, which provide information on the structure, workings and responsibilities of the main and secondary institutions of the EU. These entries delineate the evolution of these institutions from the time of their inception to their present form, as a result of the major Treaties concluded over the years. In addition, the entries deal with the procedures followed in the legislative process, as well as the obligations and rights arising from Community law.

Secondly, the dictionary deals with the long-standing and highly developed EU policies aimed at perfecting the common market and accelerating the process of integration, so as to facilitate the establishment of the Economic and Monetary Union. The way these are implemented, and the degree of responsibility the EU has vis-à-vis national governments is also addressed. Community policies are complementary to each other and most of their objectives overlap, as do the programmes and funds financing them. Nevertheless, wherever possible, this book divides the main policies into sub-policies in order to provide the reader with more detailed information on certain aspects. For instance, there are separate entries for Research and Technological Development and Trans-European Networks, although they could have been placed under the heading of Industrial Policy. The Trans-European Networks are divided further into energy, environment, telecommunications and transport policy.

Thirdly, the dictionary provides information on a number of programmes, action plans and funds of the EU that are indispensable to the implementation of Community policies. The structural funds, essential components of the Common Agricultural, Regional and Social Policy of the Community, have been given extensive coverage, but an effort has been made to include as many as possible of the lesser known funds related to culture, education, media, declining industries, etc.

Lastly, the dictionary contains entries that deal with the relations and attitudes of the EU to third parties, both within and outside Europe, including central and eastern European countries, the ACP countries, the Overseas Countries and Territories as well as a number of other countries with which the Community has signed preferential agreements. Reference is also made to the leading trading partners of the Community, especially in the context of the GATT negotiations. Other entries are devoted to broader security issues in Europe, following the sweeping changes in eastern Europe, and the new security organizations and their relation to the EU.

Part II, consists of 21 appendices providing specific and detailed information on a variety of issues. Some of the appendices are essential to individual entries. For instance, the entry on the European Commission is complete only when read in conjunction with the three appendices referring to it. Others give a bird's eye view of the general economic indicators of the EU.

Part III, consists of 300 multiple-choice questions in the style of the EU entry tests, and is divided into a number of thematic headings. The questions on the European Community revolve around the issues covered in the dictionary and are fully answered by the information provided there. It must be noted, however, that the tests also include questions belonging to the broad sphere of general knowledge, ranging from physics to literature, maths to the visual arts, from fashion modelling to history. A sample of these is given under the heading of General Knowledge Questions.

Throughout this book the terms 'Community' and 'Union' are used interchangeably, unless there is reason to differentiate between the two. The term 'Community' is used specifically when discussing matters relating to the three Communities and developments prior to the Maastricht Treaty; the term 'Union' is used when referring to the three pillars collectively or to the two intergovernmental pillars. Although the single currency, is now known as the Euro, the term ECU is still used, because this was the denomination in which funds, budget, etc.

were calculated in the past. The name 'Six' refers to: Belgium, France, Germany, Italy, Luxembourg and The Netherlands, the original members and signatories of the Treaty of Paris and Treaty of Rome.

The research for this book is based on an extensive bibliography, and on primary sources, such as Treaties, conventions, and agreements. In a number of cases where conflicting information was given by different authors, the problem was resolved through direct contact with the institution, agency or body concerned.

This book is not meant to be a critique of the functioning, efficiency, policies or purpose of the Union, nor to present the debates surrounding them. Rather, every attempt has been made to present an objective overview by describing the policies, institutions and the workings of the EU as they are claimed to be by their creators.

It is to be hoped that this Guide will make some contribution towards an understanding of the complex institutions of the EU and provide some clarification of its terminology, while also being of value to students, the general public, as well as to various organizations, journalists and EU competition entrants.

Note

The reader might find it helpful to have an overall view of the European integration, one of the remarkable events of post-war history. Unlike previous attempts to unify Europe by force, the EU is based on consent. In the post war era, the major European states were determined to establish long lasting peace and stability. As a result, the debate about European integration was resumed, and despite differences of opinion among its pioneers as to its form and content, an understanding was reached that such an objective had to be achieved through a combination of political and economic means. Amalgamation of economic interests was the primary objective, soon to be followed by political integration.

Briefly, Community integration proceeded through three main stages. The first, introduced by the Treaty of Paris of 1951, initiated the integration of coal and steel industries, essential to post-war reconstruction. This served as a paradigm for the integration of the atomic energy sector, but, above all, for the launching of the European Economic Community (EEC) by the Treaty of Rome of 1957. The EEC introduced a customs union providing for the abolition of tariffs, customs duties and quotas that member states imposed on each other's exports, as well as a common external tariff regime. Its political significance lies in the fact that it established the first supranational institutions and common policies, which were facilitated by respective funds. This stage was completed by the Six founding members of the Community in 1968.

The second stage involving the Single European Market, launched in 1987 and completed in December 1992, introduced the abolition of technical, fiscal and physical barriers to trade so as to promote free movement of goods, services and capital. During this stage, common policies were further consolidated and the notion of social Europe was ushered. Increasingly, most spheres of policy came under community competence, thus paving the way for the next stage, namely the European Union.

The third and current stage of integration, aims to achieve the Economic Monetary Union (EMU) and European Political Union (EPU). Prerequisites for the functioning of the EMU was the adoption of the Euro on 1 January 1999 with a view to actual circulation of the currency in 2002, alongside convergence of the monetary policies of member states.

The European Political Union has a threefold pillar structure, consisting of: the first, the European Communities, officially renamed European Community, which still retain their separate identities but operate as a single unit. The other two pillars, largely intergovernmental bring under Community competence the two sensitive areas of foreign and security policy, and justice and home affairs.

Throughout this publication, an effort has been made to present the reader with the manifold difficulties facing Community integration. These sprang from conflicting national interests and different attitudes, contending interests of the various groups, including the struggle between the very institutions of the Community. For example, in the institutional sphere, the EP, the only elected body, aims at acquiring more powers, and by doing so it aspires to make the EU more democratic, thus rendering legitimate the transfer of powers form national to European level. In the sphere of Community policies, funds for regional and social integration, essential components of the whole project, became available by reducing the Common Agricultural Policy expenditure, which accounted for almost 50 per cent of the budget. At the same time, increasingly more policy areas came under Community competence. Because of loss of competitiveness of European industry in global markets in the 1980s, attention was paid to industrial policy. To this end competition policy, research and technological development, and the Trans-European Networks were given additional funding. This shift in priorities met with the approval or disapproval of member states, depending on whether they were recipients or contributors. Such an approach favoured mostly the periphery countries more in need of infrastructure and funds for regional and social integration. Presently, difficulties in decision-taking and financing European integration are aggravated by the existing differences in prosperity between regions and mounting social problems, particularly high unemployment throughout Europe. Political considerations, such as the gradual surrender of national sovereignty to European institutions present an additional obstacle to further integration. It is possible that these sectional interests will be reconciled to a degree by fostering an awareness of unity. In fact, one of the dilemmas facing the European Community today is how to create and reinforce a European identity while at the same time preserving national cultures. In this respect, education and cultural policy, as well as the notion of citizenship play an instrumental role. The forthcoming enlargement of the Community is bound to exacerbate these problems.

PART I: DICTIONARY

A

ACCESSION TREATY. Treaties signed between applicant states and the members of the European Community (EC) with the objective of setting down the precise conditions of accession and specifying adjustments to the founding Treaties. New member states usually go through a transitional period in order to avoid difficulties that may arise by rapid adaptation to the EC. During this stage special provisions are made for sectors of the economy that are expected to encounter severe problems. (See also, Assent Procedure).

ACP. African, Caribbean and Pacific ocean states associated with the member states of the European Community under the Lomé Convention. Currently, 71 ACP states are associated with the EU under this convention. (See also, Lomé Convention; Appendix 18).

ACQUIS COMMUNAUTAIRE. A French term widely used in the literature of the European Community (EC) to describe the corpus of all primary and secondary EC legislation and policy commitments arising from the Treaties, and subsequently further developed. It also includes the judgements of the Court of Justice, a matter of great significance as it implies the recognition by the member states of the primacy and direct effect of Community law. Candidate states applying for membership to the European Community are required to accept the entire body of *acquis communautaire* as it stands at the time of their accession. (See also, Community Law, Direct Effect, Legislation, Primacy).

ACTION COMMITTEE FOR THE UNITED STATES OF EUROPE (ACUSE). Founded by Jean Monnet in 1955, and dissolved by him 20 years later, the Committee acted as a pressure group for closer European integration by bringing together influential personalities from the Six original member states of the Community. It played a significant role in the formation of the European Economic Community (EEC). Ten years after its dissolution, it was succeeded by the Action Committee for Europe which had the same purpose but less influence, as most of the enthusiastic advocates for European integration did not participate. (See also, The Six).

ADDITIONALITY. A term coined to denote the principle according to which sums from the Community Budget, allocated to member states in the form of both project and programme assistance, have to be additional to the relevant funding provided by national governments. However, the principle has not always been observed and often funding allocated to a specific project or programme has been used by national governments for other purposes. The principle mainly applies to structural funds. (See also, Structural Funds).

ADVISORY COMMITTEE, see **COMITOLOGY**

AGENDA 2000. Published in mid-1997, this document presents the Commission's vision of Europe for the year 2000 and beyond. It is concerned with the Community's financial framework for the period 2000-2006, the future development of its policies, especially agriculture, the structural funds and the cohesion fund, as well as the enlargement of the Community. It remains to be adopted by the Council of Ministers.

According to these proposals, the Common Agricultural Policy (CAP) will be further reformed through a continuous reduction in price support and an increase of income supports for farmers. The European Agricultural Guidance and Guarantee Fund (EAGGF) will provide for an integrated approach to the development of the countryside. A revised regime will be applied for the dairy, arable and beef sectors. More emphasis will be given to environmental issues.

The structural and the cohesion funds will be reinforced to reduce disparities at a European-wide level. In an effort to achieve greater cost-effectiveness, funding will be concentrated to improve infrastructure in the poorer regions of the Community, as well as to help areas undergoing structural difficulties. The structural funds' Objectives will be reduced from six to three. Responsibilities between the Community, member states and other actors involved in the conception and implementation of the structural funds will be further clarified. The total budget of the Community structural policies for the period 2000-2006 will amount ECU 275,000 million in 1997 prices.

Enlargement poses a challenge as it is bound to bring greater heterogeneity to the Community. Agenda 2000 proposes that the associated countries should receive pre-accession assistance through the so-called pre-accession instruments. The agricultural instruments aim at improving the efficiency of farms, processing, distribution, etc. The structural policy instruments provide assistance particularly in the environment and transport sectors. PHARE will focus on the reinforcement of administrative and judicial capacity as well as the application of the *acquis communautaire*. Action under the pre-accession instruments will be integrated into accession partnerships setting out the priorities to be pursued by each of the candidate countries. The total amount of pre-accession aid will total ECU 3,000 million a year for the period 2000-2006.

The proposals for the financial framework 2000-2006 closely follows those in Agenda 2000. The Commission proposes to keep the ceiling of own resources at the level of 1.27 per cent of the GNP over this period, leaving substantial margin to finance enlargement. (See also, CAP, Cohesion Fund, Enlargement, Own Resources, Structural Funds).

AGRICULTURAL ORGANIZATION OF THE EUROPEAN COMMUNITY, see **COMMITTEE OF PROFESSIONAL AGRICULTURAL ORGANIZATIONS (COPA)**

AGRIMONETARY SYSTEM, see **CAP**

AIRBUS. The name refers to both a type of passenger air plane and the joint venture that has undertaken its development and construction. Initially an Anglo-French proposal, the project is based on the 1967 Memorandum of Understanding signed by UK, France and Germany, and is one of the most successful collaborative European projects.

Airbus Industry was founded as a European economic interest grouping in 1970, and the first Airbus flew two years later, in 1972. The British, French and German aircraft industries are the initial major participants in the Airbus project, but at present there is a small amount of participation by Belgian, Dutch and Spanish firms. The main assembly plant is in Toulouse.

There is an increasing suspicion, especially from the American Boeing aircraft industry, that the Airbus project has been subsidized by the participating governments; this suspicion has given rise to considerable controversy since such subsidies are contrary to the General Agreement on Tariffs and Trade (GATT). (See also, GATT)

AMSTERDAM TREATY. This Treaty was concluded at the Amsterdam European Council summit of 16-18 June 1997, where the 1996 Intergovernmental Conference (IGC) presented the work carried out over a period of almost one year and a half on a number of contentious issues left unresolved by the Maastricht Treaty. It was officially signed on 2 October 1997, pending ratification by the member states. By February 1999, only France and Greece had not ratified the Treaty. The ratification process is expected to be completed within two years of the signing the Treaty, after which it will come into effect.

The Treaty addressed a number of controversial issues, which the European Union (EU) is bound to face on the threshold of the 21st century and in the light of the forthcoming enlargement. In relation to Justice and Home Affairs (JHA), commitments to fundamental rights already made by the previous Treaties are reinforced together with a new notion of freedom and security. The Treaty allows the EU to suspend the voting rights of any country, that currently violates these rights. Immigration, visa policy and political asylum has been brought under Community law and procedures, with the exception of certain visa arrangements, where a five-year transitional period applies. During the transitional period member states will have the right to initiate policy together with the Commission, and the Council of Ministers will be required to act unanimously. The Schengen Agreement, dealing with free movement of people, already established among the thirteen member states, will be incorporated into the Treaty. Britain and Ireland won an opt-out over visa, asylum and immigration policies and retain control over their borders. The removal of internal borders has been followed by a closer cooperation between police, customs and other authorities to fight transnational trafficking in drugs and human beings, in particular women, offences against children as well as cross-border fraud and the illegal arms trade. Europol, the embryo of EU police forces, will be strengthened. In addition, civilian judicial cooperation and harmonization of divorce laws will ultimately become common policy.

The Treaty dealt with a number of issues that impinge directly on citizens in an effort to make the Community more relevant and comprehensible. In this context the thorny question of unemployment in the Community was addressed. More specifically, the Council of Ministers aims to produce a coordinated strategy for employment and to establish a coordination process on employment policy at Community level. The Social Charter is to be integrated into the Treaty after it was accepted by the newly elected government of the UK at the Amsterdam summit. The provisions in this chapter have been strengthened, especially with regard to measures combating social exclusion and ensuring equal opportunities and treatment between men and women at work. Measures regarding environmental protection, public health, consumer protection, directly affecting all citizens irrespective of borders, have become a focal point of the Treaty. Furthermore, the Treaty sets out detailed, legally-binding guidelines for applying the principles of subsidiarity and proportionality, ensuring that action is taken at the most appropriate level, and is in proportion to the objectives to be achieved. The Commission has the duty to issue an annual report on the application of these principles in Community provisions.

Foreign and Security Policy remains a matter of unanimous decision, but the role of the European Council in defining common strategies has been enhanced significantly. Opposition by the UK and the five member states of the EU (Ireland, Denmark, Austria, Finland and Sweden), which hold observer status in the Western European Union (WEU), prevented the merging of the organization into the EU. Nevertheless, cooperation between the two institutions (EU and WEU), especially in humanitarian tasks, peacekeeping and crisis management, has largely been enhanced. The evolution of the Common Foreign and Security Policy (CFSP) into a common defence policy has not yet been concluded, but it was agreed that any progress in this direction would require the decision of the European Council and would be subject to agreement by member states in accordance with their constitutional arrangements.

Reforming the institutions of the EU in the light of the future enlargement was one of the main tasks of the new Treaty. In fact, agreements were reached on a number of issues, such as: a) extending the qualified majority voting (QMV) in the Council of Ministers in areas, such as freedom of establishment and research and development, previously requiring unanimity; QMV was also introduced to new areas, such as employment guidelines, incentive measures, social exclusion, equal opportunities, public health, transparency, combating fraud and customs cooperation; yet, there are few issues, including the re-balancing of the voting weightings in the Council of Ministers, which remain unresolved; b) extending the legislative powers of the European Parliament (EP) by replacing the cooperation with the co-decision procedure in areas, such as Trans-European Networks, research, development aid, employment policy, public health, transparency, combating fraud and customs cooperation; on the other hand, matters related to the Economic and Monetary Union remain under the cooperation procedure; c) introducing measures to make the role of the Commission more effective and stipulating that the number of the Commissioners following the expected enlargement will not exceed the 20, thus implying that the two commissioners of Germany, France, the UK, Spain and Italy will be reduced to one; d) enhancing the powers of the Court of Justice and especially of the Court of Auditors (COA) in an effort to fight fraud effectively.

Lastly, in the sphere of further integration, the Treaty enhanced flexibility by enabling member states to proceed with a closer union without needing to wait for all others simultaneously to do so, provided that the interests of the member states that do not wish to participate are safeguarded. Member states have to agree to such a cooperation by a qualified majority in respect to the first pillar, and by a unanimous vote in respect to the two intergovernmental pillars. Gradual integration of the Community should, however, be used as a last resort and it should be open to the rest of the members at any time.

As with the Maastricht Treaty, the Amsterdam Treaty left unresolved a number of contentious issues which need to be addressed prior to the forthcoming enlargement. To this end, it has already been agreed that an IGC will convene, at least one year before the membership of the Union exceeds 20, in order to carry out a comprehensive review of the provisions of the Treaties on the composition and functioning of the institutions. (See also, CFSP, Council of the EU, European Commission, EP, JHA, Maastricht Treaty, Schengen Agreement, Social Charter).

ANTHEM, see **EUROPEAN ANTHEM**

APOLLO. A cooperation programme between the Community and the European Space Agency (ESA) promoting collaboration in the field of high volume data transmission by satellite. The programme will facilitate the development of experimental equipment and will stimulate the creation of a European system of ground stations and receiving antennae. (See also, ESA).

APPROXIMATION, see **SINGLE EUROPEAN MARKET**

ARIANE. The name of the French-designed launcher adopted by the European Organization for the Development and Construction of Space Vehicles Launchers (ELDO). Its first test flight was successfully concluded in 1979 and its services are now available on a world wide basis. The ARIANE project was partly funded by the European Investment Bank. (See also, ELDO, ESA).

ASSENT PROCEDURE. Introduced by the Single European Act (SEA), it gives the European Parliament (EP) the right to veto certain important decisions taken by the Council of Ministers. Before a decision can be adopted by the Council of Ministers, the EP is required to give its assent by an absolute majority in favour of the act under discussion. The assent procedure is applied to two main areas: a) the accession treaties between applicant states and the member states of the European Community (EC); b) the Association Agreements between the EC and third states. The Maastricht Treaty reformed both provisions so that membership to the EC is now subject to approval by an absolute majority in the EP, while a simple majority is required for Association Agreements. In addition, the Parliament's assent is required for almost all international agreements, as well as for certain legislative matters. (See also, Co-decision, Consultation and Cooperation Procedures, Council of the EU, EP, Luns-Westerterp).

ASSIZES. Name given to meetings held between members of the national parliaments and members of the European Parliament (EP) with the purpose of exchanging information and debating certain issues. The first meeting, held in Rome in November 1990, debated the issue of the European Union (EU). It was composed of 250 national parliamentarians and a fixed number of members of the EP. The meeting was conducted under the EP procedures. Although the Maastricht Treaty provides for such meetings to convene when necessary, no such meeting has taken place since the first one.

ASSOCIATION AGREEMENT. Agreement signed between the European Community and third countries aiming at strengthening trade and economic relations between the contracting parties. It entails reciprocal arrangements for imports and exports, as well as common action and special procedures in certain areas. The first Association Agreement was signed with Greece in 1961; subsequently, Association Agreements were signed with Turkey in 1964, Malta in 1970, Cyprus in 1972 and others.

Following the changes in central and eastern Europe, further agreements, known as Europe Agreements, were signed between the Community and most of these countries, granting them tariff-free access to the Community for most of their manufactured goods, but placing restrictions on their export of textiles and agricultural products.

The European Economic Area agreement (EEA) was signed between the Community and the remaining states of EFTA, with the objective of facilitating full membership for these states to the Community. In addition, agreements signed with developing countries, such as the Maghreb, the Mashreq and the ACP countries, belong to this category.

Association Agreements, on behalf of the Community, are negotiated by the European Commission on a mandate of the Council of Ministers. Under the assent procedure, Association Agreements require the assent of the EP by simple majority vote. (See also, ACP, Assent Procedure, EEA, Europe Agreements, Maghreb, Mashreq, Small Countries).

ASSOCIATION FOR THE MONETARY UNION OF EUROPE (AMUE). A business pressure group founded in 1987. Its aim was the adoption of a single currency in Europe, which in fact came into effect in January 1999. Participation is open to all business sharing a vision of Europe as a single currency zone. (See also, Euro).

ASSOCIATION OF SOUTH-EAST ASIAN NATIONS (ASEAN). It was founded in 1967 by the declaration of Bangkok with the objective of accelerating economic progress among its members. From the original five founding members, Indonesia, Singapore, Thailand, Malaysia, Philippines, ASEAN has now expanded to include Brunei and Vietnam.

A cooperation agreement has been signed between ASEAN and the European Community; however, other countries of Asia, for example, India, Pakistan and Sri Lanka, are also benefiting by their relationship to the Community under the Generalized System of Preferences (GSP), which gives developing countries duty free access to a specified quota of finished and semi finished goods. (See also, GSP)

B

BERLAYMONT. The name of the building in Brussels where the European Commission was housed until 1992, when it was discovered that the internal walls contained asbestos. Currently, the European Commission is based in the Breydel building.

BERLIN DECLARATION. The outcome of the Conference which took place in September 1994 in Berlin with the participation of Justice and Home Affairs (JHA) ministers of the member states of the European Community and the associated countries. The document emphasised that JHA issues were a significant part of the integration process. Special reference was made to illicit drug trade, theft and illegal trade of radioactive material, traffic in human beings and illegal immigration networks. Although many meetings have taken place since, little progress has been made in regard to these problems.(See also, JHA).

BLAIR HOUSE ACCORD. An agreement between the USA and the Commission reached in 1992 in the Uruguay Round of the General Agreement on Tariffs and Trade (GATT). The accord dealt with the long-standing dispute between the two sides over their agricultural subsidies. At the time the Accord was concluded, the USA had threatened to introduce punitive tariffs on a number of Union food and agricultural products to be implemented by December 1992.

In addition to the conversion of various protectionist measures, such as variable levies into fixed tariffs, the deal reduced the volume of export subsidies by 21 per cent over six years, on the basis of the average annual volume exported between 1986-90, and internal price supports by up to 20 per cent, compared with the 1986-88 levels. Furthermore, it allowed tariff-adjustments if world market prices fell below the 1986-88 average. The deal revealed the deep rooted disagreements as well as the conflicting interests between member states of the Union, but undoubtedly it led to the successful conclusion of the GATT agreements in 1993.(See also, GATT).

BRITISH BUDGET CRISIS. This refers to the severe crisis characterising the relationship between the UK and the European Community over the 1979-84 period. The main cause of this crisis had been the high contributions of the UK to the Community Budget; the UK had been the second largest contributor to the Community Budget, while it was among the poorest member states in terms of per capita GNP. The existence of a broad consensus across the political spectrum on this matter was accompanied by the determination of the British government to resolve this problem. Agreement on this issue was reached at the Fontainebleau summit of 1984, where the finances of the Community were discussed.

The settlement for the UK was based on a yearly rebate of 66 per cent of the difference between Value-added Tax (VAT) contribution and its share of Community benefits. By the end of 1994, the cumulative amount of the rebate to the UK reached almost £16 billion. However, the UK still remains a net contributor to the Union's Budget. At the 1992 Edinburgh summit the system of calculating the rebate was renewed until 1999. (See also, Budget, Fontainebleau Agreement).

BRUSSELS TREATY, see TREATY OF BRUSSELS

BUDGET OF THE EUROPEAN COMMUNITY. It accounts for no more than 3 per cent of all the national budgets of its member states. When the European Economic Community (EEC) was formed in 1957, it was agreed to be financed by the contributions of the member states based on their individual GNP. This, however, was not implemented until 1 February 1989, when it was added to the 'own resources' system of financing the Budget, which was introduced in 1980 in conformity with the Council of Ministers Decision of 21 April 1970.

The 1997 Budget accounted for about 87.6 billion ECUs, a sum of about 1.2 per cent of the Community GNP. With regard to the contributions of the member states to the Budget in 1997, Germany still remained the largest contributor with a participation of 28.2 per cent of the total, followed by France with 17.5 per cent, the UK with 11.9 per cent, and Italy with 11.5 per cent. Luxembourg has been the smallest contributor with 0.2 per cent of the total, followed by Ireland with 0.9 per cent.

Resources
Currently the EU revenues are raised from four separate sources and belong to the Community as a right.
1. Agricultural levies on imported foodstuff from outside the community in order to raise prices of imports up to the EU level, as determined by the Common Agricultural Policy (CAP); also levies on the quantity of certain agricultural products produced within the Community but exceeding the agreed ceiling.
2. Customs duties on non-agricultural products imported from outside the EU.

3. A proportion of Value-added Tax (VAT) imposed at national level. By far the most important source of revenue, it was originally. fixed at 1 per cent of the maximum selling price on an agreed common base of goods and services. In 1986, the VAT ceiling was raised to 1.4 per cent.

4. Contributions from member states based on their share of the total GNP of the community. This source, as mentioned above, followed the agreement on budgetary reform reached at the 1988 Brussels meeting.

Expenditure
It falls under four major headings.

1. The CAP, being the most important expenditure, accounts for two thirds of the Budget. Its high costs, defined as compulsory expenditure, have undermined funding in other policy areas. Efforts have been made to curtail spending on agriculture so that more funding is diverted to non-compulsory areas.

2. Regional policy, funded through the European Regional Development Fund (ERDF), finances programmes and infrastructural projects in the poorer regions of the Community, as well as in areas that have been affected by the decline of traditional industries, such as textiles and clothing, steel and shipbuilding.

3. Social policy, funded through the European Social Fund (ESF), finances employment, training and retraining programmes.

4. External policies are directed towards Asian, Latin American, Eastern European and Mediterranean countries, in the form of food aid and assistance. This aid falls outside the European Development Fund (EDF). This fund consists of direct contributions of the member states and therefore is not part of the EU Budget.

5. All other items of expenditure, including the Commission's own administrative costs, account for less than 5% of the Budget.

Procedures
The European Parliament (EP) has acquired substantial budgetary powers by the Single European Act (SEA) in that together with the Council of Ministers it has been officially designated as a formal budgetary authority. There are three stages in the budgetary process.

a. A preliminary draft Budget is presented by the European Commission to the Council no later than 1 September of the year prior to its implementation.

b. The Council can either accept or amend the draft; it invariably tends to reduce the amount of the proposed expenditure. By 5 October the draft is submitted to the EP.

c. The EP has 45 days during which to consider the draft. The EP may suggest modifications to the compulsory expenditure, currently amounting to 66 per cent of the total expenditure; or it may suggest amendments to the non-compulsory expenditure, though not beyond the so-called maximum rate set by the Council each year. Amendments to non-compulsory expenditure require absolute majority, while modifications to compulsory expenditure require only a majority of the votes cast. The Parliament then returns the revised Budget to the Council.

d. The Council is free to reject the EP's modifications and amendments but must decide within 15 days. If the modifications to compulsory expenditure involve no increase in overall expenditure then for their rejection qualified majority, known as negative majority, is required in the Council. If increase in overall expenditure is involved, their approval requires a QMV, known as positive majority, in the Council. When the Council decides to reject EP's amendments to non-compulsory expenditure, both the EP and the Council are obliged to enter the conciliation procedure in order to reach a compromise.

e. Finally, the revised document is sent by the Council back to the EP for adoption. For the Budget to be rejected by the EP, a two-thirds majority of the votes cast, representing a majority of all members, is required.

The EP's rejection of the Budget, may result in failure to produce a Community Budget for the current calendar year. Should this occur, expenditure is restricted each month to one twelfth of the Budget approved for the previous year. So far, the Parliament has rejected the Budget only on two occasions, in 1979 and 1984. (See also, CAP, Compulsory Expenditure, Delors Packages I & II, Development Aid, Maximum Rate of Increase, Non-compulsory Expenditure, Own Resources, Regional Policy, Social Policy, VAT; Appendix 12).

C

CAIRNS GROUP. An informal association of agricultural exporting countries set up in 1986 with the objective of curtailing subsidies for agricultural production and exports. The Cairns Group consists of Australia, New Zealand, Canada, Argentina, Brazil, Chile, Uruguay, Colombia, Indonesia, Philippines, Thailand, Malaysia, Fiji and Hungary. Led by Australia, the Cairns Group played an important role during the Uruguay Round of the General Agreement for Trade and Tariffs (GATT). (See also, GATT).

CASE-LAW OF THE COURT OF JUSTICE, see **COMMUNITY LAW**

CASSIS DE DIJON, see below p. 112, n. 11

CECCHINI REPORT. This report published in 1988 under the title *1992: the European Challenge*, by a committee of experts chaired by Paolo Cecchini, a senior European Commissioner official, was an enquiry into 'the costs of non-Europe'. It estimated that completing the Single European Market (SEM) would bring the European Community a gain of around 5 per cent of its gross domestic product over the medium term. This, among others, was one of the best known indices quoted in favour of the SEM. (See also, Cockfield White Paper, SEM).

CELAD - THE EUROPEAN COMMITTEE TO COMBAT DRUGS. Set up by the Heads of State and Government in 1989, its function is to coordinate the national strategies of the member states in the struggle against drug trafficking and to implement measures taken to reduce their use. CELAD works both with the Pompidou Group to expand inter-agency cooperation, and with the European Policy Cooperation Group on Drugs. It has also contributed significantly to the political mobilization on the issue of drugs in Europe. CELAD is an *ad hoc* political group situated outside the Community structure. (See also, EMCDDA, EUROPOL, External Frontiers Convention, JHA, Public Health).

CEN, see **COMMITTEE FOR EUROPEAN NORMALISATION**

CENELEC, see **COMMITTEE FOR EUROPEAN NORMALISATION**

CENSURE MOTION. The right of the European Parliament (EP) to dismiss the European Commission on a motion of censure. For the motion to pass, a two-thirds majority of the votes cast, representing a majority of MEPs, is required. If this is achieved, the European Commission as a body has to resign. The right of censure has been granted to the EP by the Treaty of Rome, but has had very limited application. (See also, European Commission, EP).

CENTRE OF TRANSLATION, see **SYSTRAN**

CERN, see **EUROPEAN NUCLEAR RESEARCH ORGANISATION**

CHARTER OF PARIS. It was signed in November 1990 by the participants of the Conference on Security and Cooperation in Europe (CSCE). Following the collapse of the Soviet Union and the sweeping changes in central and eastern Europe, it has been widely considered as symbolising the end of the Cold War and the foundation of a New Europe based on respect and cooperation.

The Charter granted a permanent character to the CSCE process, which as a result acquired a number of structures: a Council composed of Foreign Ministers of member states, a Committee of Senior Officials assisting the Council, a permanent secretariat based in Vienna and its own Parliamentary Assembly. In addition, the Charter of Paris introduced a number of institutions, such as the Office of Democratic Institutions and Human Rights (ODIHR) based in Warsaw, the Conflict Prevention Centre based in Vienna, the High Commissioner on National Minorities operating from The Hague. (See also, CSCE).

CITIZENSHIP (EUROPEAN). The notion of European citizenship, mentioned in the Treaty of Rome, acquired substance with the Maastricht Treaty. A European citizen is defined as any person holding the nationality of a member state of the European Community. Three basic rights spring from Community citizenship: the right of residence in any European Union (EU) country, the right to move freely within the EU, and the right of political participation in the country of residence.

However, none of these rights are absolute. The right of European citizenship is determined by each member state, since residence is still largely decided by national law. The right of political participation is restricted to the right of voting and standing for the European Parliament (EP) as well as municipal elections in the country of residence, but not for national elections. A number of additional rights were introduced in the process of reinforcing the notion of citizenship. A Community citizen travelling abroad is able to avail him/herself of consular or diplomatic representation by the authorities of other EU countries in cases where his/her country of residence is not represented. A Community citizen also has the right to address a petition to the EP and refer to the Ombudsman on matters of maladministration in the Community institutions. Despite all the rights provided by the Maastricht Treaty national boundaries have not yet been transcended. (See also, Freedom of Establishment).

COCKFIELD WHITE PAPER. Drafted by Lord Cockfield, European Commissioner responsible for trade matters within the community, it was concerned with the creation of the internal market. It recommended (originally 300, subsequently 289) legislative acts aiming to remove physical, technical and fiscal barriers to trade; they were accompanied by specific deadlines for both the European Commission and the European Council. The Paper was presented in June 1985 at the meeting of the European Council in Milan and was endorsed by it. The Cockfield White Paper together with the Cecchini Report of 1988 played a very significant role in the creation of the Single European Market (SEM). (See also, Cecchini Report, SEM).

CO-DECISION PROCEDURE. Introduced by the Maastricht Treaty, it is the only procedure where the European Parliament (EP) and the Council of Ministers co-decide and pass legislation in the name of both institutions. The EP is empowered to veto, by an absolute majority at the final stage, a legislative measure on which no agreement can be reached with the Council of Ministers.

Up to the second reading in the EP, the co-decision procedure is similar to the cooperation procedure. The procedure changes, however, when the Council of Ministers fails to accept the EP's position. In such a case, if the differences between the EP and the Council of Ministers cannot be bridged in the conciliation committee and if the Council insists on adopting its common position, then the EP can prevent it by an absolute majority vote.

Some of the areas to which this procedure applies are, education, culture, health and consumer protection, Trans-European Networks (TENs), environmental action programmes, the services sectors, the free movement of workers, single market measures, and freedom of establishment. There is constant pressure from the Parliament for co-decision to be extended to other areas. (See also, Common Position, Conciliation Committee, Cooperation Procedure, Council of the EU, EP).

COHESION FUND. This was established by the Maastricht Treaty under pressure from the poorest countries of the European Community, which benefit mostly from the Fund. Together with the European Regional Development Fund (ERDF), the Cohesion Fund aims to bring about greater economic and social cohesion within the EU. The function of these funds differs in that the Cohesion Fund seeks to reduce disparities between countries, while the ERDF seeks to reduce regional disparities.

The Maastricht Treaty limited access to the cohesion fund to member states with a GDP of less than 90 per cent of the EU's average, to the four poorest members of the EU (Greece, Ireland, Spain, Portugal), and to projects of transport and environment infrastructure leading towards convergence. Among the poorest countries, Spain benefits the most from the Fund. For the period 1993-99, the budget of the fund was set to ECU 15 billion, and 70 per cent of this amount was meant to assist underdeveloped areas as defined in Objective 1 of the structural funds. (See also, Environment Policy, ERDF, Structural Funds, TENs).

COLLEGE OF EUROPE. Established in 1949 in Bruges, it offers postgraduate courses in a variety of subjects related to European integration. The College is partly financed by the Community Budget, but it is not a European Community institution. It has students of about 20 nationalities and the languages used are English and French. (See also, Cultural Policy, Education Policy).

COMETT. Scheme that stimulates the placement of university students in industrial and business sectors in order to promote cooperation between industry and university. It came into effect in 1987; since 1995 COMETT has been absorbed into the Leonardo programme. (See also, Education Policy, Leonardo).

COMITOLOGY. The word is used to signify the study and the debate surrounding the role of the numerous committees, which observe the implementation of Community law and examine a number of complex issues. The extensive role of these committees has provoked persistent disputes related directly to the balance of power between national and European Community institutions, as well as the degree to which the committees are subject to effective democratic control.

The committees consist of national experts and are headed by a European Commission official. They supervise the implementation of Community law, deriving from either the European Commission's powers of decision as a right or those conferred upon it by the Council of Ministers. Committees, charged with the study of issues, that deal mainly with technical matters, have proliferated further with the introduction of the numerous measures leading to the establishment of the Single European Market (SEM).

The 1987 decision of the Council of Ministers divided the committees into three main categories and codified their powers. The decision of the Council of Ministers is as follows:

1. An advisory committee is authorised with the power to deliver Opinions on European Commission proposals; though it is not mandatory, the European Commission has to take utmost account of the opinion delivered by the committee.

2. A management committee is also authorised with the power to deliver Opinions on European Commission proposals; however, under this procedure the Committee can block the Commission's proposals by qualified majority vote in the Committee. If the Committee agrees with the proposals, the Commission can proceed with their implementation. If, however, the Committee delivers a negative Opinion, then the Commission can still proceed with the adoption of the planned measures, but is obliged to notify the negative Opinion of the Committee to the Council of Ministers. In this case, the Council has one month to adopt a different decision by qualified majority vote. Currently, there are around 30 management committees, most of them concerned with aspects of the Common Agricultural Policy (CAP), but they have been increasingly extending their activities to other spheres.

3. A regulatory committee must give its approval to the Commission's proposals by qualified majority. If no opinion is delivered, the matter is then referred to the Council. The Council may, within three months, take a decision on the Commission's proposal by a qualified majority. If the Council does not act within three months, the proposal shall then be adopted by the Commission, unless a simple majority in the Council votes against adoption. Regulatory committees tend to be concerned with harmonisation, and therefore extend their activities to various sectional interests, consequently they are highly specialised.

All these committees meet as appropriate, in most cases, almost weekly, depending on the subject matter with which they are concerned. (See also, CAP, CEN, COR, Democratic Deficit, ESC, European Commission).

COMMISSION, see **EUROPEAN COMMISSION**

COMMITTEE FOR EUROPEAN NORMALIZATION (CEN). Founded in 1961, the Committee is responsible for laying down standard technical specifications for manufactured goods, except electrical, which come under the responsibility of CELENEC, founded in 1973. Eighteen countries participate in CEN and CELENEC, which are financed by the European Commission and contributions from industry. Both committees contribute significantly to the harmonization efforts of the Community. (See also, Comitology, Harmonization).

COMMITTEE OF PERMANENT REPRESENTATIVES (COREPER). It consists of the Permanent Ambassadors (representatives) of member states to the European Community. It prepares the agenda of the Council meetings and acts on the Council's instructions by setting up committees and working parties to study particular matters.

It is divided into COREPER I and COREPER II. The former is made up of junior civil servants (Deputy level), while the latter comprises senior officials (Ambassador level). COREPER I is primarily concerned with technical and specialized subjects, while COREPER II works with the President in planning and managing the Council's work. (See also, Council of the EU).

COMMITTEE OF PROFESSIONAL AGRICULTURAL ORGANIZATIONS (COPA). A transnational federation of national farming unions and associations which represents farmers' interests on a wide range of issues. COPA is one of the most powerful organizations acting at European Community level. (See also, Eurogroups).

COMMITTEE OF THE REGIONS (COR). The Maastricht Treaty, which established the Committee of the Regions, stipulated that the Committee must be consulted by the Council of Ministers or the Commission on areas of regional interest, as well as on issues of education, youth, culture, public health, economic and social cohesion and Trans-European Networks (TENs). The Committee can also take the initiative to give its opinion on other policy matters, given the expertise at its disposal.

The COR is comprised of 222 members who represent local and regional authorities. Its members, though not required, are elected officials from levels closest to the citizens and they serve for a four year term. The number of representatives of each member state is as follows: France, Germany, Italy and the UK, 24 each; Spain, 21; Belgium, Greece, The Netherlands, Portugal, Sweden, and Austria, 12 each; Denmark, Ireland, and Finland, 9 each; Luxembourg, 6. Located in Brussels, the COR holds five plenary meetings per year. Between the plenary meetings work is carried out by eight European Commissions and four sub-Commissions.

Since its first session in March 1994, the COR has been committed to the principle of subsidiarity, which is opposed to centralized decision-making. According to this principle decisions have to be taken by those public authorities that are as close as possible to the citizens. (See also, Comitology, Council of the EU, Subsidiarity).

COMMON AGRICULTURAL POLICY (CAP). One of the founding policies of the European Community absorbs the largest part, about two thirds, of the EU Budget and affects a large population of producers and consumers directly. Introduced by the Treaty of Rome it was first intended to ensure security in food supplies at stable and reasonable prices to the consumers, and secondly to create a fair standard of living for the agricultural community by making it independent of factors beyond man's control.

The responsibility to initiate policy with regard to CAP resides with the Commission, while the Council of Ministers takes decisions after consultation with the European Parliament (EP) and often with the Economic and Social Committee (ESC). The Council's proceedings concerning agriculture are prepared by the Special Committee on Agriculture, while the Commission has at its disposal a number of expert committees, namely the management committees, to deliver Opinions on certain aspects of the CAP.

The CAP is based on three fundamental principles:

Unity of the market: the creation of a single market for agricultural products. This requires the removal of internal barriers, the harmonization of legislation and the setting of common agricultural prices.

Community preference: the deliberate promotion of Community agricultural products over imports from external markets. Fixed prices for imported agricultural products sold in the Community market led to the introduction of a special 'levy', which increases the price of imported products to the level of the Community price.

Financial solidarity: under this principle the costs, which the market organizations necessarily entail, are raised jointly by member states. In order to raise and distribute the necessary finance the European Agricultural Guidance and Guarantee Fund (EAGGF) was set up.

A common understanding among the Six was that agriculture, unlike other sectors of the economy, needed to be subsidised and therefore to be excluded from Common Competition Policy rules. Price mechanisms rather than direct income support are applied both in the internal market and external trade. This mechanism includes three sets of prices, namely the target, the intervention and the threshold price. The target price is the maximum price and is set every year by the Council of Ministers. This is the price that the Community seeks for the producers by either intervening in the internal market or protecting them from external trade.

Intervention in the internal market is permitted at the intervention price, which is the lowest permissible price. This is carried out by intervention agencies, which either buy-in products when market prices are lower than the target price or release products when there is scarcity in the market. Intervention arrangements are often associated with high storage costs; when stocks become exorbitantly high and affect supply and demand decisively, then the intervention price is reduced. Fresh products (fruits and vegetables), which cannot be stored, are withdrawn form the market at the withdrawal price, which is the price that producers stop selling their products and send them for destruction or to charities.

Protection from external trade takes place at the threshold price, which is fixed at or just above the target price. This is the lowest price above which imports from non-members enjoy free access. Threshold price intends to protect agricultural prices from low price imports, since world prices are lower that the agreed target prices. The gap between the threshold price and the world price for import is bridged with an import levy. Unlike the customs duty, the import levy, being the difference between target and world price, varies. For products that have no target price, the threshold price is the minimum price at which a non- Community member's product can be imported.

Guaranteed prices for producers result in excessive surpluses, which, apart from being sold in the domestic market at reduced prices, are encouraged to be exported. Export refunds, which reimburse the exporter for the difference between world and Community market prices, become available. When world prices are higher than threshold prices, export levies are collected to prevent a flood of Community products onto the world markets and at the same time to ensure adequate supply and stable prices for Community consumers.

The number of products protected by means of price mechanism has increased considerably and so have the complexities of the CAP. Around 70 per cent of the agricultural production, including cereals, meat, table wine, fruits and sugar, are under price support, while around 25 per cent, including eggs, flowers, poultry, are protected from external trade. In addition, direct subsidies covering part of the production costs are provided for a few products, such as oil seeds, olive oil and tobacco. All these operations are covered by the Community Budget through the EAGGF. The agrimonetary system is an additional instrument of helping uniform and stable prices to be sustained. It is an adjustment system of the fluctuations in the values of EU currencies. This involves special exchange rates, the so-called green rates.

Undoubtedly, the CAP has succeeded in achieving its original aims, to increase agricultural productivity and sustain a high standard of living for the agricultural community. However, it has been subject to heavy criticism, not only in relation to its cost, but also in relation to its purposes. The CAP no longer needs to promote self-sufficiency in foodstuffs. This policy is perceived to have led to an accumulation of surpluses, involving massive storage costs, and to have caused waste of resources.

Resultant problems are partly solved by dumping surpluses in world markets or by destroying them. EU consumers, on the other hand, not only have to pay, through taxation, for the cost of the CAP, they often have to buy agricultural products at higher than world prices. Furthermore, the complexity of the system of the CAP leaves it vulnerable to fraud, which is difficult to eradicate mainly because of the inadequate scrutiny of national authorities. Almost half of the detected fraud in the EU relates to agricultural funds.

The CAP has also become the source of discord both between member states, which dispute the extent of benefits received by each of them, and between the EU and the outside world. The objections of the outside world to the CAP were mostly led by the USA which, backed by the Cairns Group, attacked what they perceived to be CAP's protectionist character. Less developed countries, and less able to voice their case, are also adversely affected as they find it difficult to penetrate protected markets.

Consequently, there has been a long-standing debate regarding reform of the CAP. As early as 1968 Sicco Mansholt, Vice-President of the Commission and responsible for agriculture, introduced the so-called Mansholt Plan that advocated a more prudent price policy, arguing that prices were kept artificially high, and that a drastic structural reform programme was needed to encourage a more efficient unit of production. This implied the gradual destruction of small agricultural units. Any major re-appraisal of the CAP was, however, prevented and only parts of the Plan were implemented by a Council decision of 1972.

By the early 1980s, the need for a radical reform of the CAP made itself unmistakably apparent as mountains of vegetables and dairy products, involving high costs and huge waste, revealed the major shortcomings of the CAP. The 1985 Green Paper sought to align production with consumption, to reduce price supports, introduce direct income supports, and to encourage farmers to leave their land fallow. Reform was further promoted with a decision of the European Council in February 1988 to introduce measures, such as the reform of structural funds, the extension of quotas, incentives to discourage intensive farming and direct aid for early retirement.

Difficulties in reconciling the social objectives of the CAP with market conditions undermined its drastic reform. As a result the main characteristics of the CAP remained the same and so did the necessity for its further reform. In addition, external forces, mainly American pressure, continued to clamour for change, especially after the collapse of the Uruguay Round in Brussels in 1990. As a response, the MacSharry reform of 1992 was introduced with a further reduction of price support for cereals, oil seeds and protein crops, an increase of income support linked to the set-aside land scheme and early retirement incentives. The MacSharry reforms opened the way for an agreement between the USA and the EU in 1992, known as the Blair House Accord. Internal price support and the volume of export subsidies were reduced further; import protection changed from variable levies to fixed tariffs; special reference was made to products such as sugar. France opposed the deal more than any other member state, but in the absence of adequate support against the agreement, the General Agreement on Tariffs and Trade (GATT) was finally concluded in 1993.

The cost of the CAP to the Budget still remains very high, while fresh problems loom ahead with the entry of new members to the EU. It is worth noting that the Eastern European countries have a large agricultural sector and that, currently, EU consumption accounts for over 50 per cent of agricultural exports from Eastern Europe. Once these countries accede to the European Community, the cost of the CAP to the Budget is bound to rise. The Commission has planned to mitigate this rise with further reform of the CAP to be introduced prior to future enlargement. (See also, Agenda 2000, Blair House Accord, Budget, Competition Policy, Compulsory Expenditure, Dumping, EAGGF, GATT, 'Lake', 'Lamb War', Stresa Conference).

COMMON COMMERCIAL POLICY (CCP). The Treaty of Rome, which provided for a customs union between the Six, entailed the abolition of customs duties and other charges having equivalent effect and the implementation of a common tariff and customs policy with regard to third countries. The CCP, therefore, embracing these two fundamental elements of the customs union as well as common trade agreements and a uniform application of trade policy, has been one of the Community's long-standing objectives. Harmonization of indirect taxation has also been pursued at least to the extent required for the functioning of the Common Market.

A common external tariff regime, imposing duties on goods entering the Union, was one of the very first policies of the Community and formed an indispensable part of the customs union among the Six. The Treaty of Rome also provided for the use of quotas on imports from non-European Community countries. Once such imports get customs clearance in one member state, they can move freely within the customs union. In addition to duties on imports, a number of anti-dumping measures, restrictions on imports for a temporary period, voluntary export restraints[1] have been introduced within the framework of the CCP.

The Union has signed a variety of agreements with both individual states or groups of states, some are restricted to trade matters, while others extend to political spheres. These include agreements between the EU and the EFTA countries establishing the European Economic Area (EEA), the Europe Agreements with the central and eastern European countries, involving political stipulations along with economic ones, agreements with the ACP countries under the Lomé Convention, the Mediterranean Agreements with Cyprus, Malta, Turkey and a number of Middle East countries. Agreements signed within the context of the General Agreement on Tariffs and Trade (GATT) also belong to this category.

The Commission is the chief negotiator of the EU with regard to commercial agreements and it has concluded a number of agreements with non-Community countries. It acts under the mandate of the Council of Ministers which decides on such issues by qualified majority vote (QMV), with the exemption of anti-dumping measures where a simple majority is required, and the Association Agreements where unanimity is needed. Throughout such negotiations the Commission remains in contact with the Article 113 committee of the Treaty of Rome. This committee consists of national officials and permanent representatives and is responsible for keeping the Council

---

[1] Quota agreements aimed at limiting the amount of goods exported by one country to another.

of Ministers informed on matters of external trade policy. The European Parliament (EP) has limited powers in relation to CCP, with the exception of accession, association and cooperation agreements where its assent is required.

The CCP has generally succeeded in presenting the Community's united front to the rest of the world and making it a large economic unit. There are very few exceptions where CCP has not been followed by all member states and these are cases where national interests have apparently prevailed over those of the Community. In the 1990s, the Community moved towards greater liberalization, following the completion of the single market in 1992, and the severe criticism levelled against its protectionist nature by its leading partners. (See also, ACP, Association Agreements, Customs Union, EEA, Europe Agreements, European Commission, GATT, Harmonization, Mediterranean Agreements, Taxation, Trade).

COMMON FISHERIES POLICY (CFP). Fishing is an important industry for the European Community as a whole, and particularly for some of its peripheral regions. Fisheries employ around 300,000 fishermen, 1.5 million in associated industry and 80,000 vessels. Yet, with the exception of Ireland, the EU is a net importer of fish and its products.

The CFP adheres to the principles of the Common Agricultural Policy (CAP), though the first fisheries policy was drawn up in 1971, largely to present a *fait accompli* to the new applicant states which had a substantial fishing industry. Norway refused to enter the Community mainly for this reason, whereas the other three, the UK, Denmark and Ireland succeeded in extending their six mile coastal exclusion zone to twelve miles.

In the last two decades the aims of the CFP have been beset by a number of problems, which can no longer be ignored. Scientific evidence strongly suggests that fish stocks are diminishing because of overfishing and marine pollution. At the same time, EU fishing fleets have lost traditional fishing grounds, because, since 1975, some Atlantic countries unilaterally extended their economic exclusion zones to 200 miles, confirmed by the Convention of the Law of the Sea in 1982. In consequence, the implementation of a CFP became more necessary.

In 1983, the first revised CFP involving a twelve mile exclusion zone, Total Allowance Catches (TACs), quotas, the Financial Instrument for Fisheries and Guidance (FIFG), etc, was introduced; it was also agreed that it should be revised again ten years later. In 1992, the Council of Ministers reviewed the CFP which was applicable to all member states including from 1996 Spain and Portugal, which would by then have completed their ten year transition period.

Most of the features of the CFP were retained, but certain aspects were specifically reinforced. The CFP developed to cover all activities related to resources, processing and marketing of the fisheries products; fishing licences administered by member states, and control systems of the entire sector were introduced; early retirement schemes for fishermen and modernization of fleets have also been promoted. Policies focused on achieving a balanced exploitation of resources. In this context, the Fourth Multi-annual programme (MAG IV) which has a five year duration, from 1 January 1997 to 31 December 2002, introduced a catch reduction of 20 per cent for over-fished areas and 30 per cent for areas with depleted stocks.

However, several problems are still unresolved. The enforcement of TACs and quotas, for instance, left largely in the hands of national governments, has had limited effect. Moreover, there have been incidents of confrontations at sea concerning infringement of national waters, and on the whole European Commission plans have not been perceived as very effective. On the other hand, there has been a fall from 11 to 7 per cent in the joint share of member states in world catches. Unlike the CAP, the CFP does not provide high subsidies; only a very small part of the Community Budget, around 1 per cent, is attributed to it. (See also, TACs).

COMMON FOREIGN AND SECURITY POLICY (CFSP). One of the three pillars of the European Union (EU) established by the Maastricht Treaty. The Treaty requires member states to coordinate their action in international organizations and to maintain a common position in international forums. However, neither plans involving the maximum of cooperation leading to a unified supranational foreign policy, nor the integration of the Western European Union (WEU) into the EU structure are likely to be achieved in the foreseeable future.

The CFSP is the successor of the European Political Cooperation (EPC), formally established by the Single European Act (SEA). Like its predecessor, the CFSP is based on intergovernmental cooperation and lies outside the Community's institutional framework. It represents a further step towards a common defence policy and enhances the Union's commitment to the development of joint action in foreign and security affairs. However, diverse national interests, whether of historical, political, economic or geographical origins, often undermine a common EU position or joint action. Illustrating this lack of cohesion were the stances taken during the Yugoslav crisis.

The Maastricht Treaty empowered the European Council in setting the CFSP agenda, in defining the principles and the general guidelines for the common foreign and security policy. In practice, the main decision-making body is the General Affairs Council, consisting of EU foreign ministers; this Council is empowered to decide on areas of joint action, its scope, duration and other aspects. The Council decides by unanimity on all important issues, but in some cases the Council by mutual consent agrees that a decision may be taken by qualified majority. It meets monthly but also has additional meetings when necessary. The Council presidency represents the EU on CFSP issues, and is responsible for the implementation of joint action. In this process, the General Affairs Council is assisted by representatives of the previous and next member state to hold the presidency in association with the European Commission. It is also assisted by COREPER, by senior foreign affairs officials from member states and by various working groups. The cost of any CFSP action is covered either by the Budget or directly by the member states.

As in all intergovernmental arrangements, power remains largely in the hands of national governments. Consequently, it is the Council, in this case the General Affairs Council, that plays the most decisive role in relation to the CFSP. The EP's role is limited to simple consultation, while the Commission has neither the sole right to initiate policies nor the right to monitor the CFSP. The Commission's delegations in countries around the globe, which number more than 100, by no means replace the links of each member state to those countries.

Both the CFSP and the Justice and Home Affairs (JHA) will most likely remain controversial for years to come, as their enhancement is subject to further powers being transferred to the EU institutions. Despite the various degrees of commitment to the CFSP, national governments are either not particularly willing to relinquish more powers related to such a sensitive area of policy, or have no clear idea about how this could be achieved. (See also, Common Position, COREPER, Council of the EU, EPC, European Commission, European Council, Intergovernmentalism, Joint Action, Maastricht Treaty, WEU).

COMMON POSITION. The term denotes two distinct functions in the workings of the European Community. Firstly, it is a stage in the legislative procedure of the Union related to the cooperation and co-decision procedures, requiring two-readings. A common position is reached when the Council of Ministers agrees to the European Parliament's (EP) amendments at its first reading, after the

Commission has incorporated them in the text of the proposal. The common position is sent back to the EP for the second reading and may either be approved, rejected or amended.

Secondly, the term common position is used in the Maastricht Treaty provisions on Common Foreign and Security Policy (CFSP) and Justice and Home Affairs (JHA) denoting the stance adopted by member states on a particular issue. Common positions are taken by the Council of Ministers whenever deemed necessary, and consequently member states are instructed to make sure that their national policies conform to the common positions. (See also, CFSP, Co-decision and Cooperation Procedures, JHA).

COMMON TRANSPORT POLICY (CTP). Given the importance of transport to the development of the common market, the Treaty of Rome stipulated a CTP, although with reference only to road, rail and inland waterways. The CTP implies the integration of national transport networks and seeks to organize the various means of transport in accordance with certain Community regulations, in order to eliminate barriers and ensure the free movement of haulage and transport services.

The transport sector is among the largest industries of the European Community, representing approximately 7-8 per cent of its GNP, and its size is bound to increase further due to the rise in car ownership and cross-border transport of goods and persons. In addition transport, is linked closely to other sectors of the economy, notably trade, motor and aircraft industries, ship and road building and energy.

In 1965, the Council of Ministers agreed on the harmonization of provisions affecting competition in road, rail and inland waterways transport. However, it was not until three years later in 1968, that the Treaty rules on competition policy were applied with a number of exemptions. The slow progress in the field of transport continued until 1985, when the Court of Justice ruled in favour of the European Parliament (EP) that inland transport of goods and passengers should be open to all Community firms. Moreover, the Single European Act (SEA) amended the Treaty of Rome and empowered the Council of Ministers to decide whether and how to extend a common transport policy to sea and air transport. ·

Diverse interests and priorities in national transport systems deriving from geographical reasons, differing national attitudes to state intervention and diverse preferences to certain modes of transport (Italy, Germany, France favoured railways) hindered the further development of a CTP. The wide variety of national networks and specifications presented the integration of Community transport networks with an additional obstacle, though some progress was noted as a result of certain measures being introduced in each sector:

Road transport representing 80 per cent of goods carriage between member states is essential to the free movement of people within the Community. Yet, member states were reluctant to proceed with liberalization of road transport. For many years the debate centred on the maximum height, width, weight, and weight per axle that Community road structures could take. An agreement was eventually reached in 1984 and revised in 1986.

Moreover, a system of Community quotas, although still arranged bilaterally between member states, was extended with the prospect that by 1992 freight movements within the Community would be entirely liberalised. In fact, from 1993 a Community licensing system, based on qualitative requirements, was introduced with the prospect from 1998 to be further deregulated. Cabotage is still limited to a quota of permits for road hauliers, while it is allowed for passenger transport[2]. In addition, a licence, called a *vignette*, introduced in July 1998 allows EU hauliers to pick up or deliver goods between any two locations of the Community.

Some standardization was achieved in areas such as working time for drivers, recognition of diplomas, mutual recognition of driving licences and a European driving licence and a speed limit for lorries and buses. An effort has been made to increase safety in road infrastructure through Community assistance. The so-called Pilot Actions for Combined Transport (PACT) programme, aimed at the use of different modes of transport in order to reduce pressures on the roads, has been introduced.

Railways provided their share of problems, in that most networks were either state monopolies or heavily subsidised through state aid. Initially, the Community was preoccupied with the harmonization of railway subsidies and the attainment of better transparency of state aid to railways. However, the CTP eventually adopted the position that state monopoly of railways should be removed. In fact, in many member states privatization of railways has made substantial inroads.

---

[2] Cabotage is the reservation of the internal land, sea, or air traffic of a country to its carriers. By extension within the context of the Community, cabotage refers to the opening of the member states' markets to intra-Community competition. This implies that a European Community land, sea, or air operator would be free to ply for hire in any member state's roads, railway tracks, coastal waters or air.

European railway companies have planned to build 30,000 kilometres of high speed track over the next 25 years. The CTP also tries to introduce a fairer competition between railways and other modes of transport.

Air transport is another contentious area not least because of state ownership of major airlines in most member states. It was agreed in 1987, that air transport should also be open to competition. The *Nouvelles Frontières* case had obliged the European Commission to take a clear position[3]. Two sets of regulations were issued; the first concerned air transport regulations, and the second the extent of the exemptions from the rules. The European Commission retained powers it had in other areas where a competition policy was applied. In 1992, new regulations were issued which withdrew some, but not all, of the remaining restrictions that applied to the development of new routes, access to established routes for new airlines or cabotage.

Sea transport had to follow suit, and was opened to competition not only between the member states, but also between the fleets of the EU and non-EU states. This is an important area of CTP for almost 95 per cent of the tonnage of Community trade is carried by sea; moreover, after Greece's accession, the Community became the world's leading shipping power. In 1986, a limited first package of regulations on the application of competition rules was issued, and in 1992 there were new regulations liberalising further the transport services within member states. As a result, cabotage was liberalised, though certain provisions were made for the Mediterranean countries and especially Greece which is exempted until 2002. An EU shipping register, called Euros, was introduced with the purpose of giving registered ships flying the Community flag the opportunity of enjoying certain advantages.

In the 1990s, among the main goals of the CTP have been the development of a trans-European network in transport by linking together member states' networks, and the achievement of a better balance between the modes of transport. Environmental considerations, such as the use of less polluting, more energy efficient modes of transport, have been taken into account. The aims of the CTP are

---

[3] *Nouvelles Frontières* case. A ruling of the Court of Justice declaring that air transport was not exempt from competition policy rules and that member states are not permitted to approve air fares which result from agreements between airlines. The ruling issued in 1986 gave an impetus for the further implementation of competition rules in the transport fields as it enabled the Commission to intervene more decisively.

presented fully in the 1995 European Commission's transport action programme for 1995 - 2000. In general terms its objectives are to improve the quality of transport systems, remove any remaining restrictions in the Single European Market (SEM), and develop transport links with countries outside the EU. (See also, Competition Policy, Harmonization, TENs).

COMMUNITY INITIATIVES, see **STRUCTURAL FUNDS, REGIONAL POLICY**

COMMUNITY LAW. In general, Community law has priority over any conflicting national law, and national courts are obliged to ensure its primacy and when required its direct effect. The major part of Community law consists of:

Treaties and related instruments: Treaties are often called the European Community primary legislation in that they provide its legal framework and the basis for further legislation. They define the relationships between signatory countries, and lay down policy guidelines for the future; they specify the role and the powers of each European institution; they enjoy primacy in the sense that legislation based on them takes precedence over national law, though not all their provisions have direct effect. The Treaties apply throughout the territory of member states, with the exception of the Faroe Islands, the Channel Islands and the Isle of Man, the British Base Area in Cyprus and the French overseas territories for which special arrangements operate. In addition to these, Helgoland, Bussingen in Germany and Livigno-Campione in Italy do not belong to the EU. Conversely, the French overseas departments (Guadeloupe, Guiana, Martinique and the Réunion) are considered an integral part of France and therefore of the EU; also the Finnish Åland Islands are now part of the EU.

Legislation: deriving from the Treaties, but issued by either the European Commission or the Council, it is often called secondary legislation. In the form of Directives, Regulations and Decisions, secondary legislation has a binding force on the member states. Day to day policy of the EU is carried out by means of secondary legislation. However, there are also forms of secondary legislation, such as Recommendations, Opinions and Resolutions, which do not have a binding force on the member states.

The case-law of the Court of Justice: a ruling of the Court of Justice is required in cases where either the Treaties or other forms of legislation are not precise enough to avoid problems in their implementation. It is the primary function of the Court of Justice to ensure that in the interpretation and the implementation of the Treaties the law is observed. The Court of Justice is all powerful since there is no appeal to its rulings; it may decide that certain actions of the EU institutions or of the member states are illegal when these are in conflict with European laws. (See also, Court of Justice, Direct Applicability, Direct Effect, Legislation, OCTs, Primacy).

COMMUNITY TRADE MARK, see **OFFICE FOR HARMONIZATION IN THE INTERNAL MARKET**

COMPETITION POLICY. Ever since the creation of the Community, competition has been perceived as an important component of the establishment of the single market, as well as of the European business environment and their ability to compete in global markets. In this context, the Treaty of Rome ensured that competition in the internal market should not be distorted, and for this reason it provided for a legal framework prohibiting a number of agreements and practices, such as:

anti-competitive agreements, which directly or indirectly fix purchase or selling prices, share markets or sources of supply, limit or control production, technical development or investment.

dominant positions defined as the firm or firms which by means of concentration or monopoly power exercise pressure on suppliers and buyers and act independently of other competitors. As the Treaty of Rome provided for action only after a merger had taken place, the European Commission had little authority to intervene in cross-border mergers prior to the deal becoming effective. This resulted in a large number of mergers taking place in the 1980s, especially as a response to the establishment of the Single European Market (SEM). In 1990 the Merger Control Regulation was introduced; henceforth all mergers with a world wide turnover of ECUs 5 billion require prior clearance of the Commission.

state aid refers to government subsidies that distort or threaten to distort competition and are given to enterprises in the form of direct payments, tax exemptions, debt write-offs, preferential interest rates, loans on favourable terms, and several other forms. In the 1980s, the Commission estimated that state aid to troubled key industries within the Union reached the sum of more than ECU 80 billion a year.

However, there are a number of exemptions from the general competition rules. Firstly, anti-competitive agreements or/and dominant positions, considered beneficial to consumers on the grounds that they contribute to the improvement of production, distribution of goods, promotion of technical and economic progress, are exempted. Moreover, the Commission has practically no authority to interfere with mergers below the agreed threshold, unless national governments specifically ask for its intervention. In addition, the general rules on competition are not applicable to the Common Agricultural Policy (CAP), while coal and steel industries are subject to the terms of the Treaty of Paris.

Secondly, state aid is justifiable when given to industries whose severe crisis creates acute social problems, or when it does not lead to an expansion of capacity, or is part of a restructuring package.

Thirdly, public procurement[4], accounting for more than 15 per cent of national economic activity in member states, is exempt. Provision of goods and services, such as energy supply, post, telecommunication, railways, are provided by national and local authorities. Governments also favour domestic firms undertaking certain contracts, particularly military ones. In 1992, the Commission outlined a set of reforms needed for completing the internal market in public procurement. This included opening the public sector to intra-Community trade and competition.

The Commission enjoys extensive discretionary powers with regard to the implementation of the competition rules. Firstly, the European Commission has to be provided with information on any proposed merging, on which basis it must decide within a month either to allow the deal to be carried out or to open proceedings against the merger. Any firm which fails to provide the European Commission with information, or concludes a merger without getting clearance from the European Commission, is liable to a fine of 10 per cent of its annual sales payable to the Community Budget. Secondly, the European Commission has to be notified of any state aid, given to either the public or private sector and which exceeds ECU 50,000 over three years. On the basis of the information given, the European Commission can either suppress or modify the proposal.

The Commission can investigate cases of anti-competitive behaviour on its own initiative, or if brought to its notice by interested parties. Commission decisions are subject to appeal by interested parties to the Court of Justice, which is empowered to confirm, cancel, reduce or increase fines, or to annul Commission decisions. In accordance with the 1977 resolution of the European Parliament (EP), the European

---

[4] Public procurement is the purchasing of goods and services of all kinds to cover the needs of the civil service, local and regional authorities and official bodies.

Commission is obliged to publish a report on competition policy every year. (See also, CAP, Court of Justice, European Commission, CTP).

COMPULSORY EXPENDITURE. The term refers to that section of the Community Budget spent on policies defined directly in the founding Treaties. The major expenditure is the Common Agricultural Policy (CAP), while minor costs include refunds to the member states, and those arising from existing international agreements with third countries. Compulsory expenditure constitutes almost three quarters of the Community Budget. The European Parliament (EP) has the right to modify, but not to amend, the Council's proposals on compulsory expenditure. (See also, Budget, CAP, EP).

CONCILIATION COMMITTEE. Composed of an equal number of representatives from the Council of Ministers and the European Parliament (EP), its function is to resolve disputes over proposed legislation. It was set up in 1975 as the main instrument for reaching agreement on the Budget, but since then it has become an important part of the co-decision procedure. (See also, Co-decision Procedure).

CONFERENCE ON SECURITY AND COOPERATION IN EUROPE (CSCE). It was established in the early 1970s with the purpose of promoting East-West dialogue. Representatives of all European states, apart from Albania which joined in 1991, the USA and Canada participated in the conference. In 1995, the CSCE was re-named the Organization for Security and Cooperation in Europe (OSCE) and has since acquired a more permanent character.

The first conference (1973-75) was mainly an attempt to reconcile the conflicting interests between the North Atlantic Treaty Organization (NATO) and the Warsaw Pact. Despite serious difficulties arising out of the participants' different priorities, the conference culminated in the signing of the Helsinki Final Act in 1975. The two parties recognized the inviolability of the post-World War II frontiers in Europe, committed themselves to respect human rights and fundamental freedoms, and to promote further scientific and economic cooperation.

Follow-up conferences, agreed in the first Conference, were held in Belgrade in 1977-78, Madrid in 1980-83, Ottawa in 1985, Vienna in 1986-89, Paris in 1990 and Helsinki in 1992. Of special historical importance was the 1990 Paris summit which, following the sweeping changes in Eastern Europe, formally ended the long-standing antithesis between East and West. The Charter of Paris was signed during that meeting. By 1992 the newly independent republics of the former

Soviet Union as well as Albania had become members, and a number
of institutions had been introduced.

Although the European Community signed both the Helsinki Final
Act and the Charter of Paris, it is not represented as an entity in the
OSCE. Because of this lack of representation, the EU discusses
broader security issues within the framework of the Common Foreign
and Security Policy (CFSP). (See also, Charter of Paris, Helsinki Final
Act, NATO, OSCE, Warsaw Pact, WEU).

CONSULTATION PROCEDURE. The term denotes one-stage consultation
between the Council of Ministers and the European Parliament (EP),
not to be confused with other forms of consultation among European
Community institutions. According to this procedure the EP is simply
asked to give its opinion while the Council of Ministers takes the
decision. However, the Council must wait for the Parliament's opinion,
and any parliamentary amendments that are accepted by the European
Commission can only be modified by unanimous vote in the Council.

In the 1970s the EP was granted additional powers over the Budget,
but it was not until 1979 with the Isoglucose case, that the EP acquired
more powers in respect to legislation. Since then other procedures
further empowering the EP have been developed. Nevertheless, in
some very important spheres, such as the Common Foreign and
Security Policy (CFSP), Justice and Home Affairs (JHA) and the
Economic and Monetary Union (EMU), the EP has only consultative
powers. (See also, Co-decision and Cooperation Procedures, Council
of the EU, EP, Isoglucose Case).

CONSUMER POLICY. Consumer Policy was not mentioned in the
Treaty of Rome, but in 1968 a Directorate-General was established
with the purpose of serving consumers' interests. The new body made
few contributions towards ensuring wider choice and better quality of
goods and services as it first had to deal with a variety of different
technical standards and product regulations, as well as with various
degrees of interest in matters of consumer protection in each member
state.

Further initiatives were taken in the preparatory stage for the
introduction of the Single European Market (SEM), which would
promote harmonization of quality standards. By 1981, a number of
fundamental rights on behalf of the consumer were established:
protection of consumers' health and safety, protection of their
economic interests, the right to information and education, the right to
redress, and the right to consumers' representation and participation.

Consumers' interests were incorporated in all European Community policies and dialogue between consumers, producers and distributors was promoted.

The launching of the Single European Act (SEA) enhanced Consumer Policy further and put forward the principle that essential requirements had to be met in the single market. In 1989, an independent Consumer Policy Service was set up by the European Commission, and in 1990 the Consumer's Consultative Council was established.

However, it was the Maastricht Treaty which established the legal basis for specific action to support health, safety and the economic interests of consumers and to provide information to them. The EU's consumer policy is complementary to that of national governments, and the European Commission has increasingly made an effort to advise and cooperate with consumer bodies in the member states. (See also, Harmonization, SEM).

CONVERGENCE CRITERIA. The Maastricht Treaty of 1992 made Stage III of the Economic and Monetary Union (EMU) conditional upon a number of convergence criteria, which member states had to meet in order to participate in the EMU:

inflation must be within 1.5 percentage points of the average rate of the three member states with the lowest inflation

long term interest rate must be within 2 percentage points of the average rate of the three member states with the lowest interest rates

national budget deficit must be below 3 per cent of GDP

national debt must be either below 60 per cent of GDP or heading towards it

national currency must not have been devalued in the last two years and must have remained within the fluctuation margin provided by the European Monetary System (EMS).

Only eleven member states meeting these criteria automatically proceeded to Stage III on 1 January 1999 in accordance with the Brussels summit of May 1998. Greece is excluded because she does not qualify for entry, while Sweden has chosen not to participate for the time being; on the other hand, Denmark has ruled out participation, while the UK exercises its right to opt out. (See also, EMS, EMU).

COOPERATION PROCEDURE. Introduced by the Single European Act (SEA) of 1986, the cooperation procedure is yet another mechanism of resolving disputes between the Council of Ministers and the European Parliament (EP) in the legislative process. It stipulates that the EP should be consulted twice before a legislative measure is enacted.

According to this procedure the European Commission refers a draft proposal both to the Council of Ministers and the EP. When the EP completes the first reading, it sends its 'opinion' to the Council of Ministers. The Council of Ministers decides on a common position by qualified majority vote (QMV) and sends it back to the EP for a second reading. At this stage the EP has four options:

(a) it may take no action
(b) it may adopt the common position
(c) it may amend the common position
(d) it may reject the common position

In order to adopt the common position the EP needs a simple majority, whereas for amending or rejecting it an absolute majority is required. In the case of (a) or (b) the Council may proceed to enact the proposal as defined in the common position. In the case of (d) the Council needs a unanimous decision to reinstate the common position. In the case of (c) the European Commission intervenes by examining its initial proposal, taking into consideration the EP's views and referring the new proposal to the Council, attaching to it all the EP's amendments. The Council may now do one of the following:

(i) it may amend the new proposal by a unanimous vote
(ii) it may adopt any EP amendments which the European Commission has not included in its proposals
(iii) it may adopt and enact the new proposal by QMV, or
(iv) it may fail to reach a decision within a certain deadline, in which case the proposal is abandoned

The cooperation procedure represented a shifting of power in favour of the EP, which could now influence legislation during a two-reading legislative procedure. Moreover, it opened the way for a further increase of the EP authority by the introduction of the co-decision procedure by the Maastricht Treaty. The cooperation procedure applies to areas such as the European Social Fund (ESF), social policy, development policy, certain actions in the environment policy, and certain rules governing international transport and transport safety. (See also, Common Position, Council of the EU, EP).

COREPER, see **COMMITTEE OF PERMANENT REPRESENTATIVES**

COSTA V. ENEL, see p. 155, n. 17

COUNCIL OF ECONOMIC AND FINANCE MINISTERS, see **ECOFIN COUNCIL**

COUNCIL OF EUROPE (CE). A post-war institution, established in 1949, the CE stemmed from the Brussels Treaty of 1948. It should not be confused either with the European Council or with the Council of the EU. The last two are European Community institutions, while the Council of Europe is not.

Much of its work is concerned with culture, education, human rights, environmental issues and the struggle against drugs. However, the CE is an intergovernmental organisation, and thus its decisions cannot be enforced on the states concerned. When the Committee of Ministers reaches a consensus this may take the form of a convention, which individual member states are invited to sign. Sometimes consensus does not reach the form of a convention, but is formalized as a charter or code. There have been about 150 conventions, charters or codes. The European Court of Human Rights as the judicial body of the CE has jurisdiction over a number of issues relating to human rights violations; it is based in Strasbourg. The activities of the CE in the field of human rights has been steadily increasing as a result of both the entry of new members to the Council and the growth in its areas of responsibility, such as the European Social Charter which came under its auspices in 1961.

In addition, there have been three main areas where the CE has played an important role. Firstly, its European Convention on Human Rights of 1950 marked a significant progress in this field. Secondly, it acted as a forum where non-European community members could follow developments of European integration. Thirdly, membership of the CE has gradually come to be regarded as proof that a country is democratic; it continues to play this role in relation to those countries of central and eastern Europe that consider membership in the CE as a first step towards their integration within the EU.

Currently, membership of the CE has shifted to the East with the admission of the newly formed Republics of Central and Eastern Europe. Its members include Denmark, Sweden, Norway, Germany, Italy, Spain, Portugal, Greece, UK, Ireland, Luxembourg, France, The Netherlands, Belgium, Iceland, Turkey, Austria, Cyprus, Switzerland, Malta, Liechtenstein, San Marino, Finland, Hungary, the Czech Republic, Slovakia, Albania, Andorra, Bulgaria, Estonia, Latvia, Lithuania, the Former Yugoslav Republic of Macedonia (FYROM), Moldova, Poland, Romania, Slovenia and Russia. The 'special guests' status is currently held by Croatia and Belarus, while Ukraine and

Bosnia are considering lodging applications. Yugoslavia is, at present, suspended. (See also, Council of the EU, European Council, European Social Charter, Human Rights; Appendix 17).

COUNCIL OF THE EUROPEAN UNION. Widely known as the Council of Ministers, it is the main intergovernmental institution of the European Community consisting of representatives of each member state at ministerial level. As a result, there are more than 20 'councils' named after the subject under discussion: Economic and Finance Ministers meet as the Ecofin Council, foreign affairs ministers as the General Affairs Council, agricultural ministers as the Agriculture Council, and so on.

The Council of Ministers is the principal EU legislative body, though after the introduction of the Single European Act (SEA) it increasingly shares this role with the European Parliament (EP). Normally, the Council acts on proposals forwarded to it by the Commission, after consultation with the EP and the Economic and Social Committee (ESC). However, the Council alone is the decision-making body, with the exception of decisions taken under the co-decision procedure, where the EP has the right to veto a decision of the Council by absolute majority. In fact, under the co-decision procedure the Council co-decides/co-legislates with the EP, and all final decisions are taken in the name of both institutions. The EP also has the power to frustrate the Council, with reference to the Budget. Communication between the two is essential because of the increasing share of the EP in the decision making process.

The responsibility of the Council extends to taking decisions and conferring power on the Commission to act, to coordinate member states' economic policies and implement the directions given by the European Council. In addition, the Council is responsible, more than any other EU institutions, for the Common Foreign and Security Policy (CFSP) and Justice and Home Affairs (JHA).

The Council consists of 15 ministers, one from each member state. It has, however, no fixed membership given the variety of issues and broad range of policies it has to deal with. Its headquarters are in Brussels, but certain meetings take place in Luxembourg. One member state at a time holds the presidency for a six-month term of office: January to July, July to December. The immediate past, present and future presidencies are as follows: 1998: UK, Austria; 1999: Germany, Finland; 2000: Portugal, France; 2001: Sweden, Belgium; 2002: Spain, Denmark. Rotation of the presidency is in alphabetical order, based on the name of each member state according to the language of that country. The Presidency's role has become increasingly important in that the holder of the office coordinates and presides over all meetings of the Council's business. The President puts forward acceptable compromises concerning problems submitted to the Council, seeks to ensure consistency and continuity in decision-taking process and represents the Council in its dealings with outside bodies.

Since 'Councils' meet to discuss a broad range of legislation, the necessity of safeguards to ensure coherence and continuity in decision-making is paramount. For this reason the Council's Committee of Permanent Representatives (COREPER) was created. A variety of other committees, such as the Special Committee on Agriculture, Energy Committee, Committee on Education, consisting mainly of national officials and serviced by Council administrators, assist the work of the Council. More specialized work is carried out by a large number of working parties or groups dealing with detailed analysis of formally tabled Commission proposals for Council, and EP and Council legislation; normally, working parties are of an *ad hoc* nature. The Council Secretariat, on the other hand, consisting of around 2,300 staff, provides administrative support for the work of the Council, extending from the ministerial level to the working parties.

Decisions in the Council, as prescribed in the Treaty of Rome and later Treaties, are taken in three ways: unanimity, qualified majority (QMV) and simple majority. Unanimity and qualified majority are based on a weighted voting system: France, Germany, Italy, UK 10 votes each; Spain 8 votes; Belgium, Greece, The Netherlands, Portugal 5 votes each; Austria, Sweden 4 votes each; Denmark, Ireland, Finland 3 votes each; Luxembourg 2 votes.

The weightings in the Council, as distributed at the moment, represent a serious problem, mainly because population size does not correlate with voting strength; for instance, Luxembourg has 1 vote for every 200,000 people, whereas Germany has 1 vote for every 8 million. This arrangement was established in order to prevent large states becoming dominant at the expense of small countries. However, as the number of small countries admitted to the EU increases, the large states find themselves in a position of being under-represented. The issue remains a matter of contention between member states, and this state of affairs could become worse with the forthcoming enlargement.

Unanimity had been the most common decision-making procedure in the Council of Ministers up to the SEA of 1987 and the Maastricht Treaty of 1992. The Luxembourg (1966) compromise had consolidated unanimity by giving member states the right to veto matters considered of national importance. The SEA narrowed the areas requiring unanimity and extended QMV in the Council, particularly in areas related to the dismantling of barriers, and the free movement of goods, persons, services and capital. The Maastricht Treaty, on the other hand, though it did not entirely substitute QMV for unanimity, provided for qualified majority voting in most areas that were new or subject to more extensive provisions.

The Council still has to decide unanimously on matters concerning CFSP, and in most areas of Justice and Home Affairs, particularly in the fields of entry and residence conditions of non-EU citizens, illegal immigration, political asylum, judicial and home affairs cooperation, control of drug trafficking, industrial policy, culture, research, technological and environmental development, social security, representation of enterprises, harmonization of direct taxes, conditions of employment for non-EU employees.

QMV is now required in most fields and most policy areas, including free movement of goods, capital and people, rights of non-salaried employees, aid to less developed regions of the EU, transport, health and security of workers, competition, agriculture, social funds, Economic and Monetary Union (EMU), entry visas to the EU, aid to developing countries, consumer protection, gender equality, implementation of measures in a field already agreed as subject of common action. The extension of QMV to other areas of activities was one of the main recommendations of the report of the Reflection Group.

Out of a total number of 87 votes, 62 votes, coming from at least 10 member states, are required for a QMV, making 26 votes sufficient for a blocking minority. Prior to the fourth enlargement, 23 votes out of 76 were sufficient to allow for continuation of debate on legislation for a 'reasonable period'. Before voting the Council seeks to achieve the broadest possible consensus, so that most of legislation is adopted by the largest possible majority.

Generally, decisions adopted by qualified majority vote in the Council must be submitted to the European Parliament for approval. Two options emerge from this process: firstly, the EP may reject the Council's common position in which case the Council must reach unanimity in the second reading; secondly, the EP may suggest amendments to the Council's common position. In such a case the European Commission has to re-examine the proposal and send it back to the Council.

Simple majority is used for deciding minor procedural matters and, within the context of Common Commercial Policy (CCP), dumping and anti-subsidy tariffs. Under this procedure, each member state carries one vote, and thus 8 votes out of the 15 are required for a majority.

There has been a frequent debate concerning the character and efficiency of the Council. Although it is the primary legislative body of the EU, the Council used to convene *in camera* without obligation to publish agendas, minutes and voting records. In 1993, the Council, the Commission and the EP signed an Inter-institutional Declaration on Democracy, Transparency and Subsidiarity. However, the Declaration also states that institutions that reach decisions by majority voting can refuse to disclose information. This provision has often been used by the Council to withhold official records of its meetings. With regard to the Council's efficiency, it has been argued that the rotating presidency does not guarantee policy continuity, despite the 'Troika' arrangement, i.e. discussion meetings of the president in office, the previous and the future ones. With the forthcoming enlargement a number of changes may be imminent. (See also, Co-decision, CFSP, Common Position, COREPER, Ecofin Council, European Commission, EP, Intergovermentalism, JHA, Luxembourg Compromise, Majority Voting, Veto).

COUNCIL OF MINISTERS, see **COUNCIL OF THE EUROPEAN UNION**

COURT OF AUDITORS (COA). A European Community institution whose function is to carry out: (i) the external audit of the finances of the European Community and (ii) the submission of observations and opinions on a number of financial issues.

(i) The task of the external audit of the revenue and expenditure of the Community is the examination of the documentation presented by the internal audit, but also the carrying out of independent examinations before and after the submission of the internal audit report. The previous year's report is submitted to the COA, European Parliament (EP) and the Council of Ministers, at the latest by 1 June of the following year. By undertaking an independent investigation, the COA functions as an additional safeguard against abuse of financial arrangements relating to EU policies, including questions of fraud and waste, and the adequacy of existing internal procedures. With its annual report, submitted to the Community's other institutions by 30 November at the latest, the COA assists the Council and the EP in granting discharge to the Commission in respect of a proper implementation of the Budget of the previous year.

(ii) The COA's other important activity is to submit its observations and opinions on a number of financial issues. These are submitted either: (a) when a European Community institution requests a report or the COA decides, by itself, to express its views on some specific aspect of the audit, or (b) when an EU institution asks the COA to give its opinion on a specific financial matter, e.g. concerning the possible cost of implementing some new policy under discussion, or (c) when the Council decides to introduce a new financial regulation, it must seek the opinion of the COA before reaching a decision.

The COA is located in Luxembourg and is composed of 15 members appointed for a six-year term of office by unanimous decision of the Council of Ministers after consultation with the EP. Members of the Court elect a president for a renewable three-year term of office. The COA adopts its decisions by a majority vote. Each member, however, has direct responsibility for the audit of certain sectors of the Community's activities.

The COA came into being in 1977, as a result of the 1975 Treaty, which amended certain financial provisions of the previous Treaties and replaced the European Community's existing audit bodies, namely the Audit Board of the European Economic Community (EEC) and European Atomic Energy Community (EURATOM), and the European Coal and Steel Community (ECSC) Auditor. The COA was later institutionalized fully by the Maastricht Treaty, and was given the additional responsibility of providing the EP and the Council of Ministers with a statement of assurance concerning the reliability of the accounts and the legality of the various transactions. (See also, Discharge Procedure, European Commission, External Audit, Internal Audit).

COURT OF FIRST INSTANCE (CFI). It was established in 1989, at the request of the Court of Justice, by a decision of the European Council, exercising powers conferred upon it by the Single European Act (SEA). Initially, the jurisdiction of the CFI extended to three areas: disputes between the Community and its staff; actions brought against the Commission under the European Coal and Steel Community (ECSC); and certain cases which fall under competition rules.

Later on, in 1993 and 1994, its jurisdiction was further extended, by a decision of the Council, to hear and determine, with the exception of preliminary rulings, all actions brought to it by natural or legal persons. Appeal against the decisions of the CFI may be made to the Court of Justice on points of law.

The CFI consists of 15 judges, appointed by common accord of the member states for a renewable term of six years. The judges elect a president for a three-year term. This Court sits in Luxembourg. (See also, Court of Justice).

COURT OF JUSTICE OF THE EUROPEAN COMMUNITIES. The Court of Justice is the Community's judicial institution, established in 1951 by the Treaty of Paris initially as the Court of the European Coal and Steel Community (ECSC). The Court sits in Luxembourg and has jurisdiction over a variety of judicial matters. Two types of cases can be brought before the Court:

1. Direct rulings may be brought before the Court by the European Commission, by other Community institutions or by a member state. These may take the following forms:

- Firstly, failure of a member state to fulfil its obligations under a Treaty. Most of the time, such cases are taken to the Court by the Commission rather than by another member state, since such matters have to be referred to the Commission in the first instance and member states are reluctant to come to a direct public confrontation with one another.

- Secondly, application for annulment of the legality of acts adopted by the Council of Ministers or the Commission, and certain acts of the European Parliament (EP). These acts may be declared null and void on the grounds of lack of competence, misuse of powers, infringement of essential procedural requirements of a Treaty or a rule relating to its application. Rulings under this provision have served as useful underpinnings for the commercial and competition policies.

- Thirdly, failure of the Commission, the Council of Ministers, or the EP to act on a matter provided by the Treaties, allows a member state or a Community institution, to bring a case before the Court. One of the widely known cases is the EP's action against the Commission for failure to act with regard to the Common Transport Policy (CTP).

- Finally, the Court has the exclusive jurisdiction to take action to establish liability against the institutions and the employees of the Community if they have caused damage in the performance of their duties. This, however, applies only to cases of non-contractual liability[5]. The Community was taken to Court mostly in relation to the

---

[5] Non-contractual liability refers to liabilities that are not subject to contract. The Community shall make good any damage caused by its institutions or by its servants in the performance of their duties. The personal liability of the Community employees shall be governed by the provision laid down in their

Common Agricultural Policy (CAP), but also customs unions, free movement of goods, competition rules and workers' rights. As a result, the Court became increasingly unwilling to deal with non-contractual liability cases, which presently are dealt with in national courts.

2. Preliminary rulings may be requested by courts or tribunals in the member states when they seek an interpretation of Community law in order to be able to give judgement. Preliminary rulings ensure that national laws make the 'right' legal judgements; they promote a uniform interpretation and implementation of Community law.

The Maastricht Treaty has further enlarged the authority of the Court to the extent of having the power to impose fines on member states, which failed to fulfil a Treaty obligation, or to comply with its rulings. The European Central Bank has also been brought under its jurisdiction.

The Court operates on the basis of three fundamental principles:

a. *Direct effect*: national courts have to recognize and enforce the rulings of the Court. In case of conflict with national law, the national law has to give way to the ruling of the Court. This principle applies to most treaty provisions and secondary legislation.

b. *Direct applicability*: this principle is often used interchangeably with the Direct effect; but it mainly refers to regulations, which, unlike other forms of secondary legislation, are directly applicable without the need of becoming national law through voting in the national parliaments.

c. *Primacy*: Community law cannot be overridden by domestic legal provisions. Furthermore, the Court of Justice can declare null and void any legal instrument adopted by European Community institutions which are incompatible with Community law.

The Court of Justice is composed of 15 judges and 9 advocates-general appointed by common accord of the member states for a renewable term of six years. The President of the Court is elected by the judges from among their number for a renewable term of three years. The judges' independence must be guaranteed and they must qualify for the highest judicial offices in their respective countries. There is no provision in any treaty as to the nationality of the participants, although in practice, there is one from each country. The advocates-general assist the Court by making a preliminary assessment

Staff Regulation on the conditions of employment applicable to them. Conversely, contractual liabilities of the Community shall be governed by the law applicable to the contract in question.

of any case that is coming before the Court. The Court may or may not follow their assessment.

The Court of Justice, though powerful, has certain constraints which limit its power. Its authority does not extend to all aspects of the EU, but only to those defined by the Treaties; similarly, it does not extend to all judicial matters, for instance criminal law, and has no jurisdiction over the European Council and the two intergovernmental pillars, the Common Foreign and Security Policy (CFSP) and Justice and Home Affairs (JHA), with the exception of certain aspects of JHA relating to the interpretation of conventions. (See also, Community Law, Direct Applicability, Direct Effect, Legislation, Primacy).

CROCODILE CLUB. Consisting of members of the European Parliament (EP) and led by Altiero Spinelli (an Italian resistance leader, national and European parliamentarian, a European Commissioner and an ardent federalist) the Club was established in 1980. It worked in close cooperation with the Kangaroo group and sought to accelerate the integration process. However, the Club had radical federalist ambitions, more advanced than the liberalization of the internal market sought by the Kangaroo group. The Club was especially active in the 1980s and contributed significantly to the EP proposal of the Draft Treaty establishing the European Union (DTEU). (See also, Kangaroo Group, DTEU, SEM).

CULTURAL POLICY. This policy aims at fostering national traditions within the Community and at the same time reinforcing a sense of a European identity. Only a very small percentage of the Community Budget is allocated to financing cultural programmes, such as KALEIDOSCOPE, which supports cultural events involving at least three member states; RAPHAEL, a cultural heritage programme; and MEDIA, which promotes a more integrated European audio-visual industry. So far, most of the EU's efforts have concentrated on the film and television industry, primarily because of the development of electronic media.

On the whole, the EU's contribution to the sphere of cultural policy has been very limited and unsystematic, nevertheless four main areas of activity can be discerned in the context of cultural policy. Firstly, free trade in cultural goods, involving lifting of barriers to artists exporting their talents and their products to another European country; tax-free export of tools belonging to an artist's trade; free-export of works of art, except of those strictly defined 'national art treasures'.

Secondly, the improvement of conditions for artists, including the harmonization of national laws governing copyright to creative artists; public subsidies; resale rights guaranteeing to artists a percentage every time their work is sold; limited funds to support a number of schemes for training young artists.

Thirdly, the widening of the audience with the introduction of two well known activities, the European Cultural Months and the European Culture City, sometimes taking place outside the EU. Cultural months are held in several European cities, for instance, Cracow in 1992, Graz in 1993, Budapest in 1994, Nicosia in 1995, St. Petersburg in 1996, Ljubljana in 1997, Linz, Valetta in 1998, Plovdiv in 1999. The European Culture City is designated each year by the European Commission, and involves a variety of events which were inaugurated in 1985 with Athens as the first European Culture City. More recent designated cities were Luxembourg in 1995, Copenhagen in 1996, Thessaloniki in 1997, Stockholm in 1998 and Weimar in 1999. A European Film Festival held in a different city each year has also been introduced.

Lastly, the conservation of the Community's architectural heritage has been promoted by funds made available, either through grants or loans, for the conservation of monuments of the Community or buildings in underdeveloped regions; starting in 1982 this policy benefited more than 30 archaeological sites. (See also, Media Policy).

CUSTOMS UNION. A partial form of economic integration, the customs union is a trade agreement, whereby a group of countries agree on free trade among themselves, while imposing a common set of tariffs to imports from the rest of the world.

One of the best-known customs union is the German Zollverein established in 1834, which is considered as the beginnings of German unification. Similarly, the Treaty of Rome established a customs union which prohibited any duties, tariffs and quotas among the Six, while it imposed common tariffs to third parties. This customs union led to further economic integration, taking the form of a common market which allows for free movement of capital, labour and persons as well as for enterprises to move unhindered between the participants. Its success led to a complete economic union providing for unification of monetary and fiscal policies, which in turn reinforced the tendencies for political integration.

In contrast to a customs union, a free trade area involves prohibition of duties, tariffs, etc. only among those signing the free-trade-area agreement, while each signatory retains the right to make individual arrangements with third parties. The European Free Trade Association (EFTA) is an example of such a form of economic integration. (See also, EEC, EFTA, NAFTA).

D

DAVIGNON PLAN. Issued in 1980, the Davignon Plan was meant to resolve the severe crisis in the Community's declining steel industry. Production quotas along with capacity reductions and protectionist measures were introduced in an effort to restructure the industry. The Plan, for the first time in the history of the Treaty of the European Coal and Steel Community (ECSC), put into effect Article 58 allowing the European Commission to impose quotas on steel production.

By the end of 1993, the Council of Ministers authorised state allowances to six steel making companies of four countries, which had agreed to implement reductions in production capacity. (See also, ECSC).

DAVIGNON REPORT. This report recommended that member states should consult each other on foreign policy matters, but within an intergovernmental framework. In what became known as the Davignon Procedure, it was proposed that the foreign ministers should meet twice annually and that a Political Committee, consisting of senior foreign ministry officials, should meet at least four times a year to undertake work delegated to them by foreign ministers.

The report was drawn up by a committee founded under a decision of The Hague European Council summit of 1969, presided over by the Belgian Foreign Minister Viscount Etienne Davignon, later a European Commissioner, and was accepted by the Six in 1970. (See also, CFSP, EPC).

DECISIONS, see **LEGISLATION**

DELORS, JACQUES (b. 1925). Born in Paris, Delors was engaged in French politics before his involvement in Europe, and under President Mitterrand was the Economic and Finance Minister (1981-84). A moderate socialist and a federalist, Delors was the longest serving president of the European Commission, from 1985 to 1994. Arguably the most controversial of the Commission's presidents, he is associated with at least four key achievements of his presidency: the completion of the Single European Market (SEM), the plan for Economic and Monetary Union (EMU), the addition of a social dimension in European politics and the signing of the Maastricht Treaty.

DELORS PACKAGES I & II. During the 1980s the Community Budget was regularly in deficit due to spending on common policies in excess of the income accrued from the three 'own resources'. The implementation in 1986 of the 1984 decision to increase the Value-added Tax (VAT) ceiling to 1.4 per cent provided little relief to the budgetary problems, as most of this increase was absorbed by the additional spending demanded by the accession of Portugal and Spain. The implementation of the Single European Market (SEM) programme involved a further reduction in revenues, which originated from customs duties and agricultural levies, while the Single European Act (SEA) presupposed higher spending as it introduced new areas of activity, such as economic and social cohesion, research and technological development and environment policy. These successive budgetary problems necessitated a structural reform in the Community's financial arrangements.

In 1988 the European Commission adopted the so-called Delors Package I, named after Jaques Delors. The principal element of the package was that it introduced the fourth source of revenues. This consisted of member states' direct contributions determined by their respective individual share of the total GNP of the Community. In addition, a firmer budgetary control was initiated; reform and stricter control over the Common Agricultural Policy (CAP) was introduced in order to release funds for other policy areas. These measures made available substantial sums, which more than doubled the amount allocated to structural funds in real terms over the period 1989-92. Delors Package I had a five year financial perspective, from 1987 to 1992, the year of the completion of the internal market.

The so-called Delors Package II, entitled the *Means to Match our Ambitions*, followed in 1992 and covered expenditure for the next five years. This second package promoted the goals of the previous plan and built upon its achievements. A significant increase in funding was proposed in order to meet the commitments agreed at Maastricht. It was expected that the Budget would grow by almost one third, from 66.5 million ECUs in 1992 to 87.6 million in 1997. In addition, a further change in the balance of European Community policies was introduced in order to ensure that the Maastricht Treaty objective of further integration could be achieved. In this context, several policies, such as the structural funds, contributing towards economic and social cohesion, continued to be assigned more funding. The question of Europe's industrial competitiveness in global markets was specifically addressed and three main areas of activity related to it were laid down: research and development, vocational training, development of Trans-European Networks (TENs) and environmental policies. Delors Package II also advocated an increase in the resources allocated to external policies; specifically it stressed the need for aid given to Eastern Europe and the Mediterranean countries of Africa, and focused on the ability of the Community to respond speedily to emergencies and to be in a position to provide humanitarian aid.

The Delors Packages represented a shift in policy priorities, and on the whole inaugurated a steady commitment of the Community towards the poorer member states. The reaction of member states was mixed as there were objections from the richer members concerning the financial commitment in this respect. Both packages, however, were eventually adopted by the European Council, though with some alterations. The first package was adopted by the Brussels European Council of February 1988 which agreed on the 'own resources' proposals, the doubling of structural funds over six years, capping the level of CAP expenditure and an overall Budget increase no more than 1.2 per cent of Community GDP by 1992. The second package was adopted by the Edinburgh European Council of December 1992 which agreed on a less ambitious increase of 1.27 per cent of GNP to be spread over seven years, from 1993 to 1999. This meant that an overall increase in the Budget was less than half of that originally proposed by Delors Package II. Commitments to restrict CAP expenditure and increase the structural funds were re-affirmed. (See also, Budget, CAP, Environment Policy, Industrial Policy, Own Resources, Research and Development, SEM, Structural Funds, TENs).

DELORS REPORT. The name of a document issued in April 1989 by a committee, consisting of the governors of the central banks of member states and three independent economists, chaired by Jacques Delors. The Report made recommendations on the Economic and Monetary Union (EMU), including a three-stage approach, the setting up of the European Central Bank (ECB), the European System of Central Banks (ESCB) and the European Monetary Institute (EMI). It also advocated the need for fixing exchange rates irrevocably, and a greater degree of convergence with regard to the economies of member states in order to operate the EMU successfully. In addition, it cleared the way for the establishment of the 1990-91 IGC on EMU which accepted most of its proposals. The report was discussed by the European Council meeting in Madrid in June 1989 where it provoked a rigorous debate focusing mainly on the question of national sovereignty. Most of its recommendations, however, though with a number of alterations, were included in the Maastricht Treaty. (See also, ECB, EMI, EMS, EMU, Maastricht Treaty, Sovereignty).

DEMOCRATIC DEFICIT. This term is historically associated with lack of controls and accountability in decision-making processes. In the literature of the Community, it specifically refers to the powers transferred from national to Community level, and the degree to which these powers remain subject to the democratic accountability existing at national level. Power to initiate policies at European level has always resided with an unelected Commission, while legislative powers are held by the Council. To a large extent this remains the position. However, with the introduction of the cooperation and co-decision procedures, by the Single European Act (SEA) and the Maastricht Treaty respectively, the EP, the only elected body, was given powers to amend and veto certain types of legislation.

The different nature of democratic representation in member states (different electoral systems, different political cultures, etc.), and the differing approaches of the various governing parties influence their conception of integration and the way in which they address the issue of democratic deficit. Related, but of a different substance, is the debate concerning democratic deficit at Council level, which currently focuses on the shortcomings of qualified majority voting (QMV), as it has come largely to replace unanimous voting, and therefore has curbed the right of national governments to veto certain decisions. (See also, Sovereignty, Veto, Wider *v.* Deeper Integration).

DEVELOPMENT AID. Administered by DG VIII, development aid has been financed by the Community Budget, the European Development Fund (EDF) and the European Investment Bank (EIB), and is distributed in several ways. Firstly, aid is provided to countries that have signed a special agreement with the EU in the form of trade, industrial and technical assistance. This category includes ACP, Asian, Latin American, Maghreb and Mashreq states. Secondly, aid is provided in the form of food or emergency assistance in cases of severe food shortage or natural disasters. African and Asian countries primarily belong to this category. But following the transformation in central and eastern Europe, aid falling under this category has been directed to these countries too.

The amount of EU development aid is substantial, and as a proportion of GNP is higher than that donated by either the USA or Japan. ACP countries are the largest collective recipient of aid, drawn from the EDF and the EIB. The largest single recipient of EU aid is India.

Development aid has mutual benefits for both donor and recipient countries. Developing countries are assisted to confront emergency situations and undoubtedly they receive a boost to their economies, whereas the EU reduces food surpluses and benefits the European companies, which win most of the contracts awarded under these programmes. (See also, Budget, EDF, EIB, Lomé Convention).

DEVELOPMENT POLICY. Mentioned for the first time in the Treaty of Rome, this policy was specified by the Maastricht Treaty with the addition of a new Title called Development Cooperation. Historical reasons (such as close ties existing between some Community countries and their former colonial possessions) seem to have been the most obvious incentive for the engagement of the EU in development policies. Both recipients and providers have profited from these policies. Third World countries receive some 30% of the EU's exports, while the EU is dependent on these countries for important raw materials (e.g. oil, rubber, uranium, etc.).

Among other things, the article on Development Cooperation in the Maastricht Treaty states that Community policy in this sphere shall be complementary to the policies pursued by the member states; it shall foster sustainable economic and social development, encourage the smooth and gradual integration of developing countries into world economy and campaign against poverty. Also it shall contribute towards the more general objectives of developing and consolidating democracy, and upholding human rights and fundamental freedoms.

EU aid to Third World countries is, presently, more than the combined aid of USA and Japan. The direct EU aid, together with the aid given by its member states individually, represents more than two-fifths of aid given to developing nations world wide. Assistance is usually available in the form of Generalized System of Preferences (GSP), food aid, and aid to non-governmental organizations (NGOs). Additional assistance is also provided to some developing countries that are in a special relationship with the EU, in the form of trade, industrial, and technical agreements. The Lomé Convention is one of the most important agreements of this kind. Under this convention, aid is allocated to the STABEX and SYSMIN schemes, which guarantee ACP countries against loss of export earnings.

Development is funded either by the European Development Fund (EDF), financed by special contributions from member states, or directly by the EU Budget. The latter accounts for some 5.5 per cent of the Budget and about half of this aid goes to non-ACP countries, and half to food aid purposes. The principal beneficiaries of the two funds are sub-Saharan Africa, receiving around 60 per cent (deriving mainly from the EDF), followed by South Asia and Latin America, and the Caribbean receiving 10 per cent each.

It should be noted that the EU does not enjoy exclusive competence in the development field and its role is complementary to the policies of the member states. The EU's own financial aid represents only about 15 per cent of the combined efforts of the member states. It is only the trade aspects of the development policy that the EU is entirely responsible for.

In terms of decision-making, as in other EU policies, the European Commission proposes, negotiates and implements the decision that the Council of Ministers has taken with regard to development policy. The European Parliament (EP) has limited powers to influence development policy as the EDF, the main source of finance for the EU's development policy, lies outside the Community Budget. The EP has constantly sought to incorporate the EDF in the Budget, but member states reject these proposals, being determined to retain their own policies in relation to aid to Third World countries. In June 1995 the Council of Ministers adopted a resolution on complementation, and more recently the principle of 'complementarity' between the individual member states and EU policies has been promoted further. (See also, Budget, EDF, GSP, Lomé Convention, STABEX, SYSMIN).

DIRECT APPLICABILITY. One of the principles whereby Community law is binding within member states without the need for any national legislation. Amongst various types of legal acts only regulations are always directly applicable; the rest have to satisfy certain conditions before direct applicability can be exercised. (See also, Community Law, Court of Justice, Direct Effect, Legislation, Primacy).

DIRECT EFFECT. The term refers to the principle according to which certain provisions of Community law may confer rights or impose obligations on individuals; national courts are legally bound to recognize and enforce such rights and obligations. Since 1963, when the principle was established with the *Van Gend & Loos case* (Case 26/62)[6], the Court of Justice has gradually widened its scope in order

---

[6] *Van Gend & Loos* claimed before the Dutch courts the reimbursement of a sum resulting from the increase in duties imposed on the chemical product of unreaformaldehyde they had imported to The Netherlands from West Germany. The increase was claimed to be incompatible with Article 12 of the Treaty of Rome, which ensured free movement of goods between member states. The Dutch courts referred the case to the European Court of Justice for

to make the principle applicable to secondary legislation. However, the Court has ruled out certain spheres of activity, such as free movement of capital, or cases in which discretion is explicitly granted to the addressee. Together with primacy, direct effect is one of the fundamental principles of Community law. (See also, Community Law, Court of Justice, Direct Applicability, Legislation, Primacy).

DIRECTIVES, see **LEGISLATION**

DIRECTORATE-GENERAL (DG). One of the fundamental administrative units of the European Commission. Each DG is responsible for a particular area of policy and is headed by a Director-General who is responsible to the appropriate European Commissioner or Commissioners. DGs vary in size and internal organisation. Currently, there are 24 DGs. In addition to these, there are a number of other special units and services, such as the Joint Interpretation and Conference Service, the Consumer Policy Service, the Security Office, which greatly help with the workload in the European Commission. (See also, European Commission).

DISCHARGE PROCEDURE. This is the procedure whereby the European Parliament (EP), acting on the recommendations of the Council of Ministers and the Court of Auditors (COA), accepts the annual report on the implementation of the Budget of the Community, submitted by the European Commission. The approval of the report by the EP is known as 'granting the discharge'. The discharge procedure is one of the most important powers of the EP in regard to the Budget. However, it has only been used once in 1984, when the EP refused to grant discharge with respect to the 1982 accounts. (See also, COA, European Commission, EP).

DOOGE COMMITTEE. Set up by the European Council meeting in Fontainebleau in June 1984, the Committee aimed at making suggestions for the improvement of European cooperation. This was an *ad hoc* committee, chaired by the Irish Senator James Dooge. In its final report presented in March 1985, the Committee endorsed the idea of a single market and the eventual formation of the European Union (EU); it suggested a few practical measures for the improvement of European Political Cooperation (EPC). It has to be noted that the

a preliminary ruling. The Court of Justice ruled that Community law confers rights and imposes obligations upon individuals.

Committee's first action was to reject the European Parliament's (EP) Draft Treaty establishing the European Union as being too open-ended and too advanced a document, which would perhaps alter the character of the Community.

In the institutional sphere the Committee adopted a more radical stand as it suggested: a) the augmentation of the powers of the EP through the introduction of the co-decision procedure, the approval by the EP of Accession Treaties and Association Agreements, and the sharing of responsibility in decision-making on revenues; b) the extension of majority voting in the Council of Ministers and the obligation of the presidency to put a matter to vote within 30 days at the request of at least three member states or the Commission; c) the number of Commissioners to be reduced to one for each member state; and d) the calling of an Intergovernmental Conference (IGC) to negotiate a draft for an EU Treaty.

The Danish and the Greek sides expressed several reservations about the Committee's proposals, but the rest of the European Community favoured further institutional reforms. Many of its proposals were later embodied in the Single European Act (SEA) and the Maastricht Treaty. (See also, Assent and Co-decision Procedures, Council of the EU, DTEU, EP, EPC, EU, SEM).

DRAFT TREATY ESTABLISHING THE EUROPEAN UNION (DTEU). Issued by the European Parliament (EP) in 1984, the document proposed a radical revision of the European Community structures. Its recommendations focused on a significant increase of the powers of the supranational institutions. This document was the Parliament's main contribution to the negotiations resulting in the Single European Act (SEA), although its goals were more ambitious than what was finally achieved.

The DTEU was primarily the work of Altiero Spinelli, leader of the Crocodile Club, who advocated the creation of a new European state composed of individual states that would cede their sovereignty to common democratic institutions. Such would be the democratic legitimacy of these institutions that national governments would have no objections to transferring powers to them. The document focused particularly on increasing the power of the EP. In addition, it proposed a broad expansion in the scope of Community activities.

The Treaty won a majority vote in the EP, but failed to gain wider support, as its provisions for a federalist political union went beyond anything likely to be accepted at the time. It served, however, as a focal point around which those advocating close political union could rally. The Draft Treaty establishing the EU was largely superseded by the Dooge Committee, which adopted the less ambitious task of establishing the internal market. (See also, Dooge Committee, EP, Intergovernmentalism, SEA).

DUBLIN ASYLUM CONVENTION. Signed in 1990, the Convention stipulates that requests for asylum should be examined by the member state, which first received them, unless there is good reason for the case to be handled by another member state. The Convention also empowers the authorities of member states with the right of exchanging information on asylum seekers. Under the Maastricht Treaty asylum questions fall within the jurisdiction of Justice and Home Affairs (JHA). (See also, JHA, Schengen Agreement).

DUMPING. As defined by the General Agreement on Tariffs and Trade (GATT), the term denotes the sale of certain products in international markets at prices lower than the production cost in the country of origin, or lower than the domestic sale price, or lower than the highest export price to any third country. Anti-dumping duties may be introduced with the intention of cancelling the effects of dumped imports if they cause material damage to the domestic industry of the importing country. (See also, CAP, GATT).

E

ECOFIN COUNCIL. Consisting of Economic and Finance Ministers of the member states of the European Community, the Ecofin Council meets on average once a month to discuss the macro-economic conditions in member states, to adopt legislation with regard to economic affairs of the member states and the EU, and to coordinate the EU's stance in relation to international institutions. Its responsibilities were enlarged by the Maastricht Treaty which provided for the Ecofin, in cooperation with the European Monetary Institute, to oversee the progress of member states towards Economic and Monetary Union (EMU). The Ecofin is the second most important assembly of the Council of Ministers, after the Foreign Affairs Council. (See also, Council of the EU, EMU).

ECONOMIC AND MONETARY UNION (EMU). It was seen as the means to a balanced and sustainable economic and social progress of the Community, which was to be achieved through a single monetary and exchange policy. Of paramount importance to the establishment of the EMU was the introduction of a single currency. The EMU, together with the European Political Union, was one of the dominant issues of the Maastricht Treaty. These were incorporated in the Treaty of Rome.

Paradoxically, the EMU, despite being one of the most ambitious goals of the Community, was not mentioned in any of the founding Treaties. It was as late as 1986 that reference was made for the first time in the Single European Act (SEA), which adopted the objectives of the 1969 European Council summit at The Hague. A more elaborate plan for EMU was put forward at the Intergovernmental Conference (IGC) on the EMU, decided to be convened by the Madrid European Council in 1989.

The EMU was planned to take effect in three stages:
Stage I began on 1 July 1990, prior to the signing of the Maastricht Treaty, by a decision of the Madrid European Council. Its aim was the convergence of economic performance of member states in order to make the establishment of fixed exchange rates possible. The conditions of Stage I were largely satisfied with the immediate abolition of restrictions on capital movement among member states, the introduction of closer coordination of economic policies, and the further promotion of cooperation between central banks. Most of the responsibility for achieving the objectives of Stage I was carried by the Exchange Rate Mechanism (ERM).

Stage II started on 1 January 1994. During this stage a determined effort was made to achieve a broad economic convergence. The European Monetary Institute was set up in Frankfurt to coordinate the member states' monetary policies, to encourage the use of the European Currency Unit (ECU), and to prepare the ground for entry into the final stage.

Stage III was scheduled to start on 1 January 1997 at the earliest, or on 1 January 1999 at the latest. This Stage could have started at the earliest date if the Council of Ministers had voted for it by qualified majority and if the majority of the member states had fulfilled the conditions for adoption of the single currency. Since neither of these preconditions was fulfilled, Stage III, irrespective of the number of states qualifying for entry, started on 1 January 1999. During Stage III the European Central Bank was set up, independent of the national governments, to oversee the monetary policies of the participating member states; the European System of Central Banks (ESCB) was created with the purpose of maintaining price stability, defining and implementing monetary policy; the exchange rates between the participating states were fixed almost irrevocably; and member states that did not qualify to enter Stage III of the EMU were excluded from the ECB and the ESCB. However, the Council after consultation with the European Parliament (EP) and with the advice of the Commission and the ECB may review their case every two years.

As the deadline for Stage III approached so did the fears and disagreements among member states. Denmark ruled out participation in the EMU, Britain reserved the right to opt out and did so, Sweden has chosen to remain outside for the time being, while Greece did not quite qualify yet. Increasingly, member states have been concerned with the question of a two-speed Europe as the emergence of a hard-core of member states seems to be an unavoidable reality. Moreover, there has been mounting resistance to the prospect of surrendering monetary powers to EU institutions, and especially to the ECB, which has the exclusive right to authorise the issue of Euro banknotes. The actual banknotes will be issued either by the ECB or the national central banks. Member states may issue coins subject to approval by the ECB of the volume of issue. These difficulties have been accompanied by a growing reluctance among national governments and interested parties to transfer part of their political power and sovereignty, privileges they have traditionally enjoyed, outside national borders. (See also, ECB, ECU, EMI, ERM, ESCB, Euro, Democratic Deficit, Maastricht Treaty; Appendix 13).

ECONOMIC AND SOCIAL COMMITTEE (ESC). The Treaty of Rome established the ESC with the aim of providing expert opinion to the European Commission and the Council of Ministers on certain legislative items, either at their own request, or the ESC's own initiative. It consists of 222 members drawn from a broad cross-section of the Community's economic and social interests, and of, roughly, equal numbers of employers, workers (being almost exclusively members of trade unions), and representatives of various interests (e.g. the professions, farmers, SMEs, consumer groups, public services, etc.). The number of representatives nominated to the ESC by each member state is as follows: France, Germany, Italy and the UK, 24 each; Spain 21; Belgium, Greece, The Netherlands, Portugal, Sweden, and Austria, 12 each; Denmark, Ireland, and Finland, 9 each; Luxembourg 6.

The ESC meets in Brussels, once a month; its representatives serve for a term of four years. The last term ended in September 1998. It is divided into 9 sections; it has a Secretariat of 500 employees and a Bureau of 30 members. Opinions are adopted by a simple majority vote during the monthly plenary sessions. Tom Jenkins is currently the President of the Committee.

Since its beginning, the Committee has delivered over 3000 opinions, which were published in the *Official Journal of the European Communities*. Given its well-qualified expertise, the ESC contributes directly to the growth of the single market as it constantly oversees its progress and points out its malfunctions. Twice a year, it organises a 'Single Market Forum' which brings together network correspondents in the member states to review developments.

Yet in recent times, there has been frequent questioning of the usefulness of the ESC, due mainly to new and, arguably, better ways of acquiring expert opinion and advice. To some the ESC may seem a remnant of French political ideas of cooperation between *social partners*. (See also, Comitology, Council of the EU, OJ, SEM).

ECU, see **EUROPEAN CURRENCY UNIT**

EDUCATION POLICY. Specified in the Maastricht Treaty, the education policy represents an effort of the Community to introduce a European policy in the field of education. It aims at creating a European cultural identity, while at the same time respecting the cultural and linguistic diversity of member states.

The European Commission has constantly sought to add a European dimension to the education systems of the member states. There have been around 2500 programmes promoting vocational training, inter-university cooperation and exchange of students, and learning of languages of member states. Progress has also been made with regard to the recognition of degrees and qualifications awarded after at least three years of study.

Since 1995, two major programmes, Leonardo and Socrates, came into effect replacing a number of more fragmented programmes dealing with education. For the period 1995-99, the combined budget for Leonardo and Socrates totalled ECUs 1,47 billion.

Despite the existence of the above programmes and the extension of its objectives beyond training, education policy still remains primarily the responsibility of national governments, both with regard to the teaching content and the organization of the educational system. The diversity of educational systems, the high cost of education, the subsidiarity principle are but a few of the reasons that presently limit the scope of the Community's education policy. (See also, Cultural Policy, Leonardo, Socrates, Subsidiarity).

ENERGY POLICY. The issues of energy production and consumption, which affect all sectors of the economy and social life in general, were considered of paramount importance by the founding members of the Community. Two of the original Treaties, the European Coal and Steel Community (ECSC) and EURATOM, were concerned with the coal and nuclear industries, respectively, while the European Economic Community (EEC) was allocated responsibility for oil, gas and electricity.

However, although the idea of a common market was originally based on the integration of coal and nuclear energy sectors, the Treaty of Rome made no reference to a common energy policy. Subsequent efforts, such as the 1964 Protocol Agreement on energy problems and the 1968 Commission Memorandum on the objectives of a common energy policy, failed to be adopted. Consequently, the Community is left with policies for particular energy sectors as opposed to a common energy policy.

Energy was not given a separate chapter in the Maastricht Treaty, despite the increasing significance of the energy sector in the process of European integration and the disruption caused by the sharp increase of oil prices in the 1970s. The European Community's energy dependency on external sources is around 50 per cent and it is estimated to reach 70 per cent by 2020.

The main obstacle to energy integration is that member states still prefer national solutions to common ones, largely because of the differing domestic energy resources, energy requirements, and the existence of the state owned industries in the sector. For instance, there is a long-standing dispute concerning nuclear energy which represents about a quarter of the EU's total energy production. Many members of the EU do not produce nuclear energy at all, while others, like Belgium and France produce as much as 90 and 80 per cent of total energy production, respectively. Coal also represents a problem in this respect as only the UK, France, Germany and Spain are coal producers, and so the idea of subsidising coal industries in these countries has met with opposition from other member states.

Nevertheless, a noticeable change in attitude has occurred in recent years. It has generally been acknowledged that the energy market should be liberalized and that an integrated network linking together national networks should be promoted. In this context the construction of a European system of gas pipelines and electricity interconnections has begun and been extended to countries of central and eastern Europe. The EU has introduced a number of energy programmes dealing with different aspects of energy policy, for example, SAVE promotes energy efficiency; ALTENER promotes renewable energy sources; THERMIE promotes the use of energy technology; JOULE promotes research on non-nuclear energy development. These programmes have linked energy policy to environmental problems. In addition, the 1991 European Energy Charter is an attempt to secure energy supplies sufficient for the needs of the Community, and provide funding to oil and gas producing European countries with the aim of modernising their energy infrastructure. (See also, ECSC, EURATOM, European Energy Charter, TENs).

ENLARGEMENT. This is the process whereby applicant countries join the European Community. Historically, the Community (originally comprising France, Germany, Italy, Belgium, The Netherlands and Luxembourg) has undergone four stages of enlargement beginning with Britain, Ireland and Denmark in 1973, followed by Greece in 1981, Spain and Portugal in 1986, and Austria, Finland and Sweden in 1995. The fifth enlargement of the EU is expected to take place in the year 2002, with the accession of the Czech Republic, Slovenia, Poland, Hungary, Estonia. However, many factors will determine the actual membership.

The procedure for new accessions is initiated by an application of the candidate country to the Council of Ministers, which has to act unanimously after consulting with the European Commission and after receiving the assent of the European Parliament (EP). If the Council decides to proceed, then negotiations can begin between the applicant country and the president of the Council and the Commission. Negotiations may conclude with a draft treaty, subject to the approval of the EP and the ratification by all the signatory member states. Then a formal signature of the accession treaty is required with a specific agreed date for when it comes into force, and if needs be, certain transitional stages are provided for various sectors of the economy.

Negotiations in some cases, however, may not lead to a draft treaty. In the case of Morocco, the application was rejected by the Council on the grounds of it being a non-European country. In the case of Turkey the Commission decided unfavourably on grounds of violation of human rights. Commitment to parliamentary democracy and respect of human rights were originally obstacles to the entry of Spain, Portugal and Greece to the Community.

Although theoretically there are no limits to the enlargement of the EU, there has been considerable scepticism with regard to the institutional, economic and political consequences that a further enlargement may entail. A restructuring of EU institutions seems to be necessary if more countries are to be accommodated. New members, on the other hand, are bound to introduce more diverse interests, and thus minimise the possibility of achieving a consensus, especially on matters such as Common Foreign and Security Policy (CFSP). Practical problems arise, concerning either the number of Commissioners, or the right of a country as small as Malta to veto a decision, or the increase in the number of MEPs and languages.

The differences in wealth between the existing and the future members of the EU, particularly those of central and eastern Europe, represent further challenges, especially if economic and social progress is to be promoted. Massive aid, through the structural funds, would have to be directed to those areas, in order that they may achieve sustainable economic development. This has given rise to considerable objections among the four poorest members of the Union, since it has been estimated that the new entries will receive more aid than the four member states currently receive via the structural funds. Objections have also been voiced by the sensitive industrial sectors which expect to receive community aid. Such enlargement promotes the so-called 'wider option' as opposed to a 'deeper' one. This very issue caused major disagreements in the debate concerning the enlargement of the Union.

In general, there are critical political problems that emanate from the differences in attitude and conditions of the candidate countries. Agreements and Treaties will be less likely to be applied without a plethora of derogations and exceptions, taking into consideration the peculiarities of the member states. Implementation of community law will also become more difficult. (See also, Accession, Agenda 2000, Assent Procedure, CFSP, Wider *v.* Deeper).

ENVIREG. A Community initiative concerned with the reduction of pollution and management of waste, as well as with the promotion of land-use planning and development of pollution control expertise. Envireg was directed towards the Mediterranean basin and other underdeveloped regions, and was operational for the period 1989-93, when it was replaced by LIFE. (See below, Environment Policy).

ENVIRONMENT POLICY. A policy, originally not part of the founding Treaties of the Community, was added to the Treaty of Rome by the Single European Act (SEA) under a new title on environmental policy. Interestingly, it was in connection with environmental policy that the subsidiarity principle was mentioned for the first time in the SEA, indicating that environmental issues are not the exclusive competence of the Community.

Despite the lack of a legal framework for environmental policies, the Community adopted several environment-friendly schemes in the form of Action Programmes since 1973. One of the most widely known Action Programmes established the principle, according to which, those found guilty of polluting the environment should pay a fine; the SEA gave it legal force.

In general, the objectives of the environmental policy, as mentioned in the SEA, have been preservation, protection and improvement of the quality of the environment, protection of human health, and prudent and rational utilization of natural resources. In 1990, according to the decision by the Council of Ministers, the European Environment Agency (EEA) was set up to assist the European Commission in this area.

The Maastricht Treaty further strengthened the Community's role in environment policy by promoting measures dealing with global environmental problems; fostering growth with respect to the environment; promoting integration of environmental requirements to other EU policies; providing for qualified majority voting (QMV) on most environmental issues, with the exception of town and country planning, land use, water resources, tax, and measures affecting member states' choice of energy resources which require unanimity; and establishing the Cohesion Fund, which finances environmental and transport projects in the four poorest member states.

The current Action Programme (1993-2000) marks a shift in emphasis in environment policy, for it stresses the idea of prevention rather than correction of environmental damage. The new approach requires, in the form of partnerships, the participation of a wider range of sectors, namely industry, agriculture, energy, tourism, transport, and the use of economic incentives to promote environmentally friendly policies. The Cohesion fund, LIFE and several other grants provide financial support for the implementation of Community environmental policies as well as technical assistance to non-member countries.

The European Commission seeks to ensure that environmental considerations are taken into account in all mainstream policies, particularly agriculture, transport and energy. To this end it has stipulated that each Directorate-General appoints an official in charge of this task. The DGs are also required to supply an annual report on the environmental dimensions of their policies. In general, any major project that could have an environmental impact is subjected to a 'strategic environmental impact assessment'. In 1992, an Information Directive came into force in order to improve public access to environmental information held by public bodies with responsibilities in this area.

In the context of international cooperation, the Community has agreed with the decisions taken at the Earth Summit in Rio de Janeiro in 1992. More specifically, with regard to greenhouse gases the Community has undertaken the task of stabilising the emissions of carbon dioxide at the 1990 level by the year 2000. To this end it adopted several projects promoting research and development in non-polluting, non-nuclear energy resources, as well as environment-friendly transport infrastructure. In addition, the Community proposed the introduction of an energy tax in an effort to alter the attitudes of energy users. However, following the UK opposition to the Community-wide character of this tax, its adoption was left to individual member states. (See also, Cohesion Fund, EEA, ENVIREG, LIFE, Subsidiarity, TENs).

ERASMUS. An action scheme for the Mobility of University Students. Under this scheme students can attend another University for periods of up to one year. University staff can also apply to teach or research at other Universities. The scheme was set up in 1987 and since 1995 it has become part of the Socrates programme. (See also, Education Policy, Socrates).

ESA, see **EUROPEAN SPACE AGENCY**

ESPRIT. A European Strategic programme for Research and Development, which provides help to firms, universities and institutes for projects dealing with advanced information technology. It came into effect in 1984. (See also, RTD).

ESRO, see EUROPEAN SPACE RESEARCH ORGANISATION

ETHNIC AND REGIONAL CONFLICTS AND THE ROLE OF THE EUROPEAN UNION. The post-war era experienced limited ethnic and nationalist conflicts, mainly as a result of the Cold War. However, the disintegration of the Soviet Union and the upheavals, brought about by the transition from socialism to a market economy, have re-opened old conflicts. Nationalist aspirations turned into armed conflicts in parts of the Commonwealth of Independent States (CIS) and in Yugoslavia. Since 1989, Nagorno Karabakh, Georgia, Moldova, and Chechenia, all previously part of the Soviet Union, have witnessed bloody armed conflict. Similarly, the Yugoslav constitutional crisis, originating from Slovene and Croatian demands for new confederal arrangements, finally erupted into civil war in Croatia and thereafter in Bosnia-Herzegovina. In 1998, a nationalist conflict broke out between the republic of Serbia and Kosovo, an autonomous province within Serbia, now inhabited by a majority of Albanian origin. In June 1991, the European Community became actively involved in the crisis in Yugoslavia; however, little success was observed in retaining a common position and joint action throughout the conflict. Carl Bildt and Lord Owen were the two European Union mediators in the conflict.

Czechs and Slovaks, in contrast, agreed to dissolve their federal union (former Czechoslovakia) peacefully. Two separate, independent states, the Czech Republic and Slovakia came into being on 1 January 1993. Similarly, Germany, following the fall of the Berlin wall on 9 November 1989 began a series of negotiations with the former allied powers thus paving the way to reunification by organising unified national general elections in the two parts of Germany. In accordance with the provision of Article 23 of the West German Constitution, East and West Germany were reunified on 3 October 1990 and therefore East Germany became *de facto* part of the EU.

In the changing landscape, the EU signed a number of Association Agreements with the countries of eastern and central Europe and the expected enlargement is likely to include Poland, the Czech Republic, Slovenia, Hungary and Estonia. In the sphere of security, a new European security has emerged. The disintegration of Warsaw Pact gave rise to questions about the existence and nature of the North Atlantic Treaty Organization (NATO), which in its summit of November 1991 agreed to the establishment of the North Atlantic Cooperation Council (NACC). In addition, the Conference on Security and Cooperation in Europe (CSCE) acquired further significance, as it provided opportunities for political dialogue for the continent as a whole. Yet throughout eastern Europe and the former Soviet Union, conditions are still ripe for border disputes and abuses of ethnic and national communities. This has added a sense of uncertainty about Europe's future and is a constant test of the EU's common stances. (See also, CFSP, Common Position, CSCE, Europe Agreements, NACC, Joint Action).

EURATOM, see **EUROPEAN ATOMIC ENERGY COMMUNITY**

EUREKA. The European Research Coordination Agency was initiated by the European Community, and more specifically by the French president François Mitterrand in 1985. Primarily a response to the so-called Star Wars programme launched by President Ronald Reagan in 1983, it aimed at promoting a European programme of research and development.

Several Western European countries outside the European Community agreed to participate in the programme. In fact, EUREKA has sponsored a number of transnational projects, including factory automation, lasers, etc. Most of the institutions, universities, industries involved in these projects are located within the Community, but EUREKA is not a European Community organization since most of its funding comes from private sources. (See also, RTD).

EURO. The name given to the single currency by the 1995 Madrid European Council. The new currency was introduced on 1 January 1999, starting date of Stage III of the Economic and Monetary Union (EMU). Though uniform, the Euro's legend will be written in the language of each member, a total of 11 official languages. One Euro amounts to 100 cents and is equivalent to the defunct European Currency Unit (ECU). Its introduction will take place in two stages.

The first stage, starting on the date of its introduction, is a transitional period requiring the irrevocable fixing of conversion rates, both among currencies of member states and against the Euro. During this stage, the Euro becomes the monetary policy currency of the participating member states, and foreign exchange rates are conducted in it. However, private agents will not be obliged to use the Euro.

The second stage will begin on 1 January 2002, when Euro banknotes and coins will be put in circulation alongside national currencies. Six months later at most, national currencies will be completely replaced by the Euro in all participating member states. Subsequently, national banknotes and coins will be exchanged in national central banks. (See also, ECB, ECU, EMU).

EUROBAROMETER. A term referring to surveys of public opinion carried out in member states of the European Community on behalf of the European Commission. These surveys have been regularly published since 1973 and are conducted in such a way as to trace overall trends, as well as public opinion on current affairs.

EUROCHEQUE. An intra-European system of payment established in 1968. It operates in the member states of the European Community, in eastern Europe as well as in North Africa and Israel. The USA does not accept Eurocheques.

EUROCORPS. Known as the embryo European army, Eurocorps is the outcome of a common initiative by President F. Mitterrand and Chancellor H. Kohl to form a Franco-German corps in which armed forces of other Western European Union (WEU) states could participate. In fact, since it was set up in 1992, Spain, Luxembourg and Belgium have already participated, while other members have shown an interest in doing so. At the moment it consists of about 50,000 men.

The formation of Eurocorps is in accordance with the Common Foreign and Security Policy (CFSP) introduced by the Maastricht Treaty and the decision to strengthen the WEU within the framework of North Atlantic Treaty Organization (NATO). The Eurocorps by no means constitutes a European Community defence capability which is still heavily dependent on the USA. Based in Strasbourg, France, it focuses on peace-keeping and humanitarian operations rather than straightforward deterrence. (See also, CFSP, NATO, WEU).

EUROFIGHTER. A long and expensive collaboration project (over £42 billion spent to date) based in Munich, for the creation of a fighter plane that is intended to act as the kernel of a future military aircraft company. This project aims to avoid repetition of research and wasteful competition among European countries. The partners involved are British Aerospace (BAe), Casa of Spain, Dasa (the aerospace and electronics defence arm of Daimler-Benz) of Germany and Alenia of

Italy. France participated with Dassault but the company withdrew at the initial stage and currently is engaged in making the rival Ravale fighter plane.

Nevertheless, since 1995, BAe has been collaborating with Dassault on research into fighter aircraft technology, and together they have formed a formal joint venture based in the UK, and employing around 80 engineers at BAe's site in Warton, Lancashire. In addition, BAe has already agreed with Saab of Sweden to a joint export marketing of the Gripen fighter.

EUROGROUPS. Groups which draw their membership from several countries and whose aim is to serve the interests of their members by lobbying those who are responsible for making and implementing policy at European level. To this end Eurogroups seek to exchange information both between European Community institutions and national affiliates. The number of Eurogroups amounts to approximately 550 with about 50 per cent representing industry and commerce, about 25 per cent agriculture and food, and only 5 per cent representing trade unions, environmental and other interests.

Some groups have a wide membership base and represent an entire sector or area of activity; such groups include the Committee of Professional Agricultural Organizations of the European Community (COPA) and the European Trade Union Confederation (ETUC). Most groups, however, promote the interests of a specific industry, service or product; such groups include the European Union of Fruit and Vegetable Wholesalers, Shippers, Importers and Exporters (EUCOFIL), the Federation of European Explosive Manufacturers (FEEM), and so on. Membership in most of these groups used to be through affiliation, but since the mid-1980s direct membership has been increased. Often large companies are represented directly in a group or organisation, for example, the Association of European Automobile Constructors (ACEA), which represents all the EU's major non-Japanese manufacturers apart from Peugeot.

The resources of these groups originate from their members and in most cases are very limited, to the extent that they cannot afford permanent offices or full time staff. COPA and ETUC are by far the best funded groups. (See also, COPA, ETUC).

EURONEWS. A European channel, based in Lyon, initiated by the European Community and largely subsidised by the European Commission. Currently, the channel broadcasts in Germany, the UK,

Spain, France and Italy, but countries such as Egypt and former Yugoslavia participate in the project.

EUROPE. Continent of the northern hemisphere consisting of the western part of the land mass of which Asia forms the eastern and greater part. Unlike other continents, Europe has no naturally defined borders. Originally the word Europe referred to the mainland Greece, but this changed over the centuries as ancient Greek colonization spread north and west. The acquisitions of the Roman Empire also gave Europe wider dimensions and resulted in the consolidation of the western part of the continent. However, the eastern borders of Europe have always been problematic and only recently have the Ural Mountains been accepted as its eastern frontiers.

The name of the continent originates from 'Europa', the daughter of the King of Tyre Agenor. Zeus fell in love with her and transformed himself into a beautiful bull before carrying her off to Crete where she gave birth to three sons. Minos, the builder of the Labyrinth, being one of them.

EUROPE AGREEMENTS. In the context of Association Agreements several agreements have been signed since 1991 between the Community and most central and eastern European countries, including Poland, Hungary, Czechoslovakia, Bulgaria, Romania and Slovenia, which have all requested membership to the Community. The agreement with Czechoslovakia was modified following the division of the country into two separate entities, the Czech Republic and Slovakia, in 1993. Only the agreements with the first three countries specifically stipulated eligibility for membership, though no deadline was set. Europe Agreements were also signed with the Baltic states, Albania and Ukraine.

These agreements aim to further liberalize trade between the signatories, but also to promote the greater democratization of their political systems. This is part of a general effort to prepare these countries for eventual entry into the EU. Association Agreements with Poland, the Czech Republic, Slovenia, Hungary and Estonia have resulted in official negotiations between them and the EU with the prospect of these countries joining the EU by 2002. (See also, Agenda 2000, Association Agreements, PHARE).

EUROPEAN AGENCY FOR SAFETY AND HEALTH AT WORK. Established in 1990, it has its origins in the advisory committee on safety, hygiene and health protection at work, which was set up in

1974 with the purpose of assisting the European Commission with the drafting of legislation in this field. The European Agency for Safety and Health at Work is a European Community body that aims at collecting and disseminating information on health and safety at work, coordinating national action and research programmes in this area, and providing relevant technical support. Since 1993, the Agency has been based in Bilbao, Spain. (See also, Social Charter, Workers' Rights).

EUROPEAN AGRICULTURAL GUIDANCE AND GUARANTEE FUND (EAGGF). Set up in 1962, with the purpose of financing agriculture, the fund was divided into two sections with distinct tasks in 1964. The Guidance Section of the fund is one of the structural funds and helps to reform farm structures and develop rural areas. Areas designated by the European Commission as eligible for development qualify for grants under the Guidance Section. The effectiveness of the Guidance Section is rather limited since only 5 per cent of the EAGGF is allocated to it. The European Investment Bank (EIB) may also contribute in the form of loans.

The Guarantee Section of the fund, the most criticised, is responsible for the various price and market supports. It pays for the intervention buying of products, when prices fall below target prices guaranteed annually for each product; it pays for export refunds, when prices in world market fall below those within member states. Over 95 per cent of the EAGGF expenditure constitutes the Guarantee Section, which is classified as compulsory expenditure within the Budget. (See also, Budget, CAP, Structural Funds).

EUROPEAN ANTHEM. An adaptation from the prelude to the last movement of Beethoven's *Ninth Symphony*, based on Schiller's *Ode to Joy*. It was adopted in 1972 by the Council of Europe (CE) as the European anthem, but it is also used by the European Community. (See also, European Identity).

EUROPEAN ATOMIC ENERGY COMMUNITY (EURATOM). The European Atomic Energy Community was established in 1957 by the Treaty of Rome. It was an agreement signed by the Six with the broad objectives of promoting the creation and development of the nuclear power industry in Europe through a programme of joint research and development. Nine Joint Research Centres (JRCs), were set up at four sites: Karlsruhe in Germany, Ispra in Italy, Geel in Belgium and Petten in The Netherlands.

Given the significance of atomic energy in the 1950s, the establishment of EURATOM was thought to be one of the most important agreements. The prevalent view was that the possession of nuclear weapons would be decisive in the event of war, hence French concern with the possibility of Germany's procurement of nuclear weapons. In addition, the dependence of Europe on Middle East oil, together with the uncertainty caused by the 1956 Suez crisis, forced Europe into looking for alternative or additional energy sources.

EURATOM was designed on the same model as the ECSC. It had an Assembly, a Council of Ministers, a Commission and a Court of Justice; the Assembly and the Court of Justice were institutions common to the three communities. The Economic and Social Committee (ESC) also acted as an advisory body to all communities. Until 1967, when the non-common institutions to the three communities were merged, EURATOM had a separate budget. (See also, ECSC, Energy Policy, Treaty of Rome).

EUROPEAN BANK FOR RECONSTRUCTION AND DEVELOPMENT (EBRD). Established in April 1991 and based in London, the Bank lends money for the specific purposes of reconstruction and development. Founded in the aftermath of the sweeping changes in central and eastern Europe, EBRD's operations are geared primarily to structural reform, transition to a market economy and the establishment of multiparty democracy in the ex-socialist countries.

The founding principles for the creation of the Bank were first expressed by President Mitterrand, and soon found favour with Germany. At the meeting of the European Council at Strasbourg in 1989, French and German support for the proposal prevailed over the scepticism of the other member states, and thus the EBRD became a reality.

Membership of the EBRD is open to non-European countries, but the Community, together with the European Investment Bank (EIB), contributes more than half of its capital. USA is the largest single shareholder (10 per cent), followed by Japan (8.5 per cent). The Bank is in close cooperation with other international institutions, as for example, the International Bank for Reconstruction and Development (IBRD) and the International Monetary Fund (IMF), in a common effort to promote structural reform in the countries under consideration. The first President of the EBRD, Jacques Attali, resigned in 1993 after criticism regarding waste and mismanagement; Horst Köhler is the current president. (See also, EIB, Europe Agreements).

EUROPEAN CENTRAL BANK (ECB). In accordance with the Maastricht Treaty the European System of Central Banks (ESCB) and the ECB were set up during Stage III of the Economic and Monetary Union (EMU). The ECB largely replaced the European Monetary Institute, set up at the beginning of Stage II of the EMU.

The ECB works within the framework of the ESCB and is managed by a Governing Council, consisting of central bank governors and a president who is appointed by the participating member states in consultation with the European Parliament (EP) and the Governing Council. The President of the Ecofin Council and a member of the European Commission may also participate in any Governing Council meetings, but they do not have the right to vote.

The ECB alone has the right to manage the money supply and authorise the issue of the single currency, Euro banknotes, which may be issued by both the ECB and the national central banks. Member states may issue coins subject to approval by the ECB of the volume of the issue. The ECB is obliged to draw up an annual report on the activities of the ESCB and on monetary policy for presentation to the European Council, the EP, the Council of Ministers and the European Commission. Only the participants of Stage III are represented in the ESCB and the ECB. (See also, Ecofin Council, EMU, ESCB, Euro).

EUROPEAN CENTRE FOR THE DEVELOPMENT OF VOCATIONAL TRAINING (CEDEFOP). It was established in 1975 as an advisory body to the European Commission in areas of social policy concerned with training. The Centre was initially based in Berlin but was later moved to Thessaloniki, Greece. Appointed representatives of national governments, employers' and trade unions organizations, as well as representatives of the European Commission participate in the Centre. (See also, Industrial Policy, Social Policy).

EUROPEAN COAL AND STEEL COMMUNITY (ECSC). Based on the Schuman Plan, the ECSC was established by the Treaty of Paris of 1951 and came into effect in 1952 to be valid for 50 years. The Treaty was signed by the Six, France, West Germany, Italy, Belgium, Luxembourg and The Netherlands. Had it not been for the commitment of R. Schuman and J. Monnet to the idea of European unity, it is unlikely that the formation of the ECSC would have taken place.

The ECSC was the first of the three communities to be established. Its foundation was an ambitious task as it required, so soon after the end of the war, former enemies to become partners. Its purpose was two-fold, political and economic. Political, in the sense that amalgamation of economic interests, particularly in such significant sectors as coal and steel, would render a future war not only unthinkable but perhaps impossible. It also established the first interstate organizations with significant supranational characteristics. Economic, in the sense that the coal and steel industry was essential to the recovery of post-war Europe, and European cooperation rather than protectionism was thought to be a better route to rapid recovery. Such considerations led to the foundation of a common market for coal and steel. Provisions were made with regard to growth of employment and improvement of standards of living for people working in these sectors, as well as for a common strategy for modernization of the coal and steel industry, which suffered from low productivity, excess supply and uncompetitiveness in world markets.

The Treaty of Paris established an institutional framework consisting of four main institutions: a Special Council of Ministers with its members drawn from national governments; a High Authority with Monnet as its first president, having authority on taxes and levies, production, competition and investment; a Common Assembly consisting of members of parliament of the participant states; and a Court of Justice for the settlement of disputes. With the establishment of the European Economic Community in 1957, the High Authority and the Common Assembly became the European Commission and the European Parliament (EP), respectively. A Consultative Committee, with a purely advisory role in matters relating to the coal and steel industry, was also set up by the ECSC. The ECSC had its own budget financed by a direct Community tax on coal and steel production, as well as from borrowing.

Following the signing of the Treaty, trade increased considerably in the heavy industry of the member states. Most of this increase was attributed to the establishment of the common market in this sector. As a result the ECSC served as a paradigm for further European cooperation. (See also, Energy Policy, European Coal and Steel Community Consultative Committee, Schuman Plan, Supranationalism, Treaty of Paris).

EUROPEAN COAL AND STEEL COMMUNITY CONSULTATIVE COMMITTEE. A consultative committee, representative of national interests, was formed at the time of the creation of the European Coal and Steel Community (ECSC). Currently, this advisory committee is attached to the European Commission. Its purpose is to advise the European Commission on matters related to the coal and steel industry of the European Community. It is appointed by the Council of

Ministers for two years and has 84 members who represent the interests of employers, workers and consumers in the coal and steel industry. (See also, ECSC).

EUROPEAN COMMISSION. A single European Commission of the three communities (ECSC-EURATOM-EEC) was created with the Merger Treaty of 1967. The Commission is often referred to as the civil service of the European Community. In reality, however, it is more than that, since its powers are not simply confined to executive duties, but it also participates in policy initiation and decision-making.

Based in Brussels, it was housed in the Berlaymont building until 1992 when it moved to the Breydel building. With the entry of Austria, Finland and Sweden to the EU, the number of European Commissioners increased from 17 to 20. France, Germany, Italy, Spain and the UK have two European Commissioners each, and the remaining members have only one each.

Commissioners are appointed by the member states 'by common accord' after consultation with the European Parliament (EP). The Commission is a 'college', it takes decisions collectively and holds collective responsibility, though individual members may assume responsibility for one or more portfolios. Under the Maastricht Treaty the Commission's term of office was extended to 5 years, and its appointment has to be approved by Parliament. Once approved, the Commission may nominate one or two of its members as Vice-Presidents. The President is nominated by the governments of member states after consultation with the EP. Member states are required to consult with the future president before nominating the other Commissioners.

Each Commissioner has her/his private office consisting of six or seven members[7]. In the meeting of the personal staff of the Commissioners, proposals are prepared for the weekly meeting of the Commission. In fact, the greater part of the Commission's decisions have already been agreed in these meetings and only unresolved issues go to the Commissioners themselves. The Commission agenda is prepared by the private office of the President, which consists of about 11 members. Under the Commissioners is the Commission's bureaucracy consisting of a staff of approximately 19,000, presently divided into 24 Directorates-General.

---

[7] Six members, if they are nationals of the Commissioner's country of origin, or seven if one of them is not a national of the Commissioner's country of origin.

Any member of the Commission, who no longer fulfils the conditions required for the performance of her/his duties may be declared removed from office by the Court of Justice. The Court may also provisionally suspend any member of the Commission at the request of the Council of Ministers or the Commission itself. The Commission can be removed collectively by the EP, but the Parliament has neither the right to remove individual Commissioners nor to reject the re-appointment by the Council of dismissed Commissioners.

The president of the Commission plays a major role in the its affairs as it represents it in various forums and other Community institutions. The president coordinates and guides the Commission as a whole and distributes the Commission portfolios. He/She is usually someone who has held middle to high rank posts in either the national or the international arena, for instance J. Santer and G. Thorn had held prime ministerial posts in Luxembourg. The President for 1995-99 is J. Santer.

The European Commission, as a whole, represents the Community interests and takes no instructions from the national governments. It is accountable both to the EP and the Court of Justice. However, its independence is not absolute as Commissioners are chosen by national governments, on grounds of general competence and their links to the governing party. In addition, governments are free not to re-appoint European Commissioners whose policies they dislike.

The Commission is a powerful institution and its powers may be divided into four spheres:

a. Implementation and Development of Policy: the Commission has almost exclusive power to initiate and formulate policies. This extends from general proposals related to the future of the EU to specific ones concerning even technical matters. The Commission has also the right to initiate Community legislation. Furthermore, the Council of Ministers has no right to take legislative decisions unless they are proposed by the Commission. Once the Commission has tabled a piece of legislation, it is almost certain that it will be adopted by the other institutions. Amendments to the Commission's proposals by the Council require the Commission's approval, unless the Council of Ministers has decided on an amendment by unanimous vote. In an average year the Commission sends between 600-800 proposals to the Council of Ministers.

The Commission consults with the EU institutions, the national governments and a number of consultative and expert committees before submitting a proposal. Advisory committees represent sectional interests, for instance agriculture, industry, commerce, etc. They are appointed by the Commission, whereas expert committees are nominated by national governments. Currently there are about 66 advisory committees.

b. The Guardian of the Treaties: the European Commission ensures the application of the Treaty provisions and decisions enacted by Community institutions. It supervises the every day actions of the Community and investigates violations of the Community law. It may bring member states before the Court of Justice in the event that they fail to fulfil Treaty obligations.

The Maastricht Treaty enlarged further the powers of the Commission by giving it the right to recommend that a fine be imposed on a member state that does not comply with Community law. Moreover, it can impose fines on companies for violating community law on restrictive trade practices, or state aid, and to block large cross-border mergers.

c. The Manager and Executor of the EU's policies: It supervises, monitors, coordinates and manages EU policies and finance. It is responsible for ensuring that policies are carried out, and assists in the implementation of a number of public and private organizations. Its implementation powers derive either directly from the Treaties or are conferred on it by the Council, mainly in technical matters, agriculture and completion of the internal market. The Commission is responsible for the implementation of the Common Agricultural Policy (CAP) and the Community funds, including the European Development Fund and PHARE.

d. Additional responsibilities (relations with third parties; the Budget): The Commission is responsible for negotiating on behalf of the EU all bilateral and multilateral agreements, for maintaining appropriate relations with international organizations and specialized agencies, such as the United Nations (UN) and the World Trade Organization (WTO). The Commission has delegations in all member states; by 1995 it had at least 121 delegations in countries outside the EU, including two in the USA.

The Commission manages the Budget and draws up the first draft after consultation with the other EU institutions. It is responsible for submitting a report on the accounts at the end of each financial year, as part of the discharge procedure. The Commission is also responsible for the management of the structural funds.

The Commission's powers have declined since the mid-1960s, but it still remains a strong institution with a multitude of functions and responsibilities. It can decide both the substance and the timing of a particular proposal, as well as having the right to amend these proposals, or to accept amendments put forward by the EP. It is only in relation to the Common Foreign and Security Policy (CFSP) and Justice and Home Affairs (JHA), which are essentially intergovernmental in character, that the powers of the Commission are really restricted as it has no right to initiate policy. (See also, Association Agreements, Budget, CFSP, Competition Policy, COA, Council of the EU, Court of Justice, D-G, Discharge Procedure, EP, JHA, Structural Funds; Appendices 4, 5, 6, 11).

EUROPEAN COMMUNITIES. The phrase is used to denote the collective body, that came into being with the Merger Treaty of 1967, consisting of the three communities the European Coal and Steel Community (ECSC), the European Economic Community (EEC) and the European Atomic Energy Community (EURATOM). Although the three communities have shared the same institutions since the 1967 Merger Treaty, they represent distinct entities within the European Union (EU). The singular form 'European Community' rather than the official term European Communities has been widely used as a general description of the three communities for several years. In addition to this, the EEC was officially re-named the European Community by the Maastricht Treaty. (See also, ECSC, EEC, EURATOM, Merger Treaty).

EUROPEAN COMMUNITY HUMANITARIAN OFFICE (ECHO). This office was established in 1991 as part of the European Commission structure, but it did not become operational until 1993. Its function is to promote further cooperation between the European Community and the various relief organizations, as well as to facilitate more immediate responses to emergency calls for humanitarian aid.

Together with the USA, the European Community is the largest donor of humanitarian aid. Aid is drawn both from the Community Budget and the European Development Fund (EDF). ECHO works closely with non-governmental organizations (NGOs) and the United Nations (UN) Department of Humanitarian Affairs. (See also, Development Aid, EDF).

EUROPEAN COMMUNITY STATISTICAL OFFICE (EUROSTAT). Eurostat is the EU statistical office based in Luxembourg, which publishes statistics based on information provided by the member states and related to economy, trade, agriculture, energy, etc. In most cases these statistics are compared with those of other European countries, USA and Japan.

EUROPEAN COUNCIL. This name is given to the meetings or the so-called summits of the heads of government or state of the members of the European Community. The decision for more frequent consultation at the highest level, in the form of the European Council, was taken at the summit meeting in Paris in December 1974.

The European Council was officially recognized as a European Community body by the Single European Act (SEA). It meets at least twice a year usually in the capital of the member state, currently holding the Presidency of the Council of Ministers, or in Brussels. Foreign ministers, the President of the European Commission and an additional European Commissioner also participate. Since June 1987 the President of the European Parliament (EP) addresses the meeting, though he does not participate in the main proceedings.

The Maastricht Treaty established the practice of inviting finance and economic ministers to European Council meetings when matters related to the Economic and Monetary Union (EMU) are discussed. The Maastricht Treaty clarified further the role of the European Council as being one of providing political direction to the EU, setting priorities, initiating policy recommendations, providing impetus towards the progress of the EU, and resolving contentious issues insoluble at ministerial level. The Treaty also made the European Council directly responsible for Common Foreign and Security Policy (CFSP), and Justice and Home Affairs (JHA).

The European Council remains an important focus for political activity and integration dynamics. For example, the 1985 Milan summit endorsed both the decision for an Intergovernmental Conference (IGC) to discuss institutional reform and the Cockfield White Paper which led to the SEA, the 1991 Maastricht summit agreed on the Maastricht Treaty, and the 1997 Amsterdam summit concluded the Amsterdam Treaty. (See also, CFSP, IGC, JHA, SEA).

EUROPEAN COURT FOR HUMAN RIGHTS. Set up in 1958, this is the judicial body of the Council of Europe (CE) and aims at protecting the individual against arbitrary acts of national governments. Since its formation the Court has established basic standards of behaviour to which all member states have to adhere. A case might be referred to the Court only by the European Commission of Human Rights, or by a state, and then only if the defendant state has accepted the Court's jurisdiction. The jurisdiction of the Court extends to all cases concerning the interpretation and application of the Convention of the Protection of Human Rights and Fundamental Freedoms submitted to it. Its decisions are final, but since it has no powers of enforcement the responsibility for implementing the decision rests with the Committee of the Ministers.

The Court is based in Strasbourg and should not be confused either with the Court of Justice of the European Communities, which is responsible for the interpretation of Community law, or the International Court of Justice, which is based in The Hague and is the judicial body of the United Nations (UN). (See also, CE, Human Rights).

EUROPEAN CURRENCY UNIT (ECU). Introduced in 1975, the ECU replaced the book-keeping unit known as the European Unit of Account. The ECU comprises a basket of currencies which contains specific amounts of national currencies. Each national currency has a weighting value within the basket, which represents the country's share of the Community's gross national product and internal trade.

The ECU is established in the international market as an alternative to the dollar, the Deutsch Mark, and the sterling pound. It also acts as a *numeraire* for the Exchange Rate Mechanism (ERM), a unit for all EU transactions, and a basis for a divergence indicator. The ECU is supported by the European Monetary Cooperation Fund (EMCF) to which countries participating in the EMS must make available 20 per cent of their gold and dollar reserves.

The Maastricht Treaty assigned a central role to the ECU in Stage III of the Economic and Monetary Union (EMU) as it required the 'irrevocable fixing' of exchange rates between national currencies and the ECU. During this stage the ECU was replaced by the Euro, which became the single currency in its own right, and the ECB its issuing authority.

Despite all the controversy surrounding the introduction of the EU's single currency, Euro, there will be some immediate advantages, such as the elimination of exchange rate risks, reduction in the cost of trading within the EU, convenience for travellers and the re-affirmation of a new European identity.

EUROPEAN DEFENCE COMMUNITY (EDC). In the early 1950s, the idea of greater western European cooperation in the sphere of defence was developed by politicians and defence specialists in response to the Korean war and the escalation of the Cold War. More specifically, the intention was to promote greater military cooperation in parallel with the growing economic and political cooperation among European states. Within this framework, Germany's re-armament became more acceptable to the French, since it would come under European command.

As early as October 1950, the French Prime Minister, René Pleven, suggested the creation of a common defence and a European army under the authority of the political institutions of a united Europe. By the end of 1951, the governments which had established the European Coal and Steel Community (ECSC) had agreed to the French proposal. However, as time went on, the EDC met a great deal of opposition among the Six for a number of reasons. France eventually rejected the EDC in August 1954, while Italy, waiting for French ratification, never ratified the Treaty.

Though the EDC project was later abandoned, the idea of a common western European defence remained. The alternative course put forward was the extension of the Treaty of Brussels and the creation of the Western European Union (WEU), which permitted German re-armament subject to a number of constraints. (See also, Pleven Plan, Treaty of Rome, WEU).

EUROPEAN DEVELOPMENT FUND (EDF). Established in 1958 by provision of the Treaty of Rome, this fund is an essential component of the Lomé Convention as its funds are directed to ACP countries. The Fund is not part of the Community Budget but is financed directly by member states' contributions, the percentage of which varies. This is arranged individually with ACP countries, and funding is allocated through five programmes: SYSMIN, STABEX, non-planned emergency aid for disaster relief, refugee and structural adjustment aid. Ninety per cent of the fund is allocated in the form of grants and only ten per cent in the form of loans. Around forty per cent of the fund is directed to Sub-Saharan Africa. The EDF accounts for ECUs 13.3 billion for the period 1995-2000. (See also, Development Aid, Lomé Convention, STABEX, SYSMIN).

EUROPEAN ECONOMIC AREA (EEA). A free trade area of approximately 380 million people, which accounts for around 40 per cent of world trade. Free trade of goods, free movement of persons and freedom to provide services have been extended throughout the EEA, with the exception of agriculture and fisheries. There is also a degree of cooperation in research and environment programmes. The EEA was established by a Treaty signed at Oporto on 2 May 1992 and came into effect on 1 January 1994. It consists of 18 countries, the 15 member states of the European Community plus Iceland, Liechtenstein and Norway. Switzerland signed the agreement, but rejected it in a referendum of the same year. The EEA is open to new members.

The idea of the EEA sprung from the realization that as the completion of the Single Market progressed, countries outside the EU could not indefinitely enjoy the economic benefits of free trade with the community, while at the same time continuing to enjoy certain advantages by remaining outside. As a result, a more structured partnership was developed, with the establishment of common decision-making and administrative institutions. (See also, Customs Union, EFTA)

EUROPEAN ECONOMIC COMMUNITY (EEC). An economic association established by the 1957 Treaty of Rome with the purpose of promoting European cooperation and unity. Known as the Common Market, it was based on a customs union which abolished tariffs, customs duties and quotas that members imposed on each other's exports. The EEC also introduced a common external tariff regime so that all its members can apply a uniform system of duties on goods imported from non-member states. The measures taken proved to be successful, as trade among the member states quadrupled in value between 1958 and 1968.

Arguably the EEC was more than a customs union as the Treaty of Rome made provisions for free movement of labour and capital, which are not components of a customs union. The Treaty also stipulated a common investment policy and a social policy facilitated by the European Investment Bank (EIB), the European Regional Development Fund (ERDF) and the European Social Fund (ESF), set up by it. Furthermore, provisions were made for additional common policies, including a Common Agricultural Policy (CAP), a Common Transport Policy (CTP), a system to ensure competition, as well as a progressive approximation of economic policies, an improvement of the standards of living and a closer relation between member states.

The above mentioned policies were supervised by common institutions that had to enforce common regulations for the entire community area. The four primary structural organs of the EEC were the European Commission, the Council of Ministers, the Common Assembly and the Court of Justice; the last two were also to serve the European Coal and Steel Community (ECSC), as well as EURATOM.

Although the EEC gave priority mainly to economic objectives, it also promoted political goals. It went beyond the sectorial approach of integration and proved to be the milestone of the European economic and political integration. With the Maastricht Treaty, the EEC was officially re-named the European Community, a term that had been widely used in place of the official term European Communities. The European Communities came into existence on 1 July 1967 with the Merger Treaty with the objective to describe collectively all the three Communities, namely the ECSC, the EEC and EURATOM. (See also, ECSC, European Communities, Treaty of Rome).

EUROPEAN ECONOMIC SPACE, see **EUROPEAN ECONOMIC AREA**

EUROPEAN ELECTIONS. Elections for the European Parliament (EP) are held every five years in all the member states of the Community. Until 1979, when the first direct elections took place, MEPs were nominated by national parliaments from amongst their members. This method of representation created several problems. The role of the EP was largely underestimated and as a result MEPs, who had also to serve their national parliaments, had little time for their European commitments. Political discourse was limited as there was a tendency for pro-integrationist MPs to be nominated for the EP. Furthermore, parties not represented in the national parliaments could not be represented in the EP.

Apart from the practical difficulties, lack of direct elections represented a serious legal problem for the Community, since the Treaty of Rome (establishing the EEC) made provisions for elections by direct universal suffrage in accordance with a uniform procedure in all member states. From 1979 onwards, the first part of this provision had already been implemented, but a uniform electoral system could not be agreed upon. European elections still continue to be held according to national electoral systems, differing from various forms of proportional representation to majority vote systems. Turnouts in the European elections present an additional problem as they tend to be significantly lower than in the national elections. In 1979, 63 per cent voted in the European elections, but only 56.5 per cent in 1994. Voting is compulsory in Belgium, Greece, Luxembourg and Spain. (See also, EP, Trans-national Federations).

EUROPEAN ENERGY CHARTER. Signed in 1991, the European Energy Charter is part of the broader task of establishing a pan-European energy agreement, especially between eastern and western Europe. A revised version of the Charter signed in 1994, extended membership from 38 countries to more than 50, including the USA, Canada and the countries of central and eastern Europe. The immediate aims of the Charter are the slowing down of growth in total energy consumption, and promotion of domestic energy production. The Charter also provides funding to oil and gas producing countries for the modernization of their infrastructure. (See also, Energy Policy).

EUROPEAN ENVIRONMENT AGENCY (EEA). Set up in 1990 after long delays, it became operational in 1994. Its purpose is to gather and supply information with the objective of assisting the European Commission in drawing up and implementing community policy on environmental protection and improvement. Based in Copenhagen, the agency publishes a report on the state of the environment every three years. (See also, Environment Policy).

EUROPEAN FLAG. The circle of the twelve stars on a dark blue background coincides with the twelve member states of the Community in 1985, when the flag was adopted for the general use of the community. The flag was designed by Paul Levy and is now well established as the symbol of the European Community. (See also, European Identity).

EUROPEAN FOUNDATION FOR THE IMPROVEMENT OF LIVING AND WORKING CONDITIONS. A European Community body established in 1975 to gather and disseminate information and formulate policy proposals on the living and working conditions of Community citizens. The Foundation is based in Dublin. (See also, Social Policy, Worker's Rights).

EUROPEAN FOUNDATION FOR TRAINING. The foundation was established in 1990 in Turin, with the objective of contributing to the development of vocational training systems of designated central and eastern European countries. It also provides retraining for adults and young people. Later its activities were extended to the Commonwealth of Independent States (CIS), as well as to Mongolia, Azerbaijan and Georgia. (See also, Agenda 2000, Enlargement, PHARE).

EUROPEAN FREE TRADE ASSOCIATION (EFTA). A free trade association established by the Stockholm Convention of 1960 with two main objectives: firstly, to establish the free trade area of industrial products between member countries, and, secondly, to make the whole of Western Europe into a free trade area for industrial goods. Provisions were also made for bilateral agreements to liberalize trade in agricultural products. The first of these objectives was achieved in 1967 with the removal of import duties and quantitative restrictions on most industrial goods between EFTA countries; the second was established in 1977 with the creation of a free trade area between the European Community and EFTA.

Originally, there were seven signatory countries, the UK, Austria, Denmark, Norway, Portugal, Sweden and Switzerland. Iceland joined in 1970 and Finland in 1986. The creation of EFTA was primarily a British initiative and came as a reaction to the formation of the European Economic Community (EEC). The UK government at the time was inclined towards the creation of a free trade block within Europe, which would have given the UK access to the industrial common market of Europe, while the government continued to oppose wider political cooperation likely to infringe British sovereignty.

A severe crisis followed the creation of EFTA. As early as 1961, the UK applied for EEC membership, and in 1964 violated the Stockholm Convention with the introduction of a 15 per cent surcharge on all UK industrial goods in order to shore up the pound sterling. In 1973, the UK and Denmark left EFTA on becoming members of the EEC; Portugal in 1986; and Austria, Finland and Sweden in 1995. Currently EFTA has only three members, Iceland, Norway and Switzerland (plus Liechtenstein bound to Switzerland by its Union). All, apart from Switzerland, have joined the European Economic Area.

A small number of institutions was set up by the Stockholm Convention. The EFTA Council, consisting of one representative from each member state, holds its meetings at official level every other week, and at ministerial level usually twice yearly. The Council has no executive powers and decisions are implemented by individual governments. A specialist Standing Committee to advise the Council, and a small secretariat, based in Geneva, were also established. (See also, Customs Union, EEC).

EUROPEAN IDENTITY. The theme of European identity is very complex as indeed any debate about identity, be it personal or collective. For our purposes, European identity may be defined in terms of characteristics that make people of Europe perceive themselves as Europeans.

European identity has come to the fore in recent years because of the formation of the European Community and the more extensive geopolitical changes taking place on the continent. Common historical and cultural heritage, considered as the basis of European identity, often present us with sharp diversities resulting not simply from the fragmentation of Europe into nation-states, but also from geopolitical, geographical and climatic variations, as well as from differences of race, religion and language. There are, however, certain traditions and achievements, in the fields of science, philosophy, literature, art, politics, and civil and social rights that are common to the whole of Europe.

It is this common and diverse heritage that underpins the European identity so essential for its political unity. At the same time, the task facing the European Community is how to reconcile each member state's national identity with a shared European identity. In other words, while each individual thinks in terms of his national identity, he also perceives himself as an indivisible part of the whole.

In practical terms, European identity as a political goal requires real and symbolic justifications so as to facilitate the relinquishing of national interests in favour of European ones. To this end, provisions have been made for the institutionalized sharing of responsibility and common action in such a way as to attain adequately wide consensus and loyalty.

More specifically, the theme of European identity, addressed in the European Council meeting in Copenhagen in December 1973, reinforced the unity of the nine member states of the Community and their determination to establish a united Europe. More progress was made with the two reports of the Adonnino Committee submitted to the European Council meeting in Brussels in March 1985 and Milan in June 1986. Most of the Committee's proposals have been incorporated into the Maastricht Treaty in the form of education, cultural and media policies aimed at reinforcing the notion of European identity. Constant efforts have been made to make the Community more relevant to its citizens. In addition, a number of broad educational programmes, such as Socrates and Leonardo, have contributed considerably to cross-border exchanges, language learning and vocational training. European passports, the European anthem and the European flag also help to strengthen the notion of European identity, though their value is primarily symbolic. (See also, Cultural Policy, Education Policy, European Anthem, European Flag, European Passport, Media Policy).

EUROPEAN INSTITUTE FOR PUBLIC ADMINISTRATION. Founded in 1981 in Maastricht, the Institute is a study centre for academics, lawyers and administrators concerned with European integration, especially with aspects of quality management. Despite the considerable involvement of EU member states and the Commission in its activities, the Institute is not an EU body.

EUROPEAN INVESTMENT BANK (EIB). The bank was established under the Treaty of Rome by the Six founding members of the European Economic Community in 1958. Based in Luxembourg, it was set up to finance capital investment that would contribute to the development of the Community and its associated countries.

Decisions are made by the Board of Governors, normally consisting of Finance Ministers of the member states. The Board meets once a year. Daily operations are supervised by a Board of Directors, consisting of 21 nominees from the member states and one from the European Commission. The management of operations is the responsibility of the Management Committee.

Most of the EIB's funds are raised on the international capital markets and they are available for loans, at a fixed rate of interest, for Community projects. The loans have mostly been directed to the less-developed regions of the Community as well as to those suffering from declining traditional industries; to infrastructural projects, such as communication improvements, environmental protection, promotion of urban development, support for small and medium size enterprises (SMEs), and to any other project considered to be in the interest of the Community.

National governments, regional authorities and companies may apply for EIB loans or guarantees. The EIB, however, does not undertake the entire funding of a project. Normally, it provides half of the costs, while the rest has to be met from loans from other sources, either the applicant's 'own resources', or state assistance.

Among the major beneficiaries of the EIB activity have been Italy, the UK, Portugal and Spain. Currently, its level of lending approaches that of the International Bank for Reconstruction and Development (IBRD). Most of EIB's activities take place within the European Community, but about 5 per cent of its funds go to external aid programmes, especially to ACP countries that are eligible to receive long term loans from the EIB, with the EDF contributing towards repayments by providing a 3 per cent interest rate subsidy. (See also, Regional Policy, Lomé convention, TENs).

EUROPEAN INVESTMENT FUND (EIF). Founded in 1994 by the European Investment Bank (EIB), this fund assists small and medium size enterprises (SMEs) and provides guarantees for long-term financing of European infrastructural projects, particularly in the field of transport, energy transmission and telecommunications.

EIF capital consists of 40 per cent provided by the EIB, 30 per cent by the European Community and the remaining 30 per cent by several banks and institutions throughout the European Union (EU). (See also, EIB, SMEs).

EUROPEAN MEDICINE EVALUATION AGENCY (EMEA). After lengthy deliberations among the national governments, the Agency became operational in 1995. Its main aim is to register and authorise medical drugs for both human and veterinary use within the Community. The Agency is located in London and is financed by the Community Budget and the Pharmaceutical Industry.

EUROPEAN MONETARY COOPERATION FUND (EMCF). The EMCF was established in 1973 with the purpose of facilitating currency transactions between member states as part of the Community's effort to achieve the Economic and Monetary Union (EMU). The EMCF's credit facilities were used to settle obligations deriving from interventions in the foreign exchange markets by the central banks of the member states. Participants deposited 20 per cent of their gold reserves and 20 per cent of their dollar reserves with the EMCF. At the beginning of stage II of the EMU, 1 January 1994, the EMCF was dissolved and its task was taken over by the European Monetary Institute. (See also, EMI, EMU).

EUROPEAN MONETARY INSTITUTE (EMI). The EMI was set up by the Maastricht Treaty, on 1 January 1994, at the beginning of Stage II of the Economic and Monetary Union (EMU). It is based in Frankfurt and its members are the central banks of the European Union (EU) member states. The president also heads the Governing Council of the European Central Bank (ECB), consisting of governors of national central banks[8].

The role of EMI is to strengthen cooperation between central banks and to coordinate monetary policies; to monitor the functioning of the European Monetary System (EMS); to take over the tasks of the European Monetary Cooperation Fund (EMCF), and to facilitate the use of European Currency Unit (ECU) and oversee its development.

In addition, the EMI must prepare for Stage III of the EMU. It is empowered to draw up Opinions or Recommendations regarding the orientation of the monetary and exchange-rate policy, as well as the monetary policies of the member states. (See also, ECB,EMCF, EMI, EMS, EMU).

---

[8] The current president is Alexander Lamfalussy.

EUROPEAN MONETARY SYSTEM (EMS). The EMS became operational in 1979 with the intention of creating a 'zone of monetary stability' within Europe, as well as strengthening cooperation between member states with regard to monetary policies. Currently, it is organized around the Exchange Rate Mechanism (ERM), the European Currency Unit (ECU), and since 1 January 1994, the European Monetary Institute (EMI).

All member states participate in the EMS, but they are not required to join the ERM. The pound did not join the ERM until October 1990 and left it in September 1992, while the Greek drachma joined in 1998. Preconditions for EMS participation include being part of the 'basket' of currencies that determines the value of the ECU, as well as the depositing the 20 per cent of gold and dollar reserves with the European Monetary Cooperation Fund (EMCF). (See also, EMCF, EMI, ERM).

EUROPEAN MONITORING CENTRE FOR DRUGS AND DRUG ADDICTION (EMCDDA). Based in Lisbon, the Centre provides member states with reliable information on drugs and drug addiction with the objective of combating the problem. The Centre cooperates closely with international organizations working in the field. It became operational in 1994 and published its first annual report in 1996. (See also, CELAD, EUROPOL, External Frontiers, JHA, Public Health).

EUROPEAN NUCLEAR RESEARCH ORGANIZATION (CERN). This organization was founded in 1954 under the auspices of the United Nations (UN) as a centre of research into nuclear energy and nuclear physics. It is a transnational institution consisting of 18 member countries which finance the organization by direct contributions. CERN is not formally associated with the European Union (EU). It is based in Geneva. (See also, ESA).

EUROPEAN ORGANIZATION FOR THE DEVELOPMENT AND CONSTRUCTION OF SPACE VEHICLES LAUNCHERS (ELDO). Set up in 1964 to design and build a European space launcher, ELDO was a cooperative effort between Germany, France and the UK. ELDO faced serious problems, as a result of which it was abandoned in 1975 in favour of the European Space Agency (ESA). (See also, ESA).

EUROPEAN PARLIAMENT (EP). The largest multinational parliament in the world, it has its origins in the appointed Assembly established under the European Coal and Steel Community. The term 'Parliament' formalized by the Single European Act (SEA), was first used in 1962. Originally, the EP provided mainly a democratic forum for debate, but in the course of time its legislative, supervisory and budgetary powers have gradually been widened and strengthened, first by the SEA of 1987 and then by the Maastricht Treaty of 1993.

The cooperation procedure introduced by the SEA enables the EP to amend legislation at the second parliamentary reading. This only occurs on those issues decided in the Council by majority vote. The SEA has also introduced the assent procedure, according to which the EP is required to give its assent by an absolute majority in favour of the act under discussion. Moreover, community agreements with third countries now require EP approval.

The Maastricht Treaty extended the Parliament's legislative powers further, though it did not provide the EP with full powers of joint decision-making. The right to veto legislation, the vote of approval of a new European Commission and the appointment of the European Ombudsman were among the powers granted to the EP by the Treaty.

The EP was directly elected for the first time in 1979 and is the EU's only directly elected body. Until then members of the EP were appointed from members of the national parliaments. Elections are held every 5 years in June. EMPs are elected by direct universal suffrage in every member state, but no common electoral system, as foreseen by the Treaty of Rome (establishing the EEC), has been achieved so far. All countries, except the UK (not including Northern Ireland), use forms of proportional representation, but with considerable differences in terms of procedures, voting rights and voting days. New member states must hold elections for the EP within two years of their accession to the Community; until then, they can appoint representatives from their national parliaments.

Voting turnouts in the European elections have been lower than in the national elections and have steadily decreased (63% voted in European elections in 1979, while 56.5% in 1994). Some have suggested that this could be because of the limited powers enjoyed by the EP and its relative remoteness from most citizens, while others argue that it is because the EP elections represent an opinion poll on the performance of national governments, rather than a focus on European issues.

Parliament currently has 626 members apportioned as follows: Germany 99, France, Italy, UK 87 each, Spain 64, The Netherlands 31, Belgium, Greece and Portugal 25 each, Sweden 22, Austria 21, Denmark and Finland 16 each, Ireland 15 and Luxembourg 6. MEPs come from varied backgrounds and few of them have served as members of national parliaments or as ministers. In accordance with the Treaties, MEPs can vote on an individual and personal basis.

As required by the Treaty of Rome, Parliament normally sits in the first week of each month as part of the annual session (lasting one year). These monthly meetings, referred to as plenary meetings, take place in Strasbourg. Additional sessions, as well as Committee meetings, are held in Brussels to facilitate contacts with the European Commission and the Council. The annual session begins on the second Tuesday in March, except for the year when elections are held, in which case the newly elected parliament is required to convene on the first Tuesday of the second month after the last day of the elections. The annual session is considered to be continuous for the whole year, whether the Parliament is actually sitting, or not.

The Parliament elects its President, 14 Vice-Presidents and a college of 5 Quaestors for a term of office of two and a half years. The President and the Vice-Presidents make up the Bureau of the Parliament which has the overall management of Parliament's activities. The Conference of Presidents consists of the president and the leaders of the political groups, and is responsible for organising the Parliament's work and legislative agenda. Quaestors undertake the administrative and financial decisions affecting MEPs interests. The Parliament's secretariat is located in Luxembourg. The debates of the Parliament are open to the public and are conducted in the 11 official languages of the European Community.

The EP is made up of political groups organized at Community level according to ideology and/or party affiliation. Most of its work is conducted in its 20 parliamentary committees covering all areas of the EU's activities, spanning from agricultural policy to foreign and security affairs. In addition to the parliamentary committees, there are a number of inter-parliamentary institutions, such as the ACP-EU Joint Assembly and 22 inter-parliamentary delegations through which MEPs maintain relations with parliaments and organizations outside the European Community.

The powers of the EP can be classified under four headings:

a. Legislative Powers: the legislative role of the EP is no longer purely consultative as increasingly it plays an integral role in the legislative process. Presently, it has the power to amend and, in some areas, even to veto legislation under the co-decision procedure. However, this power is limited in scope as it applies only to a few categories of legislation, while all other legislation still requires the Council's approval.

Despite its enhanced powers, the EP does not initiate legislation, nor does it have the right to consult the Commission. Policy initiation is the responsibility of the Commission. However, on the strength of an absolute majority, the EP may request the Commission to submit a proposal when it is thought that a Community act is required for implementing a Treaty. It may issue reports on its own initiative, but the Commission is not obliged to act upon them.

The debate concerning the powers of the EP is closely linked to the character of the European Community. Further enhancement of the EP's legislative powers would lead to a supranational Community; by contrast, greater restriction of these powers would result in an intergovernmental Community.

b. Supervisory Powers: a fundamental function of any parliament is to oversee the work of the executive. In the case of the EU, however, there is no single executive body. Instead, the Council of Ministers, the European Council and the Commission all play a role in the executive. As a consequence the EP lacks the necessary supervisory powers. Moreover, neither the Council of Ministers nor the European Council are accountable to the EP, for they can neither be appointed nor be dismissed by it.

The Parliament's most important supervisory power is its involvement in the appointment and dismissal of the Commission. The Maastricht Treaty gave the EP the right to approve the appointment of the Commission, including its president, within a period of 6 months of the elections of the new Parliament. The Parliament exercised this right for the first time during the election of the 1995 Commission by threatening to veto Santer's presidential nomination by the Council, and by holding rigorous interviews with most of the future Commissioners to assess their competence.

Moreover, the EP can dismiss the Commission on a motion of censure requiring a two-thirds majority of the votes cast, amounting to an absolute majority of members. However, this power has never been exercised. The close party links of the Commissioners make such a majority in the Parliament very difficult to obtain. In any case, in the event of the Commission's dismissal, the Council has the right to re-appoint the same Commissioners.

In addition to the above mentioned powers, the EP has the authority to ask members of the Council to attend the plenary sessions of the Parliament and to reply to written and oral questions from MEPs. It can require the Court of Auditors (COA) to carry out special enquiries. In common with other European Community institutions and national governments, the EP can bring an action to the Court of Justice against the Commission and the Council of Ministers for failure to act. This right was used in 1982 with reference to the Common Transport Policy (CTP). The EP may also discuss the legislative work and annual General Report of the Commission, but has no mechanism or power to act upon these matters. There is little contact between the EP and the European Council, though the EP presidency is permitted to address the latter's opening session. Similarly, the EP must be consulted on Common Foreign and Security Policy (CFSP) issues, but cannot exercise influence in this area.

The right of each individual or group to petition the EP was formalized by the Maastricht Treaty. Since 1979 the number of petitions has risen dramatically. Petitions are addressed to the Parliament's Petition Committee and must refer to a subject related to the EU's competence. After they are assessed, petitions are forwarded to the institutions responsible for the subject under discussion.

c. Budgetary powers: the Parliament's budgetary powers have grown to the extent that currently the EP and the Council are considered as a joint Budgetary authority. The EP has the right to propose modifications to the compulsory expenditure (consisting mainly of expenditure directed to the Common Agricultural Policy), and amendments to non-compulsory expenditure (expenditure deriving from the Treaties) within the context of the maximum rate of increase. Since the Council of Ministers has the last say on compulsory expenditure, no modifications proposed by the EP can increase expenditure.The Council has the power to reject them by qualified majority voting (QMV). The EP has the final word on the question of non-compulsory expenditure, accounting for less than half of the total Budget, and can even reject the draft Budget as a whole with a two thirds majority of the votes cast. This has happened twice, in 1979 and 1984, as a result of serious disagreements on spending priorities. It must be noted, however, that the Budgetary powers of the EP are severely curtailed by the fact that it has no right to increase revenue and expenditure, as well as by the fact that certain categories of expenditure, such as the European Development Fund, are excluded from the Budget.

On the other hand, the EP has been given the exclusive right of discharge, which it grants to the Commission when the implementation of the Budget has been effected[9].

d. Assent procedure: the EP must give its assent on matters of accession of new members, association and cooperation agreements and agreements with non-EU members states, before these can come

---

[9]   The Budget has been dealt with under the cooperation procedure.

into effect. For instance, the EP used the assent procedure to block agreements with Turkey and Israel on the grounds of human rights violations. The scope of the assent procedure was extended further by the Maastricht Treaty to cover other issues, such as organizations of structural and cohesion funds, changes to the statute of the European System of Central Banks (ESCB), and the uniform electoral system for the European elections.

The EP is no longer just a forum for debate. Since its establishment the EP's authority has increased significantly particularly with the acquisition of legislative and assent powers, and to a certain extent by its budgetary authority. The EP constantly seeks to increase its authority, including an extension of the co-decision procedure into new areas, the right to choose the Commission and jointly agree a five year plan, as well as the right to raise revenue and increase expenditure. Its supervisory powers, however, remain weak. (See also, Assent Procedure, Budget, CFSP, Co-decision, Cooperation Procedures, Council of the EU, Discharge Procedure, ECSC, European Commission, European Elections, JHA, Parliamentary Committees, Political Groups; Appendices 7 to 11).

EUROPEAN PASSPORT. Since 1985 European passports have been replacing national versions under the provisions made by the resolutions of June 1981 and June 1982 of the Council of Ministers. However, it is the authorities of each member state which have the right to issue passports in a uniform format agreed by all member states. The semi-soft cover of the European passport is in burgundy colour, bearing the words 'European Community' in the appropriate language together with the name of the issuing country.

European passports carry both symbolic and practical weight; symbolic in that they reinforce the notion of European identity and common citizenship; practical importance in the sense that European Community citizens can be recognized immediately and therefore avoid delays at the Community's internal frontiers, as special channels have been established for them at airports and sea ports. Moreover, all European passport holders travelling abroad are considered members of the same political entity, and receive the same treatment both at external frontiers and by the authorities within non-member states. (See also, European Identity)

EUROPEAN PATENT CONVENTION. The largest regional patent system in the world, it covers all European Community members (except Finland), Switzerland, Monaco and Liechtenstein. It provides patent protection throughout the signatory states. Its office in Munich has dealt with and granted thousand of patents. The office provides technical information and has developed contacts with national patent offices of non-signatory countries, especially in central and eastern Europe.

EUROPEAN POLITICAL COMMUNITY. A concept used to denote a process of integration that goes beyond the sectorial[10], approach which was prevalent in the 1950s. The idea of a European Political Community was most widely debated at the time when the European Defence Community (EDC) was about to be established. It was, in fact, the Common Assembly, formed under the provisions of the EDC with the purpose of studying ways of establishing federal institutions, that proposed the formation of a European Political Community. This was intended to be the beginnings of a political federation to which the European Coal and Steel Community (ECSC) and the EDC would be subordinated. A draft treaty was completed in March 1953, but France refused to ratify the EDC in August 1954, and as a result the project for a European Political Community had to be abandoned. (See also, EDC, Messina Conference, Treaty of Rome).

EUROPEAN POLITICAL COOPERATION (EPC). The official Community term for foreign policy cooperation, increasingly practised outside the Treaty framework since the early 1970s. As a result, by the mid-1980s, only a few international issues were not discussed in the context of the European Community; whenever possible a common position, but very rarely a joint action, was adopted.

Although EPC was not incorporated in the Treaties, it was given legal status by the Single European Act (SEA) under Title III. Amongst other things Title III stated that member states of the community shall endeavour jointly to formulate and implement a common foreign policy.

The SEA indicated the increasing importance of a European Community foreign policy and served as the harbinger of the Common Foreign and Security Policy (CFSP) introduced by the Maastricht Treaty. (See also, CFSP, Common Position, Fouchet Plan, Joint Action, SEA)

---

[10]   Sectorial integration denotes the integration of specific sectors of the member states of the Community. Integration was initiated by the integration of coal and steel in 1951, followed by nuclear industries in 1957.

EUROPEAN POLITICAL UNION, see **MAASTRICHT TREATY**

EUROPEAN POLICE OFFICE (EUROPOL). The creation of Europol was embodied in the Maastricht Treaty after being confirmed at a meeting of Justice and Home Affairs (JHA) Ministers in The Hague in 1991, and came into force in 1993. Europol is based in The Hague and consists of civil servants from the police forces of the member states. Its purpose is to combat illegal drug trafficking, money laundering, suspected terrorism, armed shipments, and exchange information on asylum seekers. It is an organization complementary to the existing national and international police organizations. The first of its sections to become operational was the Drug Unit in The Hague.

Like other Community organizations set up to deal with sensitive issues, Europol has faced serious difficulties in fulfilling its tasks, mainly because of restrictions exercised by national governments in the exchange of information within the EU and the different police structures in each member state. (See also, CELAD, JHA).

EUROPEAN REGIONAL DEVELOPMENT FUND (ERDF). The ERDF was established in 1975 as one of the components of the structural funds. As defined by the Maastricht Treaty in an amendment to the Treaty of Rome, the ERDF's aim is to redress the main regional imbalances of the Community by assisting in the development and structural adjustment of regions, either lagging behind and/or badly affected by the decline of traditional industry, such as steel, coal, textile, etc. Thus the ERDF is mainly directed to Objectives 1 and 2 of the structural funds. It also assists rural areas under the European Guidance Fund.

This fund is administered by the European Commission and is complementary to national sources devoted to such projects. The 1984 reforms replaced the quotas system with a system of 'minima and maxima' in an effort to increase flexibility in the share allocated to each member. In assisting underdeveloped areas, the ERDF share may not exceed 75 per cent of the total cost of the project and may be no less than 50 per cent, while in cases assisting regions with declining traditional industry these proportions are reduced to a maximum 50 per cent and a minimum 25 per cent of the total cost. The ERDF assistance is provided to projects concerned with specific objectives, as well as to programmes, concerned with broader objectives in more than one member state, e.g. inter-Community infrastructure. Increasingly, programmes have become the most commonly used method of financing regional development. Initiated by the

Commission they tend to provide a better link between the Community's regional objectives and the objectives of other Community policies. (See also, Additionality, Regional Policy, Structural Funds)

EUROPEAN SOCIAL CHARTER. Signed in 1961 by the Council of Europe (CE) and operational since 1965, the Charter is concerned with economic and social rights that were not addressed in the Convention of the Protection of Human Rights and Fundamental Freedoms.

Given the differing levels of development and social provisions between member states and the very nature of the rights to be protected, the drafting of the Charter was a matter of intense negotiations over a period of seven years. It must be noted that the rights protected by the Charter are objectives of social policy rather than rights which can be legally enforced. Nineteen rights in total are mentioned in the Charter, including the right to work, to just conditions of work, to safe and healthy working conditions, to fair remuneration, to organize and bargain collectively, and the right of migrant workers and their families to expect protection and assistance. Member states were obliged to accept a minimum of ten of the Charter provisions.

Given the nature of the rights, no judicial machinery is provided to observe implementation of the Charter; instead, an independent Committee of Experts, consisting of no more than 7 members, joined with a representative of the International Labour Organization in a consultative capacity monitors its implementation. Every two years the Committee of Experts receives and examines reports by the contracting parties regarding the implementation of the Charter. The reports of the Committee of Experts are then forwarded to a subcommittee of the Council of Europe's Governmental Social Committee, which in turn forwards it to the Council of Ministers. In extreme cases the Council of Ministers may decide to make the necessary recommendations to member states that do not comply with the Charter.

The European Social Charter should not be confused with the Social Charter adopted in 1989 by the European Council. The Social Charter was incorporated into the Maastricht Treaty in the form of a Protocol, and therefore it was given legal force. (See also, Council of Europe).

EUROPEAN SOCIAL FUND (ESF). It was established by the Treaty of Rome and set up in 1960, with the aim of promoting employment, as well as the geographical and occupational mobility of workers. Since 1993 the scope of the ESF has been widened with its involvement in combating long-term unemployment, assisting workers to adapt to technological change and training and retraining of people under 25 years of age in an effort to integrate them into the labour market. These efforts are represented primarily by Objectives 3 and 4 of the structural funds.

The ESF is administered by the European Commission; advised by a committee consisting of representatives of national governments, employers and trade unions. Help is directed more in the form of programmes rather than individual cases. The Additionality principle applies to projects supported by ESF. Consequently, funding through the ESF is complementary to national sources, the latter required to provide at least as much funding as sought from the ESF. For 1997 the Fund amounted to about ECUs 7.6 billion. (See also, Additionality, Social Policy, Structural Funds).

EUROPEAN SPACE AGENCY (ESA). It was set up in 1975 to replace the European Organization for the Development and Construction of Space Vehicles Launchers (ELDO) and European Space Research Organization (ESRO). Funded by its member states it aimed at 'providing and promoting, for exclusive peaceful purposes, cooperation among European states in space research and technology and their space applications with the view to their being used for scientific purposes and for operational space application'.

So far, ESA has launched over 20 satellites and has developed the Ariane launcher. In 1987, ESA adopted a long term programme, named 'programme 2000', to work for a manned European space flight aboard the Hermes space-shuttle. Based in Paris, ESA is not a European Community organization although the Community is greatly involved with it. (See also, ARIANE, ELDO, ESRO).

EUROPEAN SPACE RESEARCH ORGANIZATION (ESRO). Multipurpose organisation, set up in 1961 with the participation of many European countries. It aimed at carrying out research and building European satellites. Because of its limited success ESRO was replaced by the European Space Agency (ESA), set up in 1975. (See also, ESA, ESRO).

EUROPEAN SYSTEM OF CENTRAL BANKS (ESCB). Together with the European Central Bank (ECB), the ESCB was established by the Maastricht Treaty with a new article, added to the Treaty of Rome. This article provided for the creation of the two institutions during Stage III of the Economic and Monetary Union (EMU). The ECB operates within the framework of the ESCB and only member states participating in stage III of the EMU can be represented in both institutions. The main objective of the ESCB is to maintain price stability and to support the general policies of the Community. Its basic tasks are to define and implement the monetary policy of the Community; to conduct foreign exchange operations; to hold and manage the official reserves of the member states; and to promote the smooth operation of payment systems.

The ESCB is the only institution where both the governors of the central banks of the participating member states and the ECB play a role in the overall direction of the EMU. In general, the ESCB is concerned with the eventual common economic policies of the member states and their coordination in cooperation with the Council of Ministers. (See also, ECB, EMU).

EUROPEAN TRADE UNION CONFEDERATION (ETUC). This confederation is one of the Eurogroups, which represents trade union's interests on a wide range of issues. It consists of national trade union confederations from over 20 countries and took on its current structure in 1973. Because of its broad membership, the ETUC is one of the best funded groups, although it often fails to retain internal cohesion necessary to present a common front. (See also, Eurogroups).

EUROPEAN UNION (EU). The idea of an EU may be traced back to the inter-war years. The Coudenhove-Kalergi proposals on pan-Europa and the plan for a federal Europe put forward by Aristide Briand have been the most widely known of the period. The prospect was re-asserted in the Treaty of Rome of 1957, when the foundations for an ever closer Union among the peoples of Europe were laid down.

The Treaty of Rome, however, dealt primarily with economic aspects. It was the Maastricht Treaty of 1992 that created the EU, involving a higher degree of economic and political integration. This entailed a long process of evolution during which a variety of forms for a possible Union were debated. One of them, proposed by the Draft Treaty Establishing the European Union (DTEU) of 1984, was a uniform structure with a federal character, while the EU as introduced by the Maastricht Treaty is a pillared based structure. In spite of the disagreements concerning the character of the Community, the dream of the EU's pioneers for a closer Union of the peoples of Europe has largely been achieved. (See also, DTEU, European Communities, Maastricht Treaty).

EUROPEAN UNIVERSITY INSTITUTE (EUI). It was established in 1976 under the auspices of the European Communities with the objective of providing research and cultural training in postgraduate education. It carries out research with a European perspective in the fields of history, economics, law, political and social sciences. Located in Florence, it is housed in several historical buildings of the city. Its full-time staff and around 350 research students are recruited from all the countries of the European Community. Those accepted into the programmes are expected to have competence in at least two official European languages. Grants, based on Community norms, are usually provided by national governments. (See also, Cultural Policy, Education Policy).

EUROPOL, see **EUROPEAN POLICE OFFICE**

EUROSTAT, see **EUROPEAN COMMUNITY STATISTICAL OFFICE**

EXCHANGE RATE MECHANISM (ERM). The ERM was established in 1979 with the purpose of minimising the currency fluctuations of member states. As part of the European Monetary System (EMS), it serves the long term objective of the Economic and Monetary Union (EMU), namely, the replacement of the currencies of member states by a single currency. It operates on the basis of mutual support and collective action by the central banks of the member states, which intervene in the currency markets in such a way as to prevent the rise or fall in value of a currency above or below an agreed band of fluctuations. Should this happen, central banks intervene by buying or selling members' currency in order to influence its value and restore it within the agreed limits. Within the context of the ERM each currency receives a central exchange rate against the European Currency Unit (ECU). This enables the central rates between all currencies participating in the ERM to be calculated.

By 1992 the ERM had 10 members: Belgium, Denmark, France, Germany, Italy, Luxembourg, The Netherlands, Spain joining in 1987, the UK in 1990 and Portugal in 1992. Greece participated in 1998, while Luxembourg bases its franc on the Belgian Franc. ERM members allowed their currencies to fluctuate within a set margin of ±2.25 per cent within the narrow band, or ±6 per cent within the wide band in relation to every other currency in the system. The Spanish peseta, the Italian lira, the Portuguese escudo and the pound sterling were allowed to operate within the wide band.

Several realignments enabled the ERM to operate successfully until the 1992-93, when a major crisis virtually destroyed it. Following the stock market crash on 'Black Wednesday' (16 September 1992), the pound sterling and the lira left the ERM, and by the end of that year they had depreciated in value by about 15 and 16 per cent respectively; the peseta was devalued by 5 per cent and by another 6 per cent in November; the Portuguese escudo was also devalued by 6 per cent; the wide band was increased to ±15 per cent and extended to all currencies still participating in the ERM, though the German mark and the Dutch guilder decided bilaterally to retain the narrow band between the two currencies.

The crisis was the result of the increasing apprehension over the future of the Maastricht Treaty after the first Danish referendum (June 1992) resulted in a 'No' vote, and the possibility of a 'No' vote in a French referendum. Another factor, given the importance of the Deutsch Mark (DM) in the system and its close links to the ERM, may have been the German economic and monetary policy. This policy was linked to German reunification which forced Germany to opt for high interest rates and borrowing, rather than increasing taxes or revaluing the DM in an effort to counteract inflation. As a response, other members maintained high interest rates in order to avoid depreciating their currencies against the DM. In addition, there was inadequate cooperation between member states and not appropriate readjustment of parity rates.

Although the ERM has largely achieved its primary aim of creating a zone of monetary stability amongst member states, its role since 1993 in the consolidation of the EMU has diminished. Even so, new comers to the European Community must be prepared to join it. (See also, ECU, EMS, EMU)

EXTERNAL AUDIT. The external audit of the revenue and expenditure of the European Community should be distinguished from the internal audit which is carried out by Directorate-General XX, responsible for financial control. The external audit is the responsibility of the Court of Auditors (COA), a fully fledged EU institution, especially created for this task. (See also, COA, Internal Audit).

EXTERNAL FRONTIERS CONVENTION. A draft of the External Frontiers Convention was agreed by the member states of the Community in 1991, but it has not yet been ratified because of the dispute between the UK and Spain over the application of the Convention on Gibraltar. The External Frontiers Convention together with the Dublin Asylum Convention are based on the commitment of the Treaty of Rome to establish an area without internal frontiers. Under the Maastricht Treaty both Conventions are dealt with in the context of Justice and Home Affairs (JHA).

The Convention deals with the treatment of nationals of non-member states and is designed to tighten up external frontiers of the 15 members of the Community. It embraces broad areas of policies, those relating to the establishment of: a) a uniform European Union (EU) visa, covering a number of countries whose citizens must obtain a visa before entering any member state of the Community; b) a visa exemption regime, providing exemption for people resident in the European Community who are not citizens, but who want to visit other member states for a short period; c) a three-month visit visa designed for those who are neither citizens nor residents of the Community but who wish to visit the Community for a short period; d) a computerised list of known criminals, terrorists and drug traffickers who have been prohibited from entering any member state; e) a programme re-designing airports throughout the Community, so as to ensure that domestic and external arrivals are separated.

The Convention is still awaiting ratification, but meanwhile the Commission has made some progress in matters provided for in the Convention. For example, a Regulation, adopted in 1995, was issued by the Commission containing a list of third countries whose nationals need a visa to enter any member state of the European Community. Under the Maastricht Treaty decisions taken regarding visa issues have also become subject to qualified majority voting (QMV). (See also, Dublin Asylum Convention, JHA, Small Countries).

EXTERNAL TARIFF REGIME, see **CCP, EEC, TARIFFS**

F

FAILURE TO ACT, see COURT OF JUSTICE OF THE EUROPEAN COMMUNITIES

FEDERALISM. A form of political organization that unites states or other polities in such a way that each of these constituent components retains its own political integrity. There have been various types of political organization based on the principle of federalism, the most ambitious example is the USA, with fiscal, foreign and defence powers concentrated in the central federal organs of government. Within Europe there are several different types of federalist organisation, including Germany, Switzerland, Belgium, and the Benelux countries. Former Yugoslavia, Czechoslovakia and the Soviet Union were also federalist states.

In the case of the European Community, the founding Treaties and their subsequent development were overwhelmingly federal in character. The pioneers of European integration, coming out of the ashes of the Second World War, shared strong federalist ideas. These were expressed in the preamble of the 1957 Treaty of Rome, which established the European Economic Community (EEC). The Treaty clearly referred to the goal of 'an ever closer union of the European Peoples'.

The translation of this general wish into a particular institutional form, however, has been attended by conceptual and political disagreements. The European Political Community and the Draft Treaty establishing the European Union (DTEU) set out clearly the framework of a federal Community, but failed to win sufficient support from governments of the member states. Nevertheless, supranational institutions, such as the Commission, the European Parliament (EP) and the Court of Justice, designed on federal principles, were established.

The nature of the Community remains the focus of contentious debate among participants. The advocates of further integration favour the strengthening of the supranational institutions and therefore the federal character of the Community. This very argument ignited the hostility of some member states to the Maastricht Treaty, who regarded it as a threat to their sovereignty and national authority. Certain compromises, however, enabled both pro-federalists and anti-federalists to claim that the Maastricht Treaty was largely acceptable to them. This was possible because either side of the debate adduced evidence which supported either the intergovernmental or the federalist nature of the Community.

In practice, both elements exist. The Common Foreign and Security Policy (CFSP) and the Justice and Home Affairs (JHA) remain intergovernmental, although in a federal structure these would be the responsibility of the central government. On the other hand, subsidiarity, which is pre-eminently a federal principle, has been accepted; equally, the Court of Justice was given the right to impose fines on member states that fail to comply with its previous rulings, as in a federal system; but above all, the Economic and Monetary Union (EMU), which entails the surrender of a high degree of national monetary powers to European institutions, is *par excellence* a characteristic of a federal system. Despite these strong federal elements, the UK insisted that the word 'federal' be left out of the Treaty.

The issue concerning the character of the Community is likely to remain alive for years to come. What ultimately determines the character of the Union will depend on future developments, and especially the progress of the EMU, and the success of the two intergovernmental pillars of the Union in delivering concrete results. (See also, Court of Justice, EMU, Ethnic and Regional Conflicts, European Political Community, Intergovernmentalism, JHA, Maastricht Treaty, Sovereignty, Subsidiarity, Treaty of Rome).

FINANCIAL AND ECONOMIC COMMITTEE, see **MONETARY COMMITTEE**

FISHERIES POLICY, see **COMMON FISHERIES POLICY**

FLAG, see **EUROPEAN FLAG**

FONTAINEBLÉAU AGREEMENT. Signed in June 1984, it concluded the long-standing controversy over the UK contributions to the Community Budget. The UK government had maintained the position that its contributions to the Community Budget were unjustifiably high. The Fontainebleau Agreement established a rebate of 66 per cent of the difference between the UK's Value-added Tax (VAT) contributions to the European Community and its share of Community benefits. In exchange the British government agreed that the general limit of VAT contributions should be raised from 1 to 1.4 per cent. Agreement was also reached on the increase of the Communities' 'own resources' and the reduction in agricultural spending. (See also, British Budget Crisis, Budget, Own Resources).

FORTRESS EUROPE. A phrase used by the Community's leading partners to express their fears that the Community would become a protectionist block and its member states would fortify themselves against external competition. Particularly prevalent in the 1980s, these fears among non-European Community partners stem from the observation that intra-Community trade grows faster than total trade. In fact, as a result of the Single European Market (SEM) programme, the share of intra-Community trade rose from 49 to 60 per cent over the 1970-90 period.

The European Community has consistently denied the protectionist character of the SEM. In the 1988 European Council decision at Rhodes the expression 'Partner of Europe' was adopted to counter the pejorative phrase Fortress Europe. This was reinforced by the Maastricht Treaty, which mentions the Community's contribution to world trade liberalization through the benefits of the SEM to non-European Community countries. (See also, Blair House Accord, GATT, SEM, Trade).

FOUCHET PLAN. Proposals put forward by a working committee chaired by the French diplomat Christian Fouchet. The committee was set up by a decision of the Six Heads of State in Paris (February 1961), initiated by de Gaulle, with the intention of investigating a form of political cooperation to be established along with the already advancing economic cooperation.

The committee submitted a draft in November 1961 that suggested a drastic restructuring of the community's institutional framework towards an intergovernmental form of political cooperation. It also proposed cooperation in the areas of foreign policy, defence and culture. The plan was met with little enthusiasm except from France.

A subsequent attempt in the form of a second draft tabled in January 1962 was also rejected by the five members of the community on the grounds that it reiterated the former position rather than make provisions for a compromise. Negotiations were never resumed. The failure of the Fouchet Plan brought to the surface serious disagreements and differences in ideological orientation between Community partners. Charles de Gaulle's adept efforts to consolidate the intergovernmental character of the Community failed, as did his vision of a Europe with closer cooperation in foreign and security issues that would secure its independence from the North Atlantic

Treaty Organization (NATO) and the USA. (See also, CFSP, EPC, Intergovernmentalism).

FOUR FREEDOMS. An expression used to signify the essential means for the achievement of the Single European Market (SEM) defined by the Single European Act (SEA) as an area without internal frontiers. The four freedoms are: the free movement of goods, persons, services and capital. (See also, SEA, SEM).

FRAUD. There is common consent among member states that there is considerable overspending and waste in relation to the Community Budget. The sums involved give rise to suspicion of malpractice. Estimates regarding the level of fraud vary between 1.2 per cent and as much as 10 per cent of the community Budget. Most cases of fraud have occurred in relation to the Common Agricultural Policy (CAP) and structural policies.

In 1994 the Commission put forward a number of proposals with the intention of fighting fraud decisively. Firstly, a closer partnership with member states was introduced in order to overcome the limited awareness of national and regional authorities concerning the Community Budget. This aimed at ensuring that a similar need for stringency in fighting fraud was perceived both at community and national level. National and regional authorities are responsible for directing as much as 80 per cent of community funds to beneficiaries.

Secondly, European Community institutions dealing with fraud were strengthened and given more responsibilities. The Unit for the Coordination of Fraud Prevention (UCLAF) acquired more personnel and control of the anti-fraud units within the DGs for Agriculture and Customs and Indirect Taxation. The Court of Auditors (COA) was given the power to challenge the Commission or any member state should they fail to act against fraud. However, it remains questionable whether the root of the problem of excessive fraud has been tackled. (See also, COA, Discharge Procedure, EP).

FREEDOM OF ESTABLISHMENT. According to this principle, all employed and self-employed persons working within the Community are to enjoy the same rights as the nationals of the host member state. In the case of self employed persons, freedom of establishment includes the right to set up and manage any enterprise (e.g. firm or company), under the legal conditions laid down by the host country for its own nationals and subject to provisions of the Chapter relating to capital.

Freedom of establishment gives a person the right to enter and reside in the member state in which he or she wishes to engage in employment or self-employment. In fact, the right of establishment for employed and self-employed persons in a member state implies permanent residence in the country of establishment. This right extends to the spouses, children and other family members of employed and self-employed persons. Conversely, the right of establishment for providers of services does not necessarily imply permanent residence, since the provider can be established in a member state other than that of the person for whom the services are intended.

However, free movement of persons, and consequently the right of establishment, were impeded because of the numerous requirements of member states with regard to employed and self-employed persons. As a result, the Council of Ministers was empowered to issue directives for the mutual recognition of diplomas, certificates and other evidence of formal qualifications.(See also, Citizenship, SEM).

FREE MOVEMENT OF CAPITAL, see **FOUR FREEDOMS, SEM**

FREE MOVEMENT OF GOODS, see **FOUR FREEDOMS, SEM**

FREE MOVEMENT OF PERSONS, see **FOUR FREEDOMS, SEM**

FREE TRADE AREA, see **CUSTOMS UNION, EFTA**

FREEDOM TO PROVIDE SERVICES, see **FOUR FREEDOMS, SEM**

G

GENERAL AGREEMENT ON TARIFFS AND TRADE (GATT). A set of multilateral trade agreements signed in Geneva in 1947, came into force in January 1948. GATT was aimed at abolishing quotas and reducing tariff duties among the twenty-three signatories. It proved to be the most effective agent of world trade liberalization and has played a major role in the massive expansion of trade in the post-war era.

Periodically, major multilateral conferences have been held to establish tariff reductions and other related issues. Between 1947 and 1993, seven such Rounds took place. The most important among them were the so-called Kennedy Round 1964-67, the Tokyo Round 1973-79, and the Uruguay Round 1986-1994, all held in Geneva. Agreements, reducing average tariffs on the world's industrial goods from 40 per cent of their market value in 1947 to less than 5 per cent in 1993, were concluded.

During the Uruguay Round, some significant and long-lasting disagreements were finally resolved. Disputes, such as the one between the USA and the EU over agricultural subsidies were settled by the Blair House Accord with a bilateral compromise. Other disputes, such as that between France and USA over the audiovisual sector proved to be insoluble and had to be omitted from the overall conclusions. The negotiations made apparent the conflicting interests within the EU. Governments varied in their attitude. Denmark, Germany, The Netherlands and the UK, were committed to trade liberalisation. By contrast, France being the Union's leading agricultural producer and the world's second biggest agricultural exporter, opposed the deal vigorously, but failed to gain wider support for renegotiation.

In spite of its possible shortcomings the Uruguay Round was a real breakthrough in the history of trade liberalization as it reduced tariffs on industrial goods by an average 40 per cent, lessened agricultural subsidies and paved the way for new agreements in the services sector. A set of new rules on intellectual property established more guarantees for the protection of patents, and stricter controls against pirated goods and infringement of copyright. The Treaty also created a new global organisation, the World Trade Organization (WTO), to monitor and regulate international trade. At the end of the Uruguay Round, GATT ceased to exist, but most of its principles were adopted by the WTO. (See also, Blair House Accord, CAP, GSP, Multifibre Arrangement, Quotas, Tariffs, WTO).

GENERALIZED SYSTEM OF PREFERENCES (GSP). Introduced in 1971, the GSP is concerned with reductions of customs duties for imports of industrial and other processed products from developing countries to the European Community. However, quotas continue to apply to certain products allowed for import, while other products are entirely excluded.

The main beneficiaries of the system were meant to have been the poorest developing countries outside the Lomé Convention, provided that exports from these countries could be competitive. For a number of reasons, however, China, Brazil and the industrialized Asian countries have mostly profited from the system. At present, the benefits of the GSP to developing countries have diminished as a result of the general reduction of customs duties introduced by the General Agreement on Tariffs and Trade (GATT). (See also, GATT, Quotas, Tariffs, Lomé Convention).

GENSCHER-COLOMBO PLAN. A bilateral initiative taken in 1981 by the German and Italian Foreign Ministers, Hans-Dietrich Genscher and Emilio Colombo, advocating the further development of European Political Cooperation (EPC) through the adoption of a common foreign policy and the coordination of security policy. The plan also envisaged a number of institutional and procedural reforms.

The reception of the plan by member states at the European Council meeting in London (November 1981), was somewhat ambiguous, and no definite decision was taken on the proposal. Followed by long negotiations in Brussels the document was reduced to a mere declaration without any binding effect. In June 1983, most of these proposals were included in the Solemn Declaration issued formally by the European Council meeting at Stuttgart. (See also, CFSP, EPC).

GREEN RATES, see **CAP**

GROUP OF EIGHT (G8) - GROUP OF SEVEN (G7). The term G7 is used to describe the seven leading industrial nations of the world, USA, Canada, Japan, France, Germany, Italy and the UK. In the 1990s, as a result of the attendance of some summits by Russia, the G7 occasionally is referred G8. Usually, summits concerned with political issues are held by the G8, while those concerned with financial matters are held by the G7. The term G8 was used for the first time during the 23rd annual economic summit at Denver, 20-22 June 1997.

As neither Group is a formalized body, no mechanism is provided for an official name change. For the same reason, the annual summit is supported by a series of ministerial meetings that take place throughout the year. The first summit was concerned with broad economic issues and took place in 1975 with the participation of Heads of Governments and Finance Ministers of the G7 countries. The summits are also attended by the President of the Commission on behalf of the European Community.

H

HARD CORE EUROPE, see **TWO-SPEED EUROPE**

HARMONISATION. Term used to describe the efforts made by the Community to create uniformity in European standards in such a way as to ensure free movement of goods within the Community. This was one of the principal objectives of the Treaty of Rome. However, because of the diversity in scientific, safety and health standards applied in member states little was achieved in this direction.

The 1979 judgement of the Court of Justice, known as the '*Cassis de Dijon*' case[11], established the principle of mutual recognition of product standards, namely that products lawfully sold in one member country can be lawfully sold in the rest of the European Community. Mutual recognition of standards of products was a further step towards the realization of the Single European Market (SEM) in that, even when new directives could not be agreed upon, products and services could still be traded in any and every member state.

The 1985 White Paper reinforced this principle further. It called for a 'new approach' based on mutual recognition whereby only minimal standards would be harmonised, in particular those referring to health and safety. Technical details were left to be decided by specialist bodies. Harmonisation, under this new perspective, is one of the fundamental components of the SEM. (See also, Cockfield White Paper, Taxation).

HELIOS. Action plan aiming at promoting social and economic integration and an independent way of life for disabled people, by ensuring equal opportunities in employment and access to vocational training. The Plan was adopted in 1988.

---

[11] This case concerned the import of the French liqueur, *Cassis de Dijon*, into Germany. The German authorities forbade the sale of the liqueur in Germany because of its low alcoholic content (maximum strength of 20 per cent per volume). The importer claimed before the German court that this prohibition was incompatible with Community law on the grounds that it imposed restrictions to free movement of goods, or discriminated against goods produced and marketed in other member states. The national court referred the case to the European Court of Justice for a preliminary ruling. The European Court of Justice ruled that any product retailed in one member state cannot be prohibited in another, except on the grounds of public health.

HELSINKI FINAL ACT. It was signed in 1975 by 33 European states, the USA and Canada at the conclusion of the first Conference on Security and Cooperation in Europe (CSCE). The Act was primarily an effort to reduce tensions between the Soviet Union and the Western block by securing their common acceptance of the post-war status quo. It also outlined progress in economic, scientific and other fields and introduced human rights as a specific element in European interstate relations. The Helsinki Final Act is non-binding and does not have Treaty status. (See also, CSCE, Human Rights).

HIGH AUTHORITY. One of the main institutions of the European Coal and Steel Community (ECSC), which under the 1967 Merger Treaty merged with the Commissions of the European Economic Community (EEC) and EURATOM to form the new Commission of the European Communities. (See also, ECSC, EEC, EURATOM, Merger Treaty).

HUMAN RIGHTS. Human rights were of paramount priority in the post-World War II period. In 1948 the United Nations (UN) adopted the Universal Declaration of Human Rights, but no mechanism for the enforcement of the provisions of the Declaration was established. At European level, the Convention of the Protection of Human Rights and Fundamental Freedoms was adopted by the Council of Europe (CE) in 1950. The Convention came into force in 1953 and represents one of the most advanced and successful international experiments in the field of human rights by providing an elaborate control mechanism, consisting of the European Commission of Human Rights, the European Court of Human Rights and a Committee of Ministers. In addition, the Convention required signatory states to recognize that individuals have rights under international law, though it never intended to replace national law.

Complaints of human rights violations may be received by the Commission from any party member of the Convention, or any person, or group of individuals, or non-governmental organizations. If the Commission fails to provide a solution at the first level, then it draws a full report recommending action by the Committee of Ministers; it also refers the case to the European Court of Human Rights. The Committee of Ministers makes a final decision on human rights complaints in regard to cases not referred to the Court.

By comparison, human rights considerations were never given primacy by the founding Treaties of the European Community. It was not until 1977 that the Presidents of the European Parliament and the European Commission and the President in Office of the Council of

Ministers signed a Joint Declaration on Fundamental Rights in the spirit of the Convention. More recently, however, an increasing awareness of Community institutions has been observed concerning human rights; a case in point is the blocking of Turkish membership to the Union on the grounds of human rights violations. Similarly, a number of Association Agreements were delayed or never concluded for that reason. (See also, CE, European Court of Human Rights).

INDUSTRIAL POLICY. Although the idea of a common market is closely related to industry, industrial policy as such was not spelled out by either the Treaty of Rome or the Single European Act (SEA). It was in fact the Maastricht Treaty that set out the objectives of a common industrial policy aimed at speeding up the adjustment of industry to structural changes, encouraging an environment favourable to new undertakings, particularly small and medium-sized enterprises (SMEs), encouraging innovation, research and development. However, since the inception of the Community, certain policies, such as competition policy, free movement of goods and capital and the creation of the single market, have considerably affected the pattern of European industrial development.

Unlike the 1950s and 1960s, the 1970s were years of decline for traditional industries and the competitive position of European firms in world markets. The need for more decisive support of the industrial sector became imperative. As a response, the Commission launched two memoranda, under the title *Memorandum on Industrial Policy* in 1970 and 1973 respectively. Because of the differing attitudes among member states to industrial affairs, as well as the differing problems within individual states, the proposals put forward by either memoranda were largely ignored. Nevertheless, the debate concerning the necessity of a common industrial policy was inaugurated.

During the completion of the Single European Market (SEM) in 1992 special attention was paid to SMEs which it was assumed were facing both their greatest opportunity and their greatest challenge. On the one hand, the elimination of customs formalities under the SEA was largely beneficial to them; on the other, they were exposed to competition as products of any member state could be sold freely in previously protected markets, and larger enterprises were better placed to take advantage of new market opportunities. The SEA introduced an action programme aimed at simplifying administrative, financial and legal constraints for SMEs and encouraging co-operation between firms from different regions of the Community.

The 1990s marked a change in industrial policy matters. In 1990 the Commission in its effort to initiate an industrial strategy published a study entitled '*Industrial policy in an open and competitive environment*', to be followed by a chapter on industrial policy in the Maastricht Treaty. The Treaty provides for the Commission to take initiatives with regard to industrial policy, especially on aspects promoting the competitiveness of European industries. The Council of

Ministers can make decisions following the Commission's proposals, complementary to the policies of member states. Such decisions can be adopted only if based on unanimity.

Support is provided to traditional industry, such as steel, textiles, shipbuilding, and to new sectors, such as information technology and telecommunications. The structural funds and European Investment Bank (EIB) loans, Research and Technological Development (RTD) programmes, such as ESPRIT, BRITE and Research and Development in Advanced Communications Programme for Europe (RACE), are the main channels of this sort of support.

There has been a long-standing debate, both within the Community and among the national governments of the member states, about the role of state intervention in the restructuring process, the limits of the free market, and a number of similar issues revolving around these subjects. This divergence in opinion has often undermined the implementation of a common industrial policy and has allowed member states to follow their own methods in dealing with the problem. (See also, Competition Policy, RTD, SEM, SMEs, Telecommunications Policy).

INTEGRATED MEDITERRANEAN PROGRAMMES (IMP). Distinct regional programmes introduced in 1984 by a decision of the Council of Ministers. The programmes were a response to Greece's complaints about its accession terms to the Community. The IMPs embraced all Mediterranean regions including Southern France, Spain, Portugal, Italy and Greece in order to enable them to adjust under the best conditions possible, to the new situation created by their accession to the community. For the period 1986-92, the IMPs were financed mainly by the structural funds, and from 1992, mainly by the Cohesion Fund. (See also, Cohesion Fund, Regional Development).

INTERGOVERNMENTAL CONFERENCE (IGC). An IGC constitutes a series of meetings attended by representatives from the governments of member states, at which meetings amendments to the Treaties are discussed. These meetings often become forums for broader debates concerning the very future of the Community. They are convened at the request of the Council of Ministers and any decisions taken must be unanimous, although ratification by the national parliaments or electorates of the member states is required. The intergovernmental nature of these meetings and their decisions limit the range of influence of the Commission and the European Parliament (EP).

The most recent IGC began its sessions in March 1996 and ended in June 1997 in Turin, Italy. Its wide scope was confirmed by the European Council summits held in Corfu and in Essen in 1994. The Essen summit agreed on the formation of the Reflection Group to prepare for the 1996 IGC, which undertook the ambitious task of reviewing the Maastricht Treaty and of dealing with any issues left pending. The issues discussed at the time included, institutional change to prepare the Community for future enlargement, the further development of a common foreign and security policy, the extension of qualified majority voting (QMV) in the Council of Ministers, the incorporation of the Western European Union (WEU) into the European Union (EU), flexibility and citizenship.

However, only limited progress was made as each member state presented the Conference with its own priorities or was eager to include on the agenda more general questions concerning the future of the Community. France, for instance, put forward the thorny question of unemployment and poverty, accusing the Community of delaying job-creation schemes agreed in previous summits. The UK, on the other hand, insisted on retaining its right to opt out from the Social Charter, and resisted any steps towards the further development of a common foreign and security policy by its insistence on retaining unanimous voting in this field. Both France and the UK opposed further increase of the powers of the EP and the Court of Justice, while Italy was in favour. On the other hand, France and Italy favoured the gradual development and even the integration of the WEU as a component in the defence of the EU, while the UK opposed it. In addition to these divergent positions, the uncertainty over the future of the single currency and the Economic and Monetary Union (EMU) further complicated the progress of the Conference.

Most of the negotiations taking place during the 1996 IGC represented a preparation for the Amsterdam summit and the drafting of the new Amsterdam Treaty. Similarly, the two IGCs of 1990 and 1991, concerning the EMU and the European Political Union respectively, prepared the ground for the Maastricht summit and the Maastricht Treaty. Of no less importance was the 1985 IGC which resulted in the Single European Act (SEA). (See also, Intergovernmentalism, Maastricht Treaty, Reflection Group).

INTERGOVERNMENTALISM. A form of integration which is based on governments' participation in shared decision-making concerning certain areas of activities. This is contrary to supranationalism which requires a decision-making transfer from national governments to supranational bodies. Both forms of integration involve, to a degree, the erosion of the sovereignty of the participating states, but supranationalism, inevitably, more so. The difference in substance between intergovernmentalism and supranationalism has been the cause of persistent controversy among the member states of the Community.

As early as 1965, President de Gaulle opposed the rise of supranationalism by withdrawing France from most of the Community's decision-making forums. The outcome was the 1966 Luxembourg compromise, which reinforced the intergovernmental elements in the decision-making process by further containing the powers of the European Parliament (EP) and the Commission, and by replacing majority voting with unanimity in most cases in the Council of Ministers. The accession to the Community of the UK, Denmark and Greece further reinforced intergovernmentalism. Nevertheless, supranationalism could not be constrained further and the European Commission, the EP and Court of Justice continue to play a very important role in the functioning of the Community. Therefore, the EU displays both intergovernmental and supranational characteristics.

Intergovernmentalism is reflected in the Common Foreign and Security Policy (CFSP) and Justice and Home Affairs (JHA), which specifically became subject to intergovernmental cooperation under the so-called pillars of the Maastricht Treaty. Decisions related to the general direction of the Community are taken by the Heads of Governments in the European Council summits, in most cases by a unanimous vote. Most of the decisions are taken at ministerial level and in most cases consensus has to be reached.

Supranationalism, on the other hand, is reflected in the fact that the Commission is almost solely responsible for initiating legislation and most legislation is enacted in its name. As a result of the Single European Act (SEA) and the Maastricht Treaty qualified majority voting in the Council of Ministers was extended to certain areas where unanimity was previously required. The powers of the EP were enhanced with the introduction of the cooperation and assent procedures by the SEA and the co-decision procedure by the Maastricht Treaty. In the event of conflict between national and Community law, the Community law takes precedence.

The controversy over the character of the Community as supranational or intergovernmental still goes on and so does the parallel introduction and strengthening of certain aspects of institutions possessing both features. At the moment, there is no evidence to suggest that the Community may be transformed to a purely intergovernmental body, such as the Organization for Economic

Cooperation and Development (OECD) or North Atlantic Treaty Organization (NATO), or to a purely supranational body. (See also, CFSP, Community Law, Council of the EU, European Commission, EP, JHA, Maastricht Treaty, Sovereignty).

INTERNAL AUDIT. Collection and presentation of all information pertaining to the Community Budget, its assets and liabilities together with an analysis of the previous financial year submitted to the Court of Auditors (responsible for the external audit), the EP and the Council. Responsibility for the internal audit lies with the Commission and this is delegated to the Directorate-General XX, responsible for financial control. (See also, COA, External Audit).

INTERNAL MARKET. The phrase is used to indicate the economic activity within the member states of the Community as opposed to that of the European Community with third parties. The internal market was one of the fundamental goals of the Treaty of Rome, but it was substantially strengthened by the Single European Act (SEA), which introduced the necessary institutional reforms for the completion of the internal market by December 1992. (See also, SEA, SEM).

INTERNATIONAL ATOMIC ENERGY AGENCY. It was established in 1956 with the main objective of enhancing the contribution of atomic energy to the world's peace and prosperity. The agency is extremely vigilant in making sure that any assistance it gives is not used for military purposes. Its work includes research into the application of atomic energy in medicine, agriculture and industry. The agency is based in Vienna. (See also, EURATOM).

INTERNATIONAL BANK FOR RECONSTRUCTION AND DEVELOPMENT (IBRD). Widely known as the World Bank, it has its origins in the Bretton-Woods Conference of 1944. Constituted in 1945, it became operational in June 1946, with the purpose of financing productive projects that promoted economic development, particularly in Africa, Asia, Middle East and Latin America. The Bank makes loans directly to governments or to private enterprises which enjoy government guarantees. The World Bank is an organization affiliated to the United Nations (UN) and is based in Washington. (See also, IMF, UN)

INTERNATIONAL MONETARY FUND (IMF). Founded at the Bretton-Woods Conference of 1944, it was constituted in 1946 and became operational in 1947. It aims at securing international monetary cooperation, stabilising exchange rates, and expanding international liquidity. In addition, member states can be assisted in temporary balance-of-payments difficulties by Standby Arrangements, by provision of borrowing facilities by standby credit, or by compensation for losses over export receipts (Compensatory Financing of Export Fluctuations).

The IMF has gradually developed into a new multi-billion dollar pool out of which it lends money to developing countries under certain terms, sometimes regarded as too stringent by the recipient countries. The IMF is a specialized agent of the United Nations (UN) and is based in Washington. (See also, IBRD, UN).

INTERVENTION - INTERVENTION PRICE, see **CAP**

IOANNINA COMPROMISE. A compromise reached in March 1994 at the meeting of foreign ministers in Ioannina, Greece, in relation to the controversial issue of qualified majority voting (QMV) in the Council of Ministers. The dispute arose over the blocking minority question in the Council of Ministers relating to the entry of Austria, Finland, Norway and Sweden into the European Community in 1995. It was agreed that Austria and Sweden would be given 4 votes each, while Finland and Norway 3 each, thus increasing the total votes in the Council of Ministers to 90. The Greek presidency proposed that the threshold for QMV be raised from 54 to 64 votes out of a total 76 and 90, respectively. This meant that the blocking minority would be 27 rather than 23 as previously.

This proposal was opposed by the UK government on the grounds that the position of large states vis-à-vis the small ones would be further weakened, and that the correlation between population and voting strength would become even less representative, and therefore less democratic. Cooperation in this between the UK and the Spanish governments succeeded in securing an agreement with regard to QMV, which was fixed at 64 out of 90. A resolution of the blocking minority dispute and discussion of the qualified majority issue in general were postponed until the 1996 IGC. In the meantime it was agreed that if a proposal in the Council of Ministers was opposed by a minority of 23-26, then the Council was committed to do all in its power to find a satisfactory solution within a reasonable time. Since Norway did not finally accede to the Community, the qualified majority was changed to 62, the blocking minority to 26, while a minority of 23-25 was sufficient to commit the Council to discuss the matter under consideration further. (See also, Council of the EU, Luxembourg Compromise, Majority Voting).

ISOGLUCOSE CASE. In 1980 the Court of Justice annulled a piece of legislation on the grounds that the European Parliament (EP) had not given an opinion. The case concerned isoglucose, a form of sugar extracted from cereals. The case was taken to the Court by a firm that was affected by the production quota on isoglucose as laid down by the Council. The decision of the Council was declared null and void on the grounds of formality, in that the EP was not consulted in this case. The significance of the isoglucose judgement, issued just one year after the first EP elections, lies in the fact that it enhanced further Parliament's prestige and influence in respect to legislation. (See also, Co-decision and Cooperation Procedure, EP).

J

JOINT ACTION. The two intergovernmental pillars of the EU, the Common Foreign and Security Policy (CFSP) and Justice and Home Affairs (JHA), are not subject to procedures applied in other spheres of Union policies. This means that they are not subject to Community law; nor has the Commission the sole right to initiate policy, or the European Parliament (EP) the scrutiny powers, which it enjoys in other areas.

Instead, as specified by the Maastricht Treaty, the Council of Ministers may adopt a common position and may take a joint action within the framework of CFSP and JHA. Member states have to adopt the stance taken by the Council of Ministers. With reference to the CFSP, the Council of Ministers is empowered to take decisions by unanimity under the direction of the European Council. While in the context of JHA any individual member state, and in some cases the Commission, may propose joint action. The Council again decides by unanimity. Any follow-up decisions related to both policies are taken by qualified majority voting (QMV). (See also, CFSP, Common Position, Council of the EU, JHA).

JOINT EUROPEAN TORUS (JET). A joint undertaking set up in 1978 with the purpose of constructing and operating the world's largest magnetic confinement fusion experiment, which aims at confirming the scientific theory of fusion and the scientific feasibility of nuclear fusion for power generation. In November 1991, JET achieved the first ever production of fusion power.

Eighty per cent of the JET programme is financed by the European Atomic Energy Community (EURATOM); the remaining expense is shared between the countries associated with the European fusion programme. The JET site is located at Culham, Oxfordshire, and the team of scientists is recruited from the participating countries. (See also, EURATOM, JRC, NET).

JOINT RESEARCH CENTRE (JRC). A scientific and research centre of the Community set up in 1958 under the auspices of the European Atomic Energy Community (EURATOM). It has four sites in Geel (Belgium), Karlsruhe (Germany), Ispra (Italy) and Petten (Netherlands). It consists of nine different institutes, each with its own focus of expertise. The JRC performs scientific research and technology development for the European Commission, national agencies, universities from member states and other countries.

Scientific provisions, referring to material, database services, environmental protection, research on nuclear safety that may be applied throughout Europe, are available at the Centre. (See also, EURATOM, JET, NET).

JUSTICE AND HOME AFFAIRS (JHA). One of the two intergovernmental pillars of the European Union (EU) established by the Maastricht Treaty. With regard to JHA, the Treaty requires that in areas of common interest member states must inform and consult each other within the Council of Ministers. These areas include asylum policy, control of the Union's external frontiers, immigration policy, combating drug addiction and fraud on an international scale, judicial cooperation in civil and criminal matters, customs cooperation, and police cooperation to combat and prevent terrorism, drug trafficking and other serious forms of international crime.

It must be noted that visa policy was not included in the areas of common interest, but is dealt with by a separate article, 100c, added to the Treaty of Rome by the Maastricht Treaty of 1992, with effect from 1996. By replacing unanimity with qualified majority in the Council of Ministers, this article enabled a visa policy to be put into effect. Nevertheless, the Council of Ministers, after consultation with the EP, continues to be responsible for drawing up a list of those countries whose nationals must be in possession of a visa when crossing the external borders of the member states.

In the context of JHA, members inform and consult each other in matters of common interest in order to adopt a joint action, or common position, or to draw up conventions which will be recommended to member states for adoption. To this end, institutional provisions are made by the Maastricht Treaty. At the administrative level, Article K4 establishes a committee of senior officials to coordinate and prepare the Council's work and to give opinions on matters of JHA. At the political level, this committee is supervised by the Council of Ministers, consisting of Justice and Home Affairs ministers. Administrative costs for the JHA are charged to the Budget of the Community, but operational ones are borne either by the Budget or directly by member states.

As in all intergovernmental arrangements, so in JHA, power lies with the national governments. Consequently, the Council of Ministers is the principal decision-making body. The European Parliament's (EP) role is limited to simple consultation, although it has the right to ask questions, or to make recommendations to the Council and be kept informed by the Presidency of the Council. Similarly, the Commission does not have the exclusive right of policy initiation in JHA as it has in other policy areas, and it is obliged to consider requests from member states. Moreover, JHA is not under the jurisdiction of the Court of Justice.

The provisions made by the Maastricht Treaty for JHA represent a continuity of the *ad hoc* procedures long employed by the Community. Since the 1970s there has been increasing cooperation among member states in matters relating to terrorism, drugs and organized crime. The so-called Trevi process brought together officials from Interior and Justice ministries, senior police and intelligence officers on a confidential basis, with the purpose of exchanging information on these matters. The need to develop a more extensive cooperation in this sphere increased with the Single European Market (SEM) programme, which pre-supposes the dismantling of internal borders.

It is likely that the role of the JHA, together with the Common Foreign and Security Policy (CFSP), will remain contentious for years to come, for any strengthening of its powers will require further transfer of powers to European Community institutions. Despite varying degrees of commitment to the JHA, no national government is willing to release more powers related to such a sensitive area of policy. (See also, Berlin Declaration, Common Position, Council of the EU, European Commission, European Council, Intergovernmentalism, Joint Action, Maastricht Treaty).

K

KANGAROO GROUP. Consisting of members of the European Parliament (EP) of every political orientation and symbolically named after the ability of Kangaroo to 'hop over borders', the Group sought to speed up the integration process by removing the non-tariff barriers[12] to trade between member states. It played a very significant role in the perception and implementation of the Single Market programme, but it neither advocated a federalist Community nor aimed at broader institutional reform. One of the most successful pressure groups was particularly active in the 1980s. (See also, SEM).

KARLSRUHE JUDGEMENT. A judgement of the German Federal Constitutional Court in Karlsruhe on the case brought against the German government by an action group opposing the Maastricht Treaty. A ruling in favour of the opposition group, advocating that the Treaty was incompatible with German law, would have had complex political implications and may have prevented ratification of the Maastricht Treaty in Germany.

However, the judgement of the Constitutional Court took into consideration the intergovernmental character of the European Union (EU), which was ensured by the Treaty with the establishment of the Common Foreign and Security Policy (CFSP) and Justice and Home Affairs (JHA). It was on these grounds that the compatibility of the Treaty with German law was demonstrated, since the latter permits sovereign powers to be transferred to intergovernmental institutions. The Karlsruhe judgement therefore enabled Germany to ratify the Treaty. A similar problem was faced by the Irish government concerning the ratification of the Single European Act (SEA) of 1987. On that occasion, however, the Supreme Court of Ireland ruled the Treaty unconstitutional, and only constitutional reform made possible its ratification. (See also, CFSP, Intergovernmentalism, JHA).

KONVER. A Community initiative developed to help regions faced with a decline in defence spending. Funds are utilized for the conversion of

---

[12] The term denotes trade barriers arising from different norms and technical product specifications between member states, different regulations for plant and animal products, border controls and customs formalities, market distorting pricing and subsidies, and different tax rates. Non-tariff barriers should not be confused with tariffs, quotas, or levies imposed on imports and exports.

defence industries. The main beneficiaries are Germany, France and the UK. (See also, Regional Policy).

L

'**LAKE**'. The name used to describe a severe dispute between France and Italy over trade in wine. In 1975 this dispute developed into a major Community crisis when the French authorities, following widespread demonstrations by French wine producers banned all wine imports. The protest was against cheap wine imports, mainly Italian, which had caused a fall in the price of French wine under the level guaranteed by the Common Agricultural Policy (CAP). As a result, intervention buying had built up a 'lake' of wine surpluses, mainly French. A compromise was eventually reached. The French government agreed to end its import ban and to introduce ways of reducing French wine production; in return the Council of Ministers agreed that an additional 460 million litres of stored wine could be distilled. The name 'lake' and 'mountain' have been used more widely to describe any surpluses created within the Union, largely as a result of the CAP. (See also, CAP).

'**LAMB WAR**'. A dispute arising between France and the UK in 1979-80 because of French fears that unrestricted British lamb imports would damage French producers. Since lamb was not covered by the Common Agricultural Policy (CAP), the French unilaterally restricted these imports. As a result of the dispute, lamb and mutton came under regulation of the CAP, which was principally applied by imposing limitations on New Zealand imports. (See also, CAP).

LANGUAGE. The increase in the number of official languages in the European Community has kept pace with its enlargement. At its creation it had only four languages, French, German, Dutch and Italian; by 1973, they increased to six with the addition of English and Danish; by 1981, Greek was added and by 1986, Spanish and Portuguese; by 1995, the Community had acquired a total of eleven languages, the last being Swedish and Finnish.

Official documents must be available in all languages at meetings, and full interpretation is provided. The Commission uses a fully mechanized method, the so-called SYSTRAN, for translating. The European Parliament (EP) is the institution most affected by the use of so many languages and runs the risk of creating numerous misunderstandings. Only the Court of Justice out of the five main institutions of the European Community is not obliged to follow this rule, but can choose a procedural language for each case.

It has been suggested that the number of working languages be reduced to three or four, while leaving the number of official languages as they are. However, there is considerable opposition to such a solution as member states refuse to place their national language into a secondary position. Furthermore, such a solution will not contribute to the reduction of languages used in the EP as elected politicians cannot be required to work in a language other than their own. No viable alternative has yet been found and the problem is expected to worsen with the Community's future enlargement and the increase of official languages to 15, if all five prospective countries are admitted. (See also, SYSTRAN).

LEAGUE OF NATIONS. An international organization established at the end of the World War I by the victorious Allied Powers. Based in Geneva, the organization aimed at international cooperation. The League Covenant, included in the Versailles Treaty of 1919, incorporated the principle of collective security, arbitration of international disputes, reduction of armaments and open diplomacy. The Covenant also established the League's directing bodies, an assembly composed of representatives of all members, a council composed of permanent and non-permanent representatives, and a secretariat, presided over by a secretary general. It also provided for a Permanent Court of International Justice and for a system whereby colonies in Asia and Africa would be distributed among the Allied Powers in the form of mandates.

The League was weakened from the beginning of its creation, because of the failure of the USA Congress to ratify the Versailles Treaty containing the League Covenant; as a result, the USA never became a member of the League. But the final blow came in the 1930s when Germany, Japan and Italy, dissatisfied with the Versailles Treaty, challenged the *status quo* by a number of aggressive actions, such as Italy's annexation of Abyssinia (modern Ethiopia), the expansion of Japan into Manchuria, and the repudiation of the Versailles Treaty by Hitler. The League found itself in a weak position as it had no means to enforce its will, other than through its member states.

The League ceased its activities during World War II. In 1946 it was replaced by the United Nations (UN), which inherited many of its purposes and methods and much of its structure. (See also, UN).

LEGISLATION (TYPES OF). Legislation, also known as secondary legislation, forms and is a part of Community law derived from the Treaties but enacted by Community institutions. It is to be distinguished from the Treaties and the case-law of the Court of Justice. The most common types of secondary legislation are Regulations, Decisions, Directives, Recommendations and Opinions. A Regulation is binding in all its elements and is directly applicable in member states. A Decision, on the other hand, is binding in all its elements upon those to whom it is addressed. Regulations and Decisions may be issued by the Council of Ministers or the European Commission and must be based on one or more Treaties. A Regulation substitutes Community law for national law and consequently is the most effective legal instrument provided by the Treaty. Regulations take effect on a set date, or, if no date is set, on the twentieth day following their publication in the *Official Journal of the European Communities* (OJ). Decisions, on the other hand, take effect from the date of their communication to the addressee rather than the date of their publication in the OJ.

A Directive is binding upon each member state to which it is addressed, but the form and methods by which it is to be achieved is left to the national authority. Like the Regulations and Decisions, Directives must be based on one or more Treaties, but for their application they must be enacted as national laws in conformity with the procedures of each member state. Directives referring to all member states must be published in the OJ, but do not take effect until the member states to which they are addressed have been notified.

As to the Opinions and Recommendations there is no common consent as to whether they constitute forms of secondary legislation, since they have no binding force on the member states. Their principal aim is to assist in the interpretation and implementation of legal acts. This also applies to Resolutions, Action programmes, Guidelines, etc. through which the Council and the European Commission may express their wishes in a certain policy area. (See also, Community Law, Direct Applicability, Direct Effect, OJ, Primacy).

LEONARDO. An education programme introduced in 1995 with the purpose of promoting vocational training schemes and language skills in member states, as well as fostering innovation in training programmes. It replaced a number of more fragmented programmes, such as COMETT, PETRA, FORCE and LINGUA. For the period 1995-99 Leonardo has a budget of ECU 620 million, assigned to it by the Community Budget, although the programme also covers non-European Community members. (See also, COMETT, Education Policy, LINGUA, PETRA, Socrates).

LEVY. In general a levy is a form of duty. In the literature of the Community, and more specifically in relation to the Common Agricultural Policy (CAP), it is an adjustable levy imposed on agricultural commodities imported into the Community from third countries when world prices are lower than Community prices. A levy accounts for the difference between the import price and the target price operating in the European Community. Levies are extensively used for cereals, dairy products, sugar and olive oil. The operation of levies not only offers protection to the European agricultural sector from low cost imports, but it also accounts for a source of income to the Community's Budget. (See also, Budget, CAP).

LIFE. A programme that funds various actions on the environment, such as projects promoting nature-protection clean technologies, waste management and protection of natural habitats. Its budget over the period 1996-9 amounts to ECU 450 million. (See also, Environment Policy).

LINGUA. Operational since 1990, the programme aimed at promoting the learning of foreign languages among students and teachers in the European Community through exchanges and improvement of learning techniques. In 1995, the programme was merged with Socrates and Leonardo. (see also, Education Policy, Leonardo, Socrates).

LOME CONVENTION. A Treaty on cooperation and development signed in 1975 at Lomé, the capital of Togo, between member states of the European Community and the ACP countries. So far it has been renewed three times. The Lomé convention revived relations that the ACP countries enjoyed with individual member states of the Community prior to their accession. With the exception of Ethiopia and Liberia, the ACP countries were ex-colonies of former European powers. Currently, 71 ACP countries have signed the Convention.

The Treaty arranged for a non-reciprocal trading relationship between the European Community and ACP countries. ACP countries were not obliged to offer access to European Economic Community (EEC) exports, while ACP exports were granted duty-free access for almost all their products, including as much as 96 per cent of their agricultural produce (usually not produced in the European Community). Products which came under the marketing arrangements of the Common Agricultural Policy (CAP) were excluded from duty-free treatment; nevertheless they enjoyed preferential treatment. Special provisions were made for products, such as sugar, bananas, rum, beef, tomatoes, these being of special importance to the economies of certain ACP countries.

Moreover, a system, known as STABEX, concerning stabilization of export earnings of ACP countries, was introduced. It was designed to ensure export revenues for ACP countries against any shortfall of earnings, resulting from production difficulties caused by natural conditions or changes in the overall economic situation.

In terms of institutions, the Lomé Convention set up a Joint Council of Ministers, a Joint Committee of Ambassadors, a Joint Consultative Assembly and an ACP Secretariat based at Brussels. It also introduced the European Development Fund (EDF), a special fund financed directly by the member states.

Lomé II was signed in 1979 and largely retained the same provisions as Lomé I. In addition, it introduced a complementary scheme known as SYSMIN, also referred to as MINEX, which aimed at maintaining the export capacity of mineral products of ACP countries.

Lomé III, signed in 1984, emphasized the use of development aid and laid down stricter controls on how money received under STABEX and SYSMIN was spent.

Lomé IV, signed in 1989, reformed the STABEX scheme and provided for a separate fund to help those ACP countries undertaking an International Monetary Fund (IMF) structural adjustment plan. The current Convention made available 26 billion ECU for the period 1990-2000. Special reference is made to industrial cooperation in an effort to encourage ACP countries to give priority to the development of their industrial sector. Negotiations for a post-Lomé convention between the European Community and the ACP countries began in September 1998. (See also, Development Aid, EDF, STABEX, SYSMIN).

LUNS-WESTERTERP PROCEDURE. Named after Luns and Westerterp, Dutch ministers, the procedure deals with the enhancement of the European Parliament's (EP) powers. Joseph Luns' initiative of 1964 aimed at strengthening the provisions of the Treaty of Rome that dealt with the powers of the EP over Association Agreements. It stipulated that the EP be kept informed throughout the negotiation process and be informed of its outcome before an Association Agreement was actually signed.

Under Westerterp's initiative in 1973 this procedure was expanded to include trade agreements. Luns-Westerterp procedure was embodied both in the Single European Act (SEA) and the Maastricht Treaty that

further empowered the EP. Currently, membership of the European
Community and Association Agreements are subject to approval by the
EP, while its assent is also required for almost all international
agreements and certain legislative matters. (See also, Assent Procedure,
EP).

LUXEMBOURG COMPROMISE. Reached in 1966, it established a
convention according to which member states could veto matters of
vital importance to them. As a result, discussions were to continue in
the Council of Ministers until consensus was reached. The
Luxembourg compromise came as a solution to an acute crisis, which
in the 1960s brought community developments to a standstill. The
crisis was initiated by President de Gaulle's refusal to accept any
enhancement of the powers of the Commission or the Council of
Ministers. He opposed proposals for the extension of majority voting
in the Council of Ministers, which amounted to member states having
to accept majority rather than unanimous decisions. He also opposed
proposals relating to a Community Budget, based on its 'own
resources' belonging to it as a right. The crisis culminated with the
'empty chair' policy, i.e. France's refusal to attend Council meetings
during this period.

The Luxembourg compromise was of great political significance for
it advocated integration at a pace acceptable to the most reluctant
member states. In practice, it slowed down decision-making in the
Council of Ministers as it became customary to insist on a unanimous
vote even in cases where the Treaties had provided for majority voting.
In fact, decisions that could not possibly gain unanimous support were
stored for an unlimited period.

By 1982, it had become apparent that action had to be taken if
progress was to be made in Community affairs. The
Genscher-Colombo Plan limited the use of the Luxembourg
compromise to matters purely of national interest and was followed by
the European Parliament (EP) proposals, which called upon members
to respect provisions made by the Treaties on voting methods in the
Council of Ministers. The Solemn Declaration reinforced the position
of the EP further, although it avoided specifying the degree to which
the Luxembourg compromise could be used.

The turning point, however, was the Single European Act (SEA),
which extended qualified majority voting (QMV) in the Council of

Ministers[13]. This led to the Luxembourg compromise falling into abeyance. In fact, since then it has rarely been invoked. It is worth noting that the Luxembourg compromise was never enshrined in any Community Treaty, nor did it have any legal force. Furthermore, the Court of Justice on many occasions ruled that Declaration of political will by the Council, or by member states collectively, cannot prevail against rules contained in the Treaties. (See also, Council of the EU, EP, Ioannina Compromise, Majority Voting, SEA, Solemn Declaration).

[13] QMV was instrumental to the completion of the Single European Market, though this had a decisive effect on the Luxembourg Compromise.

M

MAASTRICHT TREATY. Formally known as the Treaty on the European Union (EU), it was signed in Maastricht on 7 February 1992 and came into force in November 1993, after being ratified by all member states. The Treaty brought into being the long-standing objective of the formation of an EU, which had not been realized by any of the earlier Treaties, including the Treaty of Rome and the Single European Act (SEA), or by the Solemn Declaration, or the Draft Treaty on the European Union (DTEU).

Despite this long term objective, there was no clear vision as to the nature of the Union. As a result, in the European Council meeting in Dublin in June 1990, the divisions between governments of member states were exposed, as each government came to the meeting with its own agenda and demands. Both main issues under discussion, the European Political Union (EPU) and the Economic and Monetary Union (EMU) turned out to be deeply controversial. The issue of political union proved extremely contentious as Germany and France favoured a federal union, while the UK opposed such an idea. Since no conclusion could be reached on this, the Dublin meeting decided to establish an Intergovernmental Conference (IGC) on European Political Union to run parallel with the IGC on the EMU.

Both conferences opened at the European Council summit in Rome in December 1990. By then the Commission had already expressed its opinion on political union in favour of the French-German proposals for a union that was federal in character so preventing the Community from disintegrating. However, any reference to federalism was dropped on the first day of the Maastricht summit, held in December 1991. Moreover, other contentious issues, not clarified, were included in the Treaty. As a result the final document was left open to interpretation.

The Treaty comprises 7 Titles, 17 Protocols and 33 Declarations. The Titles refer to common provisions and form the main body of the text. The Protocols are appended to, and form a part of, the Treaty and are legally binding on member states. The most important Protocols deal with social policy, the operational aspects of the EMU, economic and social cohesion, the Social Charter and the British and Danish opt-outs on EMU. Declarations are appended to the Treaty, but unlike the Protocols, do not form part of it and have no legal force. Nevertheless, the Court of Justice may be asked to interpret them. The most important of the Declarations refer to the role of the national parliaments, police cooperation in the context of Justice and Home Affairs (JHA), and the future of Western European Union (WEU).

In the framework of the EPU, a temple structure was established, consisting of three pillars; the first being the European Communities, and the other two, largely intergovernmental in character, are the Common Foreign and Security Policy (CFSP) and Justice and Home Affairs (JHA). In addition, the Treaty of Rome was amended and the term European Communities was officially replaced by the term European Community, a term already in use. At the same time, the Treaty introduced the term Union, although without abolishing the term Community or explicitly replacing it with the term 'Union'. Although these terms seem confusing their meanings can be differentiated. The term 'Community' should still be used when matters solely relating to the European Community are discussed, while the term 'Union' should be used when reference is made to either the three pillars collectively or to the two intergovernmental pillars. If there is no reason to be specific about the one or the other, however, the two terms can be used interchangeably.

Disagreements over the EMU were no less severe. Both the speed with which it would progress and the institutions which would be responsible for its management raised fears even among its most fervent advocates. Germany, for instance, was worried by the large sums that would have to be directed towards the poorer member states, as well as by the possible reaction of the German electorate as the time for replacing the Deutsch Mark approached. Nevertheless, a final compromise was reached when it was agreed that the EMU would be completed in three stages. Britain retained the right to opt out of Stage III, while Denmark ruled out the possibility of participating. Denmark also gained an opt-out from European citizenship and defence, while the UK refused to sign a separate agreement on social policy, based on the Social Charter of 1989[14].

In addition to the establishment of the EPU and EMU, the Treaty included the following important institutional provisions: a) powers of co-decision were accorded to the EP, thus giving it the right to veto certain decisions, while the assent procedure was extended; b) the cooperation procedure was extended to new subject areas; c) the EP was to have a decisive say in the appointment of the members and the President of the Commission; d) the EP would appoint the Ombudsman; e) the Court of Justice could impose fines on member states which failed to comply with its previous rulings; f) the Court of Auditors (COA) was upgraded to a full community institution; g) the

---

[14] On UK participation see Social Charter.

use of qualified majority voting (QMV) in the Council of Ministers was extended to new areas.

Furthermore, the Treaty established the principle of subsidiarity and created the notion of European citizenship; it introduced community action in the fields of culture, education, vocational training, consumer protection, Trans-European Networks (TENs), industrial policy, environment and development policy.

Despite all the obstacles apparent during the negotiations, the Maastricht Treaty was finalized for an unlimited time. However, more problems appeared during its ratification. The Danish Parliament failed to secure the necessary majority to ratify the Treaty and was narrowly defeated by a 50.7 per cent majority vote in the first referendum (June 1992); after further concessions to the Danish government, a second referendum (May 1993) resulted in favour of the Treaty with a 56.8 per cent majority vote. The British Parliament ratified the Treaty by a narrow majority and even in France only a small majority of 51.05 per cent voted in favour of the Treaty. In Germany anti-Maastricht campaigners succeeded in taking the issue to the German Constitutional Court, but were defeated by the Karlsruhe judgement; The Treaty was eventually ratified on 12 October 1993.

The Maastricht Treaty represents a landmark in the political and economic integration of the EU. However, given various inherent weaknesses the Treaty provided for its revision by the 1996 IGC. These weaknesses result from efforts made to bridge numerous deep-seated disagreements among the member states, as well as the need to address a multitude of issues. An eloquent example of the difficulties involved in drawing up the Treaty was the omission of the term 'federalism' from the text of the agreement, despite provisions for a common currency, a central bank and a CFSP, which clearly point to a federal entity. On the whole, the agreement left a number of general and institutional issues unresolved. (See also, CFSP, Citizenship, DTEU, EMU, European Communities, EU, Federalism, IGC, JHA, Karlsruhe Judgement, Subsidiarity; Appendix 14).

MacSharry reform, see **CAP**

Maghreb Countries. The name describes the group of Maghreb countries, consisting of Morocco, Algeria, Tunisia and Libya. Bilateral trade and aid agreements, signed with the European Community, provide duty free access for most industrial Maghreb commodities, while making special provisions for certain agricultural products. These countries also have access to European development aid, as well as to low-interest loans from the European Investment Bank (EIB). (See also, Development Aid, EIB).

MAJORITY VOTING. The most commonly used method in the Council of Ministers, majority voting may take two forms:
simple majority requires the votes of 8 member states out of 15. This kind of voting is restricted to minor procedural matters and to certain aspects of the Common Commercial Policy (CCP). According to this procedure each member state is given one vote.
qualified majority gives a 'weighting' to the votes of each member state, though at present, 'weightings' inadequately reflect the size of the population of member states. This is the most widely used method of voting in the Council of Ministers, especially after the introduction of the Single European Act (SEA) and the Maastricht Treaty[15]. (See also, Council of the EU, Ioannina Compromise, Luxembourg Compromise).

MANAGEMENT COMMITTEE, see **COMITOLOGY**

MANSHOLT PLAN, see **CAP, STRESA CONFERENCE**

MARSHALL PLAN. Formally called the European Recovery programme, it was launched by the USA in April 1948 with the objective of helping the rehabilitation of the European economies. The programme was originally offered to all European countries, but the tense political climate prevailing in the post-war era led the USSR and the countries within its sphere of influence to withdraw from the programme. Consequently, only the countries which sided with the West, namely, Austria, Belgium, Denmark, France, Greece, Iceland, Ireland, Italy, Luxembourg, The Netherlands, Norway, Portugal, Sweden, Switzerland, Turkey and the United Kingdom, took part.
    The total amount distributed to the above mentioned countries over the 1948-51 period reached $13 billion. The assistance was mainly directed towards the restoration of industrial and agricultural production, the reestablishment of financial stability and the expansion of trade. It also became a means of stemming the expansion of Communism. Most of the aid was given in the form of grants, the remainder in the form of loans. The programme was coordinated by the Organization for European Economic Cooperation (OEEC) founded

---

[15] Each member state is allocated a number of votes which tends to correspond to its population. See Council of the European Union.

in 1948, the predecessor of the Organization for Economic Cooperation and Development. (See also, OEEC).

MASHREQ COUNTRIES. The name given to the geographic region extending from the western border of Egypt to the western border of Iran. It includes Egypt, the Sudan, Saudi Arabia, Yemen, Oman, Kuwait, United Arab Emirates, Israel, Jordan, Lebanon, Syria, and Iraq. Bilateral agreements in the fields of trade, economic policy, aid and finance have been signed between the European Community and the Mashreq countries. Exports are free to enter into the Community, barring products covered by the Common Agricultural Policy (CAP) for which there is a tariff preference. These countries are recipients of development aid, as well as low-interest rate loans from the European Investment Bank. (See also, Association Agreements, Development Aid, EIB).

MATTHAEUS. The programme was adopted by the European Commission in April 1989 with the purpose of training national customs officials and, more specifically, preparing them for the realization of the internal market. (See also, SEM).

MAXIMUM RATE OF INCREASE. A defined limit of increase of non-compulsory expenditure set up by the European Commission annually, and calculated on the basis of economic growth, government exchange rates, and inflation in the member states. The rate can be changed only by agreement between the European Parliament (EP) and the Council of Ministers. (See also, Budget, Non-compulsory Expenditure).

MEDA. A programme of cooperation with the Mediterranean countries. It finances projects concerned with socio-economic development, environment and education. Its budget for the period 1995-99 will reach ECU 5.5 million. (See also, Mediterranean Policy).

MEDIA POLICY. Part of the cultural policy of the European Community, media policy is related mainly to film and television. The European Community has grown extremely active in this area of cultural policy, among other reasons because of the prospects offered by the rapid and continuous technological developments. The main concern in this field is whether the expected explosion in demand for audiovisual material will largely be met by EU produced programs,

The European Community has in recent years introduced a series of measures in an effort to redress this imbalance and to set the guidelines of a media policy. The most notable among them are the two directives: a) The 'MAC Packet', issued in 1985, which sets out television standards developed by the European film industry and the European Broadcasting Union. b) The 'Television without Frontiers', issued in 1989, which came into force in 1991, is designed to create a single market for television broadcasts in Europe. It also calls on member states to try to ensure that at least 60 per cent of air time is devoted to programmes of European Community origin, and 10 per cent of their programming budget is devoted to European works from independent producers.

With the objective of supporting the production and distribution of the European film industry, the European Commission launched in 1987 an action plan entitled MEDIA. A second programme entitled SCRIPT followed in 1988 in order to contribute to the financing, production and distribution of cooperative multilingual European broadcasting.

Further progress towards a Community media policy was made with the 1997 European Commission Green Paper on the convergence of Telecommunications, Media and Information Sectors. This was based on the report of the High Policy Group set up in 1997 with the objective to reflect on a Community audiovisual policy guidelines. Both documents focused on the need to ensure a balance between market forces and public interest, establish digital broadcasting, develop a high-performance distribution and add the European dimension. The Community undertook the responsibility to work with central and eastern European countries for the development of their broadcasting system. The MEDIA programme was renewed with a budget of 310 MEC. (See also, Cultural Policy, Telecommunications).

MEDITERRANEAN POLICY. The countries of the Mediterranean have always been regarded as being of special importance to the Community and to Western Europe as a whole, for economic, political and strategic reasons. Greece was the first country of the Mediterranean to sign an Association Agreement and to become a member of the Community. Portugal and Spain acceded to the Community in 1986. Association Agreements were subsequently signed with other Mediterranean countries, including the Maghreb and Mashreq groups, Turkey, Cyprus, Malta, and the countries of former Yugoslavia, known as Mediterranean regions.

However, it was not until 1994 that the European Council meeting at Corfu decided to draw up a comprehensive policy covering the area. This was the result of a conspicuous shifting of trade and aid towards central and eastern Europe. In October 1994, the Commission launched an ambitious proposal for a 'European-Mediterranean Partnership' with the objective of establishing the largest free trade area in the world by 2010, covering the EU, the countries of central and eastern Europe, those of the Mediterranean, including the Middle East, Cyprus, Malta, Turkey, Albania and the former Yugoslavia. The level of investment up to 1999 will reach 5.5 billion ECUs. Cooperation in foreign and security policy, in combating drugs and crime, and the introduction of measures for the protection of the environment have already been agreed. In June 1995, the Cannes meeting of the European Council endorsed the Commission's proposals. (See also, Association Agreements, Maghreb, Mashreq, MEDA, Small Countries).

MERGER CONTROL, see **COMPETITION POLICY**

MERGER TREATY. The first treaty to amend the Treaty of Paris and Treaty of Rome was signed in 1965 and came into force in July 1967. It merged the separate executives of the three Communities, namely, the High Authority of the ECSC, the Commission of the European Economic Community (EEC) and EURATOM, to a single Commission which took charge of the affairs of all three communities. In addition, a common Council of Ministers was formed. There was no need to amalgamate the Common Assembly, the Court of Justice and the Economic and Social Committee (ESC), as in accordance with the 1957 'Convention on Certain Institutions Common to the European Communities', they were already serving the three communities jointly.

The Merger Treaty also provided for a common Budget of the Communities, as well as for a single administration, consisting of the officials of the three original Communities. As a result of the Merger Treaty, the three Communities came together officially to become the European Communities, although the term European Community is more widely used. Even within the framework of the European Union (EU), where the latter term was formally established and the three communities operate as a single unit in all respects, they still retain their separate identities and constitute the first pillar of the European Union. (See also, European Communities, Treaty of Rome, Treaty of Paris).

MESSINA CONFERENCE. Meeting of the Foreign Ministers of the Six which took place in June 1955, following the rejection of the European Defence Community (EDC) by the French National Assembly in August 1954. At the conference the Six signatories of the Treaty of Paris re-affirmed their commitment to a closer economic integration of the European States. Under the chairmanship of Paul-Henri Spaak, the Belgian Prime Minister, a committee was formed to investigate the feasibility of establishing a common market. On that occasion, the Treaty of Rome, creating the European Atomic Energy Community (EURATOM) and the European Economic Community (EEC), was negotiated. (See also, EDC, European Political Community, Treaty of Rome).

MESSINA II
In 1995, forty years after the Messina Conference, the 15 member states of the European Community formed a group based at Messina in order to prepare the IGC of 1996. The group consisted of one representative from each Member State, two EMPs and a European Commissioner. The report prepared by the group was presented at the Madrid summit in December 1995. (See also, IGC).

MINEX, see **SYSMIN**

MONETARY COMMITTEE. Established by the Treaty of Rome and further consolidated by the Maastricht Treaty, the Committee is an advisory body to the Council of Ministers in the economic and financial fields. It promotes coordination of policies of the member states with respect to the internal market, the European Monetary System (EMS), capital movements, international monetary relations and any issue relating to the Economic and Monetary Union (EMU).

Since its creation the Committee meets at least once a month, normally before the Ecofin Council; its chairman reports directly to the Ecofin Council on the Committee's work several times a year. The Committee has privileged access not only to the Ecofin Council, but also to the Commission.

It is composed of two high-ranking officials from each member state and two members from the Commission - mostly senior and influential personalities from Finance Ministries and Central Banks. Although the members of the Committee are appointed on their own merit, they largely express the point of view of their respective governments, and in this way prepare the ground for agreement in the Ecofin Council.

The Monetary Committee was replaced by the Financial and Economic Committee at the beginning of the third stage of the EMU, on 1 January 1999. The new Committee undertook more extensive duties in the context of EMU. (See also, Comitology, Council of the EU, Ecofin Council, EMS, EMU, European Commission).

MONNET, JEAN (1888-1979). Born in Cognac, France, he began his political career during the First World War working in London in the field of economic cooperation amongst the Allies. In 1920, he was appointed Deputy Secretary General of the League of Nations. He left the League in 1923 to pursue private business in Cognac, but on the eve of the Second World War he was back in politics, assuming responsibility for the planning of economic cooperation between the UK, France and the USA. He spent the war years in Washington.

After the war, he was in charge of the *Commissariat du Plan* responsible for the economic recovery of France. Originator of the Schuman Plan, Monnet developed an alternative approach to that of the European federalists, which, in the 1948 Congress at The Hague, ended in failure. As it was made clear by the participants, European governments at the time were not prepared to proceed with a federal Europe. Although Monnet remained faithful to the federalist ideal, he put forward the idea of sectorial integration aimed at creating a united Europe in a piecemeal way by encouraging cooperation between European countries in specific areas. His proposals resulted in the formation of the European Coal and Steel Community (ECSC) with Monnet as the first President of the High Authority.

However, following the collapse of his other great plan, the European Defence Community (EDC), in November 1954, he resigned from the High Authority and devoted himself to freelance campaigning for European unity. Monnet sought to maintain the impetus of integration and continued to campaign for sectorial integration along the lines of the ECSC. He saw atomic energy as the second sector to be integrated. In February 1955, Monnet became head of the Action Committee for the United States of Europe (ACUSE). (See also, ACUSE, ECSC, EDC, Federalism, Schuman Plan, Footnote 10).

MULTIFIBRE ARRANGEMENT. An agreement signed in 1974 as part of the General Agreement on Tariffs and Trade (GATT) with the objective of protecting the textile industry of the developed world. The European Community (EC) participated in the negotiations as a single entity. Export quota restrictions and export restraint agreements were imposed on developing countries in a period when the textile sector in

Europe was either phased out or drastically restructured. (See also, GATT).

N

NEUTRALITY. Neutrality as a principle is abstention from taking any part in conflict between states. The status of neutrality can be obtained by either constitutional provisions, as in the case of Switzerland, Austria and Malta, or by long-standing policies, as in the case of Sweden and Finland. The rights and duties of neutral states were defined in 1907 in two conventions signed in The Hague.

The status of neutrality within the European Union (EU) presents a problem, in particular with regard to the Common Foreign and Security Policy (CFSP). Neutrality will pose an even greater problem if the development of a common defence policy, as put forward in the Maastricht Treaty is to be realised. For the admission of more neutral countries into the Community will make the adoption of a common position and joint action, and the introduction of a common defence policy, more difficult to pursue. (See also, CFSP).

NEWS AGENCY. There are many news agencies which gather, write and distribute news from around the world to radio and television broadcasters, newspapers, periodicals and other means of mass communication.

The four largest world agencies are the United Press International and Associated Press based in New York, Reuters in the UK, and Agence France-Presse in France. In most countries, however, this service is mainly provided by national news agencies, such as Agenzia Nazionale Stampa Associata (ANSA) in Italy, Deutsche-Presse Agentur in Germany, Press Association in the UK, and Ritzaus Bureau in Denmark.

NEXT EUROPEAN TORUS (NET). The name given to a planned follow-up to the Joint European Torus (JET) in the research programme on nuclear fusion. The two programmes work in parallel, but NET focuses more on the technological feasibility of fusion. Its main priority is to set the scientific and technical foundations and to prepare industry for the construction of a more advanced experimental fusion reactor. The NET team at Garching carries out most of the research, but several Community Joint Research Centres (JRC) also participate. (See also, JET, JRC).

NON-COMPULSORY EXPENDITURE. The term refers to that section of the Community Budget, which relates to policies not directly stipulated by the founding Treaties. This section, in fact, covers virtually all EU expenditure with the exception of agriculture, refunds to member states, and expenditure arising from international agreements. The European Parliament (EP) possesses extensive powers in relation to non-compulsory expenditure as it is in a position to amend this section of the Budget, although not beyond the limits of the overall maximum rate calculated by the Commission annually. The non-compulsory expenditure, however, constitutes the smallest percentage of the Budget, less than 40 per cent. There has been a constant effort by the EP to increase this percentage, which in turn will increase its influence. (See also, Budget, Compulsory Expenditure, EP, Maximum Rate of Increase).

NON-PROLIFERATION OF NUCLEAR WEAPONS TREATY (NPT). Signed on 1 July 1968, by the UK, the USA, the Soviet Union and 59 other states, it came into force in March 1970 for a limited 25-year period. According to the Treaty, the three major signatories agreed not to assist states, which do not possess nuclear explosives in obtaining or producing them. Subsequently, other nations ratified the Treaty, including France and China in 1992. The European Council agreed at the Corfu meeting of June 1994 on the indefinite and unconditional acceptance of the NPT from as many countries as possible. A year later in 1995, the Treaty was extended indefinitely by a consensus vote of 174 countries at the United Nations (UN).

NON-TARIFF BARRIERS, see p. 125, n. 12

NORDIC COUNCIL OF MINISTERS. Its establishment in 1971, under the amendment of the Helsinki Convention, rendered official a variety of long-standing relations between the Nordic states of Denmark, Finland, Iceland, Norway, and Sweden. Its general objective is to promote consultation and cooperation on matters of common interest, such as transport and communications, scientific research and development, protection of the environment, culture, education, judicial affairs and social welfare; it also finances joint projects in the Third World.

It consists of the ministers of state of the member countries, as well as other ministers with responsibility for a specific subject under discussion. Formal decisions are usually binding on the member governments. The Council of Ministers oversees the work and provides funds for a large number of joint Nordic institutions, such as the Nordic Investment Bank, and the Cultural Fund. However, it did not succeed in establishing the Nordic Economic Union, a long-standing aim of the Nordic countries.

NORTH AMERICA FREE TRADE AREA (NAFTA). A trade pact signed by the USA, Canada and Mexico in December 1992; it came into effect on 1 June 1994, with the task of creating a free-trade zone among the three largest countries of North America. Its main provision called for the reduction in tariffs, customs duties and other barriers between the three members, with some tariffs being removed immediately, and others over a longer period. (See also, Customs Union).

NORTH ATLANTIC COOPERATION COUNCIL (NACC). It was founded in December 1991 in order to provide for the participation of Eastern European countries in non-military activities of the North Atlantic Treaty Organization (NATO). Austria, Finland, Ireland and Sweden, being non-NATO members, also participate. The formation of the NACC was the outcome of the initiative taken by the US Secretary of State, James Baker, and the German Foreign Minister, Hans-Dietrich Genscher, based on NATO's declaration that the security of Eastern Europe is inseparably linked with NATO.

NACC currently consists of 38 countries: 16 NATO members, the former Warsaw Pact members, all successor members of the USSR and Albania. Austria, Finland, Ireland, Sweden, and Slovenia have observer status.

Following the launching of the Partnership for Peace (PFP) initiative by President Clinton at NATO's summit in Brussels in January 1994, the role of NACC has been largely transformed. PFP involves a higher degree of collaboration than was initially envisaged within the NACC framework, as it provides for participation in the political and military bodies at NATO headquarters. Joint NATO-PFP exercises are also conducted. The number of PFP signatories is constantly increasing to include Russia and even Austria and Sweden. (See also, NATO, Warsaw Pact; Appendix 17).

NORTH ATLANTIC TREATY ORGANIZATION (NATO). It was set up by a Treaty signed in Washington on 4 April 1949 and came into effect on 24 August 1949, as a military organization opposing the presence of the Soviet Union and providing collective security for the entire North Atlantic area.

The original signatories of the Treaty were Belgium, Canada, Denmark, France, Iceland, Italy, Luxembourg, The Netherlands,

Norway, Portugal, the UK and the USA; Greece and Turkey joined in February 1952, West Germany in May 1955 and Spain in May 1982. France and Spain withdrew from the integrated military command of NATO in 1966 and 1986, respectively. In 1966, the NATO headquarters were moved from Paris to Brussels following France's withdrawal from the integrated military command.

The sweeping events of 1989-90 in Eastern Europe removed the threat of communist expansion and forced the re-appraisal of NATO's role and structure. Proposals have been made for transforming the organization from a military to a political one, devoted to maintaining international stability. There have also been conflicting views among European states as to whether the strengthening of the Western European Union (WEU), with the ultimate aim of taking over NATO's role in European security, would be preferable to the transatlantic link provided by NATO. For instance, the British and Italian governments are more keen to maintain the transatlantic link, while France and Germany stand for a more Europe orientated security policy.

In the present circumstances the organization is open to new members, including countries of central and eastern Europe and the former Soviet Union, which are in the process of joining. Hungary, the Czech Republic and Poland are the first to join. NATO's approach towards new entries is gradualist in order to prevent a drastic shift in the balance of power within the organisation. The formation of the North Atlantic Cooperation Council (NACC) has, among other things, served as a preparatory platform for the admission of Eastern European countries. The NATO summit of 1994 has also agreed to the formation of Combined Joint Task Forces (CJTFS), which would operate within the NATO framework, while leaving open the participation of non-NATO forces. (See also, CFSP, NACC, Warsaw Pact, WEU; Appendix 17).

NOUVELLES FRONTIÈRES see p.31, n. 3

O

OFFICE FOR HARMONIZATION IN THE INTERNAL MARKET. An autonomous body of the European Community, responsible for the harmonization of the Community's Trade Marks and Designs. Created by a decision of the Council of Ministers on 29 October 1993, it became operational in September 1994; it is based in Alicante, Spain. Business may secure trade mark protection throughout the European Economic Area (EEA) by registering their trade mark with this Office. The same regulation applies to designs and models. The Office has, at present, a personnel of approximately 350 officials from every country of the Community. (See also, Harmonization, SEM).

***OFFICIAL JOURNAL OF THE EUROPEAN COMMUNITIES* (OJ).** Published on most working days throughout the year and in all official languages, the Journal is divided into three sections, L, C, S and Annex. The L (Legislation) series contains the full text of all legislation and acts which, according to the Treaty of Rome, the European Community is obliged to publish. It provides information regarding Directives, Regulations and other legal acts. The C (Communications) series, including Information and Notices, covers proposals for legislation put forward by the Commission, written questions put forward by the European Parliament (EP), a list of cases brought before the Court of Justice, ECU/Euro exchange rates in the currencies of the member states, EU job vacancies and other official notices. The S (Supplements) series contains notices of public works and public supply contracts tendered to competition. The Annex contains transcriptions of debates conducted in the EP. (See also, Legislation).

OFFICIAL LANGUAGES OF THE EUROPEAN COMMUNITY, see **LANGUAGES**

OMBUDSMAN. The Ombudsman is empowered to receive complaints from any citizen of the Community or any resident, legal or natural person, in a member state concerning maladministration in the activities of the community institutions and bodies, excluding the Court of Justice and the Court of First Instance (CFI).

Appointed by the European Parliament (EP), the Ombudsman is independent and can only be dismissed by the Court of Justice. He acts either on his own initiative or on complaints forwarded to him by the MEPs. However, the Treaty cannot force European institutions to act on the Ombudsman's findings. Only the EP, at the request of a quarter of its members, may set up a Committee of Inquiry to investigate instances of maladministration in the implementation of Community law.

Based in Strasbourg the first Ombudsman, Jacob Soderman from Finland, was appointed in June 1995. The Ombudsman was introduced by the Maastricht Treaty with a new article added to the Treaty of Rome. (See also, EP, Fraud).

OPINIONS, see **LEGISLATION**

OPT-OUT. A phrase used to describe the decision of a member state not to participate in a Community activity covered by Treaty provisions. The most widely known is the opt-out of the UK from the Social Charter and the Economic and Monetary Union (EMU), and Denmark's opt-out from the latter. (See also, EMU, Maastricht Treaty, Social Charter).

ORGANIZATION FOR ECONOMIC COOPERATION AND DEVELOPMENT (OECD). Established in 1961, it replaced the Organization for European Economic Cooperation (OEEC). It is not only concerned with the domestic economies of its members, but also with the broader and long-term problems of the international economic system. Based in Paris, it has at its disposal a large number of expertise and has often contributed to the development and implementation of new economic concepts and policies. However, it has no statutory right to enforce its policy upon its members.

Unlike its predecessor, the OECD is not confined to Europe, but extends to the advanced industrial nations which have never been part of the communist world. It currently consists of 24 countries: Australia, Austria, Belgium, Canada, Denmark, Finland, France, Germany, Greece, Iceland, Ireland, Italy, Japan, Luxembourg, Malta, The Netherlands, New Zealand, Norway, Portugal, Spain, Sweden, Switzerland, Turkey, UK and USA. (See also, OEEC).

ORGANIZATION FOR EUROPEAN ECONOMIC COOPERATION (OEEC). It was established in 1947 under USA leadership with the purpose of channelling USA aid under the Marshall Plan to the countries of Western Europe. The OEEC continued to exist, even after the completion of the Marshall Plan, primarily as a forum promoting economic cooperation among Western European countries. In 1961 the OEEC was replaced by the Organization for Economic Cooperation and Development (OECD). (See also, Marshall Plan, OECD).

Organization for Security and Cooperation in Europe (OSCE). In January 1995 the Conference on Security and Cooperation in Europe (CSCE) was re-named OSCE. The former organization was founded in the 1970s with the purpose of promoting dialogue between the North Atlantic Treaty Organization (NATO) and the Warsaw Pact, while the present body OSCE, in the post-cold war context, provides a number of opportunities for member states to discuss issues relating to security.

It consists of a total of 53 members, the USA, Canada, and all European states, even those which do not participate in any other security organisation. It has developed preventive diplomacy and has been involved in withdrawal missions and crisis management, as well as in sanction assistance. However, it largely remains a forum for debate rather than a decision-making or policy implementing body. All decisions have to be taken by unanimous vote. (See also, CSCE, NATO, Warsaw Pact; Appendix 17).

Organization of Petroleum Exporting Countries (OPEC). A multinational organization established in 1960, which became operational in 1961 with the purpose of coordinating the petroleum policies of its members and of providing them with technical and economic support. The founding members were Iran, Iraq, Kuwait, Saudi Arabia and Venezuela; later, Qatar, Indonesia, Libya, Abu Dhabi, Algeria, Nigeria, Ecuador and Gabon were also admitted. The Headquarters of OPEC are currently in Vienna.

Overseas Countries and Territories (OCTs). The Treaty of Rome makes provisions for the non-European territories, which have special relations with certain member states, and whose external relations are on the whole the responsibility of a Community member. OCTs have been divided into four categories, French, British, Dutch and Danish. OCTs are not part of the Community, but are associated with it and as a result enjoy certain rights[16].

The main objective of the relationship between the Community and the OCTs, as mentioned in the Treaty of Rome, has been their economic and social development, and the establishment of relations between each one of them and the Community as a whole. To this end, they enjoy privileged access to the Community market with the

---

[16] Conversely, the French overseas departments (Guadeloupe, Guiana, Martinique and the Réunion) constitute an integral part of France and consequently of the EU.

exception of products covered by the Common Agricultural Policy (CAP), for which special provisions are made. Export stabilization schemes similar to that of STABEX and SYSMIN are implemented. They receive financial assistance through the European Development Fund (EDF) in the form of grants, as well as through the European Investment Bank (EIB) in the form of loans. For the 1990-5 period the amount allocated to the OCTs through the EDF reached ECUs 140 million, while the amount allocated through the European Investment Bank to ECUs 25 million.

Given the diversity of the OCTs in terms of geography, history, population, size, climate and prosperity, European law and policies are difficult to apply in an even way. In general, European law applies only to European territories of member states, but not to their OCTs. However, the development of trade between the European Community and the OCTs has followed the same pattern as trade between the individual member state and its own OCT. In addition, since 1996, nationals of the OCTs, by virtue of being nationals of a Community member state, become citizens of the Community. As a result, they enjoy a number of privileges, though not all of them have been clearly defined. Constant efforts have been made to improve the rights of individuals and the status of OCTs nationals in the Community. Furthermore, the Council of Ministers has undertaken the task of reviewing the Association Agreements by February 2000 with the objective of promoting social and economic development of the OCTs more effectively.

Although both ACP countries and OCTs enjoy a special relationship with the Community, there is little cooperation between the two. Efforts have been made to redress this, and in 1991, a partnership arrangement to include the provisions made in the Fourth Lomé Convention was introduced. (See also, ACP, Development Policy, EDF, EIB, STABEX, SYSMIN; Appendix 19).

'OWN RESOURCES'. A term used to denote certain revenues that by right belong to the European Community (EC) and are to be distinguished from the contributions of member states to the Budget before the 1970 Decision of the Council of Ministers. The 'own resources' consisted of agricultural levies, customs duties and 1 per cent of national revenues from Value-added Tax (VAT) applied to a uniform base. The new system was to be applied on 1 January 1975, but was ultimately introduced in 1980 because of the difficulties in implementing a uniform VAT base.

In 1987, the revenues raised by the 'own resources' system were found to be inadequate in financing the policies introduced by the 1986 Single European Act (SEA). This was partly the outcome of tariff reductions and concessionary trade agreements implemented in the process of the Single European Market (SEM). The Decision of the Council of Ministers of 24 June 1988, based on the Delors Package I, added a fourth source of revenue, namely contributions from each member state related to its gross national product. The 1988 Decision of the Council came into force on 1 February 1989 with effect from 1 January 1988.

The 'own resources' system makes the Community to a great degree independent of member states, although any relevant decisions of the Council of Ministers are subject to ratification by national parliaments. Unlike the expenditure of the Budget, the European Parliament's (EP) powers with regard to the revenues are confined to simple consultation. (See also, Budget, Delors Packages I and II, SEM, VAT).

P

PARLIAMENTARY COMMITTEES. Specialized standing committees that carry out most of the work of the European Parliament (EP). There are currently 20 committees, 3 subcommittees and a temporary committee on employment. Each MEP is a full member of one committee, while he often participates in more than one, though not as a full member. Committees have been a central part of the Parliament's work since its inception, but as a result of the expansion of the community's fields of responsibility, their numbers have increased since the 1979 direct elections.

Committees meet during the so-called 'Committee Weeks', which immediately follow the plenary sessions of the EP; the busier Committees meet at least twice a month, usually in the Parliament building in Brussels. A Committee's work is organized by its Bureau, which consists of a chairman and four vice-chairmen. Both posts are elective, but in reality all these posts are divided by agreement among the political groups, taking into consideration the prestige of the Committee and the political benefits that a Group can derive from it.

Committees present their work in the form of reports or opinions, either as a consultation on draft legislation at the formal request of the Council of Ministers or the European Commission, or as a resolution tabled by individual members, or on their own initiative either on a subject that it has not been consulted, or on an entirely new subject. Once the Committee is ready to draw up a report or opinion, it nominates a *rapporteur* and a draftsman. (See also, EP).

PETRA. An action programme for the vocational training of young people and their preparation for adult and working life. Operational in 1989 the programme was financed by the Community Budget and it was complementary to national sources assigned to these objectives. Since 1995, it has merged together with Lingua, COMETT and Force into the Leonardo programme. (See also, LEONARDO).

PHARE. Aid for Economic Restructuring was set up by the Group of Seven (G7) in 1989, and became operational in June 1990. Initially, it aimed at providing aid to Poland and Hungary, but shortly after it was extended to Albania, Bulgaria, Slovakia, the Czech Republic, East Germany and Romania, as well as to the Baltic States.

It is administered by the European Commission, even though aid additional to that of the European Community comes from Australia, Canada, Iceland, Japan, New Zealand, Norway, Switzerland, Turkey and USA. PHARE gives priority to the privatization and re-structuring of state-owned enterprises, and to the private and services sectors. Modernization of fiscal, financial and welfare systems is also facilitated by PHARE. In 1994, the programme amounted to ECUs 963 million. (See also, Agenda 2000, Europe Agreement).

PILLARS OF THE EUROPEAN UNION, see **CFSP, COURT OF JUSTICE, JHA, MAASTRICHT TREATY**

PLEVEN PLAN. Plan put forward in October 1950 by the French Premier Pleven for the creation of a European Defence Community (EDC). The new structure would have placed a re-armed Germany within a European defence system, thus limiting its ability to act independently. (See also, EDC).

POLITICAL GROUPS. MEPs constitute political groups, which support their respective political parties in accordance with their ideology and/or political affiliation. The minimum number of MEPs to form a political group is 29 if the members come from one member state, 23 if they come from two, 18 if they come from three, and 14 if they come from four or more member states.

No MEP can be a member of more than one political group, but no MEP is obliged to be a member either. Some MEPs are not full members of a political group and call themselves associate members. They are not bound by the common manifesto of the pan-European political party, if their national political party is not a member of it. Nevertheless, political groups derive their orientation from their respective pan-European party. On the other hand, there is a very small number of MEPs, who call themselves independent by not being attached to any political group. Currently, these MEPs belong to French, Austrian, Italian nationalists and to the Unionist Party of Northern Ireland.

Nevertheless, most MEPs belong to a political group, usually at the cost of their own political orientation, on the grounds that their influence is maximised on almost all matters which are discussed in the European Parliament (EP). Political groups are also entitled to a proportionate share of all posts in the EP, posts within the Committees and the rapporteurs.

Other benefits provide further incentives to the political group formation. Once a group is formally recognised, funds for administration and research purposes are distributed as a fixed amount, plus an additional sum for each member. Although unattached members of Parliament are also recipients of these funds, there is no doubt that for funding purposes the larger the group the more easily it can afford good services.

Political groups existed from the inception of the Community. Even in the Common Assembly of the ECSC, representatives were grouped according to party affiliation in three political groups, Socialists, Christian Democrats and Liberals. However, the enlargement of the community introduced a considerable increase in the number of political groups. Currently, there are nine political groups in the EP, the largest being the socialist, while the smallest is made up of the so-called unattached members. (See, also EP).

PRIMACY. The Treaties do not make any provision for the primacy of Community law over national law. However, the Court of Justice from an early stage took an active part in establishing the primacy of Community law, in an effort to consolidate a uniform and consistent legal order. The Court has stated that national courts must apply Community law in the event of conflict, even if the domestic law is part of the national constitution. The Court can also declare void any legal instrument adopted by Community institutions, which is not compatible with community law. Among the most important legal cases establishing the principle of primacy were the *Costa* v. *ENEL* (Case 6/64)[17], and the *Simmenthal* v. *European Commission* (Case 92/78)[18]. (See also, Community Law, Court of Justice of the European Communities, Direct Applicability, Direct Effect).

PROPORTIONALITY. The principle of proportionality was incorporated into the Treaty of Rome by the Maastricht Treaty and requires that any

---

[17]   *Costa* v. *ENEL* concerned the nationalisation of private electricity companies by the Italian government. ENEL, the company that acquired the assets, was taken to the Court of Justice by Costa, a lawyer and a former shareholder, who objected to the nationalisation measures on the grounds that is went counter to the various Treaty articles. The Court stated that Community law binds both member states and individuals as well as national courts.

[18]   *Simmenthal* v. *European Commission* concerned several regulations and notices issued by the Commission with regard to import of meat. The case was brought to the Court of Justice directly by an Italian meat importer on the grounds that the Commission's decisions were not in line with article 184 of the Treaty of Rome. The Court annulled the decision of the Commission only in relation to the applicant.

action of the Community should not go beyond what is necessary for
the achievement of its objectives. This, together with subsidiarity, is
yet another principle aimed at restraining the Commission's tendency
towards excessive regulation. (See also, Subsidiarity).

PUBLIC HEALTH. The Maastricht Treaty provided the Union with legal
competence on the subject of public health and granted it authority to
take preventive action. In addition, a Resolution of the Council of
Ministers of 2 June 1994 set up a framework for action. The need for
closer coordination between the European Community, the appropriate
national institutions and international organizations was stressed, giving
priority to cancer research, Aids, drug addiction, and other contagious
diseases. The Community's role, however, still remains largely
complementary to that of the national governments.

Q

QUOTAS. A form of governmental restrictions imposed on quantity over a specified period of time, or in exceptional cases, on the value of goods or services that may be exported or imported. In the context of intra-Community trade, quotas were abolished by the Treaty of Rome. On the other hand, quotas have been used extensively with the objective of reducing the production of certain agricultural products in the European Community. Quotas have been used, especially in the dairy sector, as the means of limiting the production of milk, excess of which does not qualify for price-support. (See also, CAP, Treaty of Rome).

R

RECOMMENDATIONS, see LEGISLATION

REFLECTION GROUP. Formed by a decision of the 1994 Essen Council in preparation for the 1996 Intergovernmental Conference (IGC), the group was charged with the task of investigating the necessary institutional reforms in the light of future enlargement.

Consisting of 18 members and chaired by the Spanish Minister Carlos Westendorp, the Reflection Group began its work in June 1995. The Group's final report was presented to the European Council summit in Madrid in December 1995, and was published in the same month. The report revealed many differences in outlook on a wide range of issues between representatives. (See also, IGC).

REGIONAL POLICY. This is a major policy which addresses a variety of complex problems relating to the even development of the European Community as a whole. For this purpose, it must deal with extensive regional disparities between member states as well as with those within individual member states. Regional disparities manifest themselves in the form of underdeveloped rural areas, industrial decline, congested cities and frontier regions, originating from the differing socio-economic and geographical backgrounds of member states, often aggravated by the integration process itself.

An eloquent illustration of the above problems is presented by the 1995 Eurostat Report, which found that none of the regions in Greece or Portugal reached the average GDP per capita of the EU, and that only one region in Spain did so. On the other hand, Germany, after its reunification in 1990, has one fifth of its population living in regions with GDP per capita of less than 35 per cent of the Community's average, while areas like Bavaria, Hamburg and Bremen have a GDP per capita of more than 1.5 times of the Community average. Some inner-city areas face severe deprivation; some of the poorest areas have high unemployment, whereas other poor areas have low unemployment (mainly in Greece and Portugal). The decline of traditional industries, such as textiles, coal, or of a particular agricultural sector, often concentrated on specific regions of the Community, contribute further to regional inequalities.

Until the creation of the European Regional Development Fund (ERDF) in 1975, regional policy was largely the responsibility of national governments. However, with the accession to the European Community of the UK and Ireland, and subsequently of Greece,

Portugal and Spain, regional policy became a matter of greater interest, having until then been the concern of Italy alone. Regional policy was reinforced with the establishment of the Committee of the Regions (COR) by the Maastricht Treaty. The disparities were accentuated later with the accession of Finland, Sweden and Austria, the first two with their remote and sparsely populated areas and Austria with its Alpine region.

It is now accepted that regional policies are linked with the majority of the Community's policies. Telecommunication Policy, Transport Policy and Energy Policy have contributed greatly to the elimination of regional disparities. However, certain regional policies may be required in order to counterbalance the adverse effects caused by some Community policies. For instance, the Economic Monetary Union (EMU) will affect poorer countries adversely, at least in the short term.

For this purpose the ERDF, which constitutes part of the structural funds, has developed into the principal instrument of regional policy. In addition to the ERDF, the Community uses a number of mechanisms and procedures in order to implement regional policy, such as:

Community initiatives: targeting specific geographical areas, industries, groups and issues. These initiatives include programmes, such as RECHAR, RESIDER, RETEX, INTERREG, REGIS, YOUTHSTART, HORIZON, NOW, LEADER, KONVER, ADAPT, PESCA and URBAN. For the period 1994-99 ECU 13.77 billion has been allocated to such initiatives.

Community support framework: commonly agreed policies between the European Commission and national and regional authorities in accordance with a development plan, which is initiated by national and regional authorities. Once a plan is agreed, member states have to present the Commission with operational programmes.

Community pilot projects: explore a possible solution to a regional problem.

Integrated Mediterranean Programmes (IMP): involve grants and loans to help towards the adjustment of Mediterranean regions to EU integration.

Regional policy has constantly tried to deal with serious problems affecting the lives of a large number of people. A Commission report estimated that by 1993 the ERDF money amounted to only about 6% of gross fixed capital formation of the poorest member states. This small amount has not succeeded in reducing unemployment or improving living standards noticeably. An effort has to be made to generate adequate resources in order to face the constantly increasing regional problems. The reluctance of the more prosperous member states to increase the ERDF may compound further these problems. Moreover, closer monitoring of funds is required if a more efficient utilization of these resources is to be achieved. (See also, ERDF, EUREKA, KONVER, HORIZON, IMP, STAR, TENs).

REGULATIONS, see **LEGISLATION**

REGULATORY COMMITTEE, see **COMITOLOGY**

RESEARCH AND DEVELOPMENT IN ADVANCED COMMUNICATIONS PROGRAMME FOR EUROPE (RACE). Introduced in 1987, the programme's main objective is to promote the technologies required for the introduction of integrated broadband communications in the 1990s. It is concerned with several aspects of the telecommunications sector, such as network compatibility, image and data transmission, and mobile equipment. (See also, Telecommunications Policy).

RESEARCH AND TECHNOLOGICAL DEVELOPMENT POLICY. Research in general has been one of the Community concerns ever since its creation, as mentioned in all the founding Treaties. However, no coherent policy was ever attempted until the Resolution of the Council of Ministers in January 1974 and the document produced in 1979 by Vicomte Davignon, the Commissioner responsible for RTD, which advocated a European research strategy.

The efforts made for the development of a more effective RTD were in response to the crisis that manifested itself in the 1970s, caused principally by Europe's industrial decline and the loss of European competitiveness in world markets. This was largely attributed to Europe's slow pace in technological progress for the following reasons, low investment, accounting for only 2 per cent of the GDP in the Community, in contrast to 3 per cent of the GDP in Japan; low application, in that Europe is more advanced in pure science than in applied research, and produces fewer saleable products than Japan and USA; fragmentation in research activities as national research programmes took precedence over those undertaken on behalf of the EU.

So far the European Community has introduced several research and technological programmes by the Single European Act (SEA) and the Maastricht Treaty. These programmes, far from aiming at transferring all research to the European level, support cross-border cooperation of projects which are less costly than if conducted on a national level, and at the same time avoid duplication of research. In addition to the Community's Joint Research Centre (JRC), the European Commission has established (CORDIS) a centralized information service on Community RTD developments.

Major European research projects, such as EUREKA, European Nuclear Research Organization (CERN), Joint European Torus (JET), COST, DIANE, European Space Agency (ESA), are not simply confined to the European Community, as non-Community members can also participate. However, there are others, the so-called framework programmes, which are centred around the Community's RTD policy. The Fourth Framework programme valid for the period 1994-98 has a budget of ECU 13,16 billion. It aims to transfer the Community's research effort to newer technologies, such as biotechnology, biomedicine and health, eco-technology and IT. It also seeks better cooperation between national, EU and pan-European research developments. (See also, CERN, ESA, EUREKA, JET, JRC).

RESOLUTIONS, see **LEGISLATION**

S

SCHENGEN AGREEMENT. Signed on 14 June 1985 by France, Germany, Belgium, Luxembourg and The Netherlands, this agreement has its origins in the Saarbrücken Agreement of 1984 between France and Germany. Italy signed the agreement in November 1990, Spain and Portugal in June 1991, and Greece and Austria in 1997.

The signatories committed themselves to the gradual abolition of internal land, sea and air border controls, so that citizens of signatory countries are able to travel freely within the Schengen zone. However, the Agreement does not constitute part of the Community policy to abolish border controls, although only Community members can join the Schengen zone.

The Schengen Convention, signed in June 1990, dealt with the implementation of the Agreement, including rules governing non-European nationals, although a system of common border controls, replacing the internal controls, was not implemented until March 1995. Since then, in order to eliminate illegal immigration non-European Community nationals face tighter controls at borders of all signatory countries. Asylum seekers, if refused asylum in one Schengen country, are deemed to have been refused in all the others. Constant efforts have also been made towards the implementation of a common set of visa requirements; a Schengen Information System (SIS) exchanging information between police and immigration authorities on illegal drugs, weapons, etc. has also been established.

The Schengen Agreement, dealing with sensitive issues, has often given rise to serious disagreements among the participants, and has made non-participants reluctant to join. In June 1995 France cancelled full participation as a response to the large numbers of East Germans entering the Union. Greece and Italy did not participate until 1997 because of the difficulties of controlling their long coastal borders. The UK's wish to retain control over its borders, resulted in Ireland not joining, as this could have led to stricter border controls between the two countries. Denmark, Sweden and Finland represent a problem too as they are joined to Norway and Iceland in a passport union. (See also, Amsterdam Treaty, SEM).

SCHUMAN, ROBERT (1886-1963). Born in Luxembourg, he made his career in France. As a member of the Movement Républicain Populaire, he became Prime Minister in 1947-48 and Foreign Minister in 1948-53. The adoption of the Schuman Plan made him one of the founders of the European Community. The anniversary of this day, 9

May 1950, is still celebrated within the Community institutions as a holiday. Schuman's name is also given to medals awarded annually by the Schuman Foundation to persons committed to the cause of European unity.

SCHUMAN PLAN. Presented by Robert Schuman in May 1950, the Plan aimed at placing the Franco-German coal and steel production under a common High Authority. The organisation, open to other countries of Europe, was to oversee the reduction of coal and steel trade barriers between the participating states. In this way the fate of Germany and France was bound together and, in Schuman's words, aversion or aggression between the two states would become 'not merely unthinkable, but materially impossible'.

In addition, the Schuman Plan was the first step towards a much wider enterprise promoting the establishment of a federal Europe, named the United States of Europe. The plan was originally an idea of Monnet. (See also, ECSC).

SIMMENTHAL v. EUROPEAN COMMISSION, see p. 155, n. 18

SINGLE ADMINISTRATIVE DOCUMENT (SAD). This is a multi-purpose document introduced with the objective of simplifying customs formalities. On 1 January 1993, the Community abolished SAD for intra-Community trade, thus causing the elimination of about 60 million documents a year. SAD still applies to trade with third countries. (See also, SEM).

SINGLE EUROPEAN ACT (SEA). The SEA came into force on 1 July 1987 and was the first significant amendment to the founding Treaties, as it further promoted the long-standing objective of the internal market. It also introduced considerable institutional reform and addressed the theme of European Political Cooperation (EPC). Because the Act revised the founding Treaties, it required ratification by the member states. In February 1986 the document was officially signed by all the member states with the exception of Denmark, Greece and Italy. The SEA was subject to a referendum in Denmark and Ireland[19].

---

[19] The Irish government's initial signing of the SEA was ruled unconstitutional by the Supreme Court of Ireland after the matter was brought before it by an Irish citizen, on the grounds that it went counter to Ireland's foreign policy, embedded in its constitution. As a result, Ireland had to amend

In the sphere of the internal market, an immediate goal of the Treaty of Rome, the implications of the SEA were enormous. The firm political will for the implementation of the Cockfield White Paper was expressed. Customs barriers and formalities for the transit of goods, from one member state to another, were simplified; tax harmonization measures, especially with regard to indirect taxation, were introduced; harmonization of excise duties for products such as tobacco, alcohol, etc., was achieved. In addition, the role of the Community was specifically strengthened with regard to economic and financial policy, environment policy, social policy and research and development.

Institutional reforms, accommodating proposals of the Genscher-Colombo Plan, the Solemn Declaration and the Draft Treaty establishing the European Union (DTEU), prepared the Community for the accession of Portugal and Spain. Moreover, these reforms were instrumental to the implementation of the single market programme. In the Council of Ministers, qualified majority voting (QMV) was extended to matters which previously had required unanimity and were principally related to the establishment of the internal market; the cooperation and assent procedures which increased the powers of the European Parliament (EP) were introduced; the Court of First Instance (CFI) was established; and the European Council was formally recognised.

A brief, but not insignificant, reference was made to the EPC, the forerunner of a common foreign and security policy. Title III of the SEA gave recognition to the EPC and stated that member states would endeavour jointly to formulate and implement a European foreign policy. The Act also provided for a permanent secretariat to serve the EPC.

The SEA has been revised and most of its provisions have been superseded by the later Treaties. But it contributed substantially to the goal of the internal market and the closer European integration. (See also, Assent Procedure, Cockfield White Paper, Co-operation Procedure, Council of Ministers, DTEU, EPC, Genscher-Colombo Plan, Harmonization, Internal Market, SEM, Taxation, VAT).

SINGLE EUROPEAN MARKET (SEM). Defined by the Single European Act (SEA) as an area without internal frontiers within which free movement of goods, persons, services and capital is ensured.

its constitution through a referendum held in May 1987. The referendum became a yes or no vote to Ireland's continuing membership to the Community.

Sometimes it is referred to as the internal market in order to distinguish it from the Community external trade. The Single European Market should not be confused with the European Economic Area (EEA), though since 1 January 1994 most SEM legislation has applied throughout the EEA.

Although an immediate objective of the Treaty of Rome, the SEM took a long time to be realised, as the Commission's initiatives on economic liberalization were delayed or blocked in the Council of Ministers. The stalemate was broken at the European Council meeting at Brussels in March 1985, where the principle of establishing the SEM within a specified deadline was adopted. The Commission was instructed to draw up a programme whereby the single market would be completed by December 1992. Lord Cockfield, who was given the task of drafting this programme, issued a document in which the legal and institutional framework of the SEM was embodied in 289 measures, to be implemented within a specified timetable. A further impetus to the implementation of the SEM was given by the Milan summit of June 1985, which endorsed the Cockfield White Paper, and the Luxembourg summit of December 1985, which reached other agreements instrumental to its completion. All measures mentioned in the Cockfield White Paper contributed to the establishment of the SEM, but those specified below were considered indispensable to its consolidation.

1. Free movement of goods may be considered one of the cornerstones of the internal market to be achieved by the removal of various barriers to trade:

a. technical barriers, arising out of the different national technical specifications, were removed. Unable at the time to implement a uniform standard throughout the Community, the adoption of two strategies was accepted: the mutual recognition of national standards, and approximation, which insists on minimum requirements, such as minimum health and safety standards.

b. fiscal barriers, arising out of the differing rates of indirect taxes, particularly Value-added Tax (VAT) and excise duties, slowed down cross-borders trade appreciably. In 1992, an agreement was eventually concluded, introducing a standard VAT rate of at least 15 per cent with the exception of certain goods. In addition, a minimum rate of excise duties for tobacco, cigarettes, alcohol and mineral oil products was agreed. On the other hand, 'duty free' shops were to have no place in a borderless Community, but were given a respite until 30 June 1999, pressure being brought to bear by airports.

c. physical barriers, such as frontier formalities for goods transported across Community borders were simplified with the introduction of the 1988 Single Administrative Document (SAD). Since January 1993, even these remaining formalities were abolished.

2. Free movement of persons refers to the right of any citizen of the Community to move and reside freely within the member states, including the right to seek and obtain work and enjoy the same treatment as any national of the host country. Moreover, professionals in most occupations would have the right to have their qualifications recognized in any member state. Because of the importance of labour in the internal market, initial legislation focused on the rights of those seeking employment in another member state, and addressed the issue in a Regulation and a Directive as early as 1968.

In 1990 the Council of Ministers adopted a Directive on the right of residence for students, retired people and nationals of member states. According to this directive, they are free to reside in any member state provided they are covered by sickness insurance and that they are in receipt of an income sufficient to prevent them from burdening the welfare system of the host member state.

Theoretically, free movement of persons was not to be limited to European Community citizens in so far as the Treaty was also committed to the relaxation or removal of controls for non-European nationals. Common arrangements on asylum seekers and immigration rules have sprung out of this commitment, but to date neither the Schengen Agreement, nor the External Frontiers Convention, or the Dublin Asylum Convention has been signed by all member states of the Community. Well-established differences in attitudes among member states, as well as the determination of the Community to fight terrorism, drug trafficking and crime, serve as one of the many obstacles to a fuller implementation of the free movement of people.

3. Free provision of services is also essential for the establishment of the internal market. Services may be provided in any member state of the Community without requiring permanent residence of the provider in the country where the service is provided.

The Treaty of Rome extends the freedom of provision of services to non-Community nationals. But special arrangements have been introduced for transport and financial services. In the 1980s impetus was given to the free provision of services by the mutual recognition of qualifications. However, the services sector still accounts for only 18 per cent of internal trade, but as much as 65 per cent of the GDP within the Community.

3. Freedom of capital movement, implying abolition of restrictions on the movement of capital belonging to persons resident in the Community, is stipulated by the Treaty of Rome. However, freedom of capital movement was not applied until the adoption of a Directive in 1988, providing for full liberalization capital movement by July 1990. Greece, Ireland, Portugal and Spain were excluded at that time.

The Maastricht Treaty placed capital movement legislation within the Economic and Monetary Union (EMU) framework with the European Monetary Institute as the supervisory body. Since 1 January 1995 free movement of capital exists in all member states of the Community, and it also extends to the European Economic Area. (See also, Cockfield White Paper, Dublin Asylum Convention, EEA, External Frontiers Convention, Freedom of Establishment, Internal Market, SAD, Schengen Agreement, SEA, Taxation, VAT).

SIX (THE). An expression used to describe the Six founding members, France, Germany, Italy, Belgium, The Netherlands and Luxembourg, of the European Coal and Steel Community founded by the Treaty of Paris of 1951, and the European Economic Community and the EURATOM founded by the Treaty of Rome of 1957. (See also, ECSC, EEC, EURATOM).

SMALL AND MEDIUM-SIZED ENTERPRISES (SMES). Any undertaking with a workforce of less than 250 employees is defined as an SME. According to the Commission's estimate around 90 per cent of Community industry belongs to this category. In contrast, only 1 per cent of all Community undertakings employ more than 500 employees. (See also, EIF, Industrial Policy).

SMALL COUNTRIES. These are very small states in size and population, often past protectorates of or closely linked to a European Community member state. Their relationship to the Community is usually determined by their special relationship to a member state. These are: Andorra, Channel Islands, Cyprus, Gibraltar, Liechtenstein, Malta, Monaco, San Marino and the Vatican city. Presently, none of them is a member of the EU in its own right, although Cyprus and Malta have signed Association Agreements with the Community.

Cyprus became a republic in 1960. It signed an association agreement with the Community in 1973. Since the 1974 Turkish invasion one third of the island remains under occupation. In July 1990, the Republic of Cyprus, the only recognized authority, applied for full membership to the Community. However, an obstacle remains in the Turkish objection on the authority of the Republic of Cyprus to negotiate on behalf of the whole island.

Malta, a former British dependency, became a republic in 1974. It signed an association agreement with the European Community in 1976 and submitted an application for full membership in 1990. However, internal political factors and a rather cautious approach by the EU have impeded further progress.

Gibraltar is a British dependency since 1713, but is a disputed territory between UK and Spain. The UK is responsible for its external relations, defence and internal security. Having this special relationship to the UK and being a European territory, Gibraltar is covered by the Treaty of Rome.

The Channel Islands and the Isle of Man are not part of the European Community, but have a special relationship with the UK. On these grounds, free movement of agricultural products and industrial goods between them and the Community is guaranteed under the United Kingdom's Accession Treaty of 1972.

Andorra joined the custom's union in 1986 as a result of Spain's entry into the European Community, although special arrangements apply to its agricultural products. Monaco's customs union with the European Community dates from 1963, the date of the latest convention governing Monaco's customs union with France, while San Marino joined on the date of the amendment of its 1939 customs union agreement with Italy. In 1992, an agreement on customs union and cooperation was concluded directly between the EU and San Marino. Relations between the EU and San Marino are the responsibility of a Cooperation Committee.

Liechtenstein first joined in a customs union with Switzerland in 1923. Following a second referendum in 1995 Liechtenstein took the radical step of joining the European Economic Area (EEA). Switzerland, on the other hand, had voted against participation in the EEA in December 1992.

The Vatican City does not participate in a customs union either with Italy or with the EU. It is the smallest political entity in the world and has a permanent observer status at the United Nations (UN) and the Council of Europe (CE).

All small political entities present the international organizations, and even more so the EU, with serious institutional, political and economic problems. In general, special forms have to be devised for small countries to be accommodated in the EU. (See also, Association Agreements, External Frontiers Convention).

SNAKE. The term applied to an agreement signed in 1972 by several European states in order to establish a European System of Exchange Rates. The Snake was to 'operate in a tunnel' represented by the fluctuation margins of 4.5 per cent between Community currencies and the dollar as authorised by the Washington Agreement. It proved an unsuccessful instrument of exchange rates control. Only Germany, Denmark and the Benelux countries were able to stay within the fixed framework. The UK, Denmark, Ireland left in 1972 and Italy in 1973; France left in 1974, rejoined in 1975, and left again in 1976. Snake was abandoned in the late 1970s only to be replaced by the European Monetary System (EMS), which became operational in March 1979. (See also, EMS)

SOCIAL CHARTER. Adopted in December 1989 in the context of social Europe as advocated by Delors, the Social Charter was attached to the Maastricht Treaty in the form of a protocol on social policy. The UK is widely known for winning an opt-out, on the grounds that the Charter represented a purely continental approach to industrial relations and granted privileges which went counter both to employers and employees.

The Protocol on social policy consists of seven articles. All, except article 2, refer to the objectives of the Charter, as well as to certain rights provided by the Protocol. The Social Charter introduces a number of rights including the right to work in a European Community country of one's choice; the freedom to choose an occupation and the right to a fair wage; the right to improved living and working conditions; the right to social protection under prevailing national conditions; the right to freedom of association and collective bargaining; the right to vocational training; the right of men and women to equal treatment; the right of workers to access of information, consultation and participation; the right to health and safety at work; protection of children and adolescents; decent living standards for the elderly; improved social and professional integration for the disabled. Article 2 addresses the Council's voting procedures, according to which the Council decides by qualified majority voting (QMV) or unanimity in areas of social policy defined by the Single European Act (SEA).

The Charter has no direct legal force, but most of its principles have been put into effect through Community legislation. By 1993, the Commission had forwarded 47 detailed proposals, including 29 that required legislative action. Among them there were some highly controversial proposals, such as the Working Time Directive, which was eventually approved by the Council in 1993, with the UK abstaining despite the many concessions it won. Adoption of these proposals has been an important factor in shaping the Community's social dimension.

The British opt-out put the social policy in an awkward position as it had to be based on two legal frameworks, the *acquis communautaire* applicable to all member states, and the Protocol applicable to all with the exception of the UK. However, the UK was not exempted from other commitments to social policy made at Maastricht, or in the SEA or Treaty of Rome. The British opt-out was revoked by the newly elected Labour government, which accepted the Social Charter at the Amsterdam summit on 16-18 June 1997. As a result, the Social Charter will be embodied in the new Amsterdam Treaty which is in the process of ratification. (See also, *Acquis Communautaire*, Delors, Opt-out, Social Policy, Workers Rights).

SOCIAL EXCLUSION. A term used in the literature of the Community to denote poverty and marginalisation. It has been estimated that more than 50 million people within the Community live in households with an income of less than half the average of their country. Poverty is still addressed primarily at national level, but since 1975 the Commission has launched the so-called poverty programmes in an effort to contribute to the solution of this problem. The third programme of 1989-93, although considerably higher than its predecessors, only amounted to ECUs 121 million. As the richer member states of the Union have grown increasingly reluctant to undertake commitments in this field, the adoption of a fourth programme was blocked by the UK and Germany in 1995. (See also, Regional Policy, Social Policy).

SOCIAL POLICY. Social policy, addressing employment matters, was one of the policies of the Community to be introduced at an early stage. In 1951, the European Coal and Steel Community (ECSC) sought the improvement of living and working conditions of those employed in the coal and steel industry. By contrast the European Economic Community (EEC) addressed wider issues, such as labour mobility, equal pay between men and women, as well as introducing the European Social Fund (ESF). In the framework of Social Policy, the Commission, as in other sectors, is empowered to deliver Opinions after consultation with the Economic and Social Committee (ESC), to encourage cooperation between social partners (management and labour) and to administer the ESF.

In the early 1970s, after a long period of stagnation, social policy extended to other spheres relating to broader social issues than simply labour. In 1972 a Social Action Programme was introduced with the intention of addressing the growing problem of unemployment, and in 1989 President Delors added a social dimension to the emerging single market with the introduction of the Social Charter.

The Single European Act (SEA) provided for qualified majority voting in the Council of Ministers for aspects of the Social Policy, such as health and safety at work, working conditions, information and consultation of workers, equal opportunities between men and women, integration of people excluded from the labour market. Nevertheless, unanimity is required for issues of social security, social protection of workers, protection of redundant workers, representation and collective defence of workers and employers, employment conditions of third country nationals, and finance and employment generation.

The Maastricht Treaty reinforced further the attitudes and practices of the SEA with particular emphasis on welfare and employment policies. Legal competence with regard to public health is specified, so that preventive action may now be taken. The Maastricht Treaty also introduced two sets of policy provisions: one, based on the Treaty of Rome, applicable to all member states, and the other, based on the 'Protocol on Social Policy', applicable to all member states with the exception of the UK. This is to change with the ratification of the Amsterdam Treaty by the UK.

A Commission Green Paper on Social Policy, published in 1993, stimulated an overall discussion concerning social policy issues; and the 1994 Commission White Paper on Social Policy acknowledged that the European Community's social goals are the following: a high level of employment and social protection, raising of the standard of living and quality of life, together with economic and social cohesion. Yet, these were clearly high goals to achieve in a Community that had an estimated 18 million unemployed in 1995 (some 11.6% of the work force). In the last 20 years, only 3 million jobs have been created in the member states of the Community, compared with some 30 million jobs created in the USA in the same period. The Community's goal to create 15 million new jobs before the year 2000 is unlikely to be achieved.

In general, social policy remains largely fragmented as it is mostly the social policies of national governments which continue to affect the lives of Community citizens. European Community expenditure on social policy is still a very small proportion of national spending on welfare and employment creation. National governments provide pensions, unemployment, sickness, child benefits and other welfare benefits. Even in the field of employment 90 per cent of legislation is still the responsibility of national governments. (See also, CEDEFOP, Delors Package I, ESF, Public Health, Social Charter).

SOCRATES. An education programme introduced in 1995 by a decision of the Council of Ministers. It covers the work of Erasmus and Lingua, programmes dealing with cross-border inter-university cooperation and student exchange, respectively. Socrates also covers the work of both Eurydice and Arion, concerned with information exchanges on education systems and study visits for educational specialists, respectively. It supports the cooperation between educational institutions and provides funds for students willing to study at an institution in another member state. More than half of its funds are related to higher education and a smaller amount is directed towards school education, language teaching and distant studying. For the period 1995-99, Socrates has a budget of ECUs 850 million. (See also, Education Policy, Erasmus, Lingua).

SOLEMN DECLARATION. Also known as Stuttgart Declaration after the European Council meeting in Stuttgart on 17-19 June 1983, which issued a statement concerned with a wide range of issues related to the institutions and policies of the European Community. The text expressed the will of the participants to transform the existing relations between their states into some form of European Union.

The Solemn Declaration reflected many of the proposals of the 1981 Genscher-Colombo Plan. It stressed the role of the European Council in promoting closer integration; it addressed the importance of European Political Cooperation (EPC); it favoured the enlargement of the powers of the European Parliament (EP); it supported the extension of Community activity to new areas.

The Solemn Declaration had no legal force and consequently none of its proposals could be enforced. However, its significance lies in that it largely provided for many aspects of the Single European Act (SEA) signed three years later, in 1986. (See also, EPC, Genscher-Colombo Plan, SEA).

SOVEREIGNTY. The concept of sovereignty originates from the Latin term *superanus* and is taken to mean supreme power. It has, however, departed from its original meaning and there is a further semantic problem deriving from the fact that the term can be given only an approximate equivalent, when translated into contemporary political theory. Over time, sovereignty has acquired several successive interpretations, such as popular, parliamentary, constitutional and pluralistic sovereignty, in each case indicating the different body or group in which sovereignty resides. It remains one of the most controversial concepts in political science and international law.

The doctrine of sovereignty has influenced developments within states considerably, but its greatest impact has been on relations between states. With reference to the 20th century, important restrictions on the freedom of action of states began to appear with the formation of international organizations, such as the League of Nations, the North Atlantic Treaty Organization (NATO), the United Nations (UN), and the European Court of Human Rights, which set up rules concerning the conduct of nations. As a result, the term sovereignty is no longer synonymous with supreme, unrestricted power. Such restrictions on sovereignty are usually based on consent or on the binding provisions of international law.

The signing of the Treaty of Rome implied that member states voluntarily transferred a part of their sovereignty to the new entity, which is called upon to achieve certain objectives in accordance with the conditions and timetable set by them. At this initial stage, the transfer of power had been limited and confined into the framework provided by the constituent Treaties. It must, however, be noted that this transfer is a dynamic process; the more the Community evolved and undertook new functions and policy areas, the more the transfer of state powers ensued. As a consequence, member states had to overcome their reluctance to grant additional powers to the Community and to conclude new treaties to legalize the situation.

This transfer of powers inevitably enhanced the partly supranational character of the Community. Supranationalism has to fulfil at least four conditions including, exclusive competence, internal independent institutions, capability to enact binding decisions to the member states and the presence of a mechanism, which compels the member states to obey the decisions of the organisation. The European Communities meet all four conditions, and as a consequence a further erosion of sovereignty of member states is involved. To an extent, however, national sovereignty is protected by the principle of subsidiarity, in which decisions for action have to be taken at the lowest possible level, except in those areas where the Community has exclusive competence.

The Court of Justice has probably enjoyed the most significant expansion of its authority, especially as it claims the exclusive right to interpret and implement the Treaties. It is therefore the unique supreme court, which is entitled to judge Community disputes. In addition, the existence of an elected European Parliament (EP) has legitimately taken away the exclusive right of national parliaments to legislate. Community law is binding on member states and enjoys both primacy and direct effect over national law, so that in a number of cases it has overturned previous judicial rulings in member states.

The implications of loss of sovereignty have become the source of much disagreement in the political debate, especially within member states. Euro-sceptics and anti-Europeans claim that the 'deepening option' of integration in particular tends to lead to a loss of sovereignty and the ability of a government to act in the national interests[20]. The counter-argument maintains that such a loss does not represent a real threat to national interests and identity, and that political and economic benefits of a united Europe outweigh other drawbacks. The whole argument seems to rest on the different emphasis that each side attributes to the advantages and disadvantages of the transfer of powers to a supranational centre. (See also, Direct Effect, Community Law, Court of Justice,Intergovernmentalism, Maastricht Treaty, Primacy, Subsidiarity, Wider v. Deeper Integration)

SPAAK COMMITTEE. Consisting of government delegates, the Spaak Committee put forward suggestions for closer economic integration among the Six. It was chaired by Paul-Henri Spaak, the Belgian Prime Minister, and presented its final report to the foreign ministers of the Six in March 1956.

The report provided the foundations for the Treaty of Rome establishing the European Economic Community (EEC) and European Atomic Energy Community (EURATOM). It dealt very little with institutional matters, but focused almost entirely on the common market, nuclear energy and a number of priority sectors, such as transport and telecommunications.

The report accepted by the Six, after minor reservations, is still considered a turning point in the history of the Community. For this reason the 1984 Dooge Committee was modelled on it. (See also, Dooge Committee, Treaty of Rome).

STABEX. A stabilization scheme of export revenue earnings of ACP countries heavily dependent on exports of primary products, such as tea, cocoa and cotton. In accordance with this scheme, ACP countries were to be reimbursed if their loss of export earnings was more than

---

[20] See wider versus deeper.

approximately 7.5 per cent, or in the case of the poorest among them if their losses were over 2.5 per cent. STABEX, like the rest of the programmes relating to the ACP countries, is funded by the EDF. Under the 1989 Lomé Convention, STABEX was reformed and money disbursed for lost revenues no longer requires repayment to the European Community. (See also, Lomé Convention).

STAR. Special Telecommunications Action for Regional Development, a programme which coordinates regional policy and research and development policies of the European Community. Its task is to help the less developed regions of the Community through construction of advanced telecommunication technologies and services. (See also, Regional Policy, Telecommunications Policy).

STRESA CONFERENCE. Taking place at Stresa, Italy, in July 1958, the Conference was concerned with the implementation of the Common Agricultural Policy (CAP). It was convened under the initiative of Sicco Manshlot, the Dutch Vice-President of the European Commission, who was also responsible for the CAP. European Commission officials, national experts and representatives of farmers' organizations assembled to decide how to accomplish the objectives of the CAP, as set out by the Treaty of Rome. (See also, CAP).

STRUCTURAL FUNDS. Devoted to structural change, and thus primarily directed towards the less developed areas of the Community, these funds became instrumental in the structural policies of the Community, especially after the introduction of the Single European Market (SEM), which called for disparities between centre and periphery to be reduced. The Cohesion Fund also shares the same aim. It is expected that by the year 2000 the structural funds will represent one third of the Community's Budget.

Since 1989, common objectives were set up for a better coordination of the various structural policies. In this context six objectives are identified:
Objective 1: assisting underdeveloped areas
Objective 2 : assisting regions affected by the decline of traditional industry
Objective 3: assisting long term unemployment and the integration of young people into the labour market
Objective 4: helping workers to adapt to technological change
Objective 5: assisting structural reform in agriculture and helping rural areas

Objective 6 : assisting the development of the thinly populated Arctic regions

The structural funds comprise the European Social Fund (ESF), the European Regional Development Fund (ERDF), the Guidance section of the European Agricultural Guidance and Guarantee Fund (EAGGF) and the Financial Instrument for Fisheries Guidance (FIFG). The ESF supports Objective 3 and 4 entirely, and Objectives 1, 2 and 5 partly. The ERDF supports Objectives 1 and 2 primarily, and to a lesser degree Objective 5. The EAGGF Guidance Section and FIFG mainly supports Objective 5, and to a lesser degree Objective 1. Objective 6 has been added recently and provides assistance to remote and sparsely populated areas of Sweden and Finland.

Funding is usually distributed in the form of Community Support Frameworks which are drawn up by the Commission after consultation with member states on the basis of a development plan, the use of structural assistance and the expected impact of the project. In all cases financial assistance is given in the form of grants, additional to national assistance. In certain cases assistance may be given in the form of loans by the European Investment Bank (EIB). For the period 1994-99 the total amount assigned to the structural funds has been ECUs 150 billion with 74 per cent going to Objective 1, 11 per cent going to Objectives 3 and 4, and the rest distributed about equally between the other objectives. (See also, Additionality, CAP, CFP, Cohesion Fund, EAGGF, EIB, ERDF, ESF, FIFG, Regional Policy, Social Policy).

SUBSIDIARITY. This is the principle intended to draw boundaries between national and community levels in policy making responsibility. It was stated for the first time in the Single European Act (SEA), specifically with reference to environmental policy, but it was introduced into the Treaty of Rome by a new article of the Maastricht Treaty, both as a principle and a means of steering action in the Community on matters of non-exclusive competence. Being related to central issues, it is regarded, together with proportionality, as the most important principle to European integration.

Despite its significance, the principle of subsidiarity remains far from clear and begs a number of questions. The difficulty with the concept arises partly from different definitions given to it, and partly from the difficulty that exists in implementing it, since the spheres of action of the Community vis-à-vis the member states are not clearly defined. It is usually interpreted as the principle by which decisions should be taken at the lowest possible level, i.e national, regional or local, rather than at European level, unless there is good reason to do otherwise. In other words, the European Community should not intervene in every sphere of activity carried out by member states.

Given its imprecise meaning, subsidiarity has raised suspicions even among federalists, though it is primarily a federal principle. They argue that national governments might use it as a stepping stone for avoiding their commitments to the Union, and as a consequence the very principle could turn against the Union's attempts to progress further with integration.

To clarify these perplexities the Commission issued a paper on subsidiarity in October 1992, stating that national rather than Community authority should be preeminent. It listed five criteria to guide the exercise of power under subsidiarity: need, effectiveness, proportionality, consistence and communication. In addition to this, the European Council in Birmingham in November 1992 stated that decisions have to be taken as closely as possible to the citizens, and called for the subsidiarity principle to be taken into consideration during the preparation of legislation. Furthermore, the Edinburgh council of December 1992 set the guidelines for the implementation of the principle. Since October 1993, an inter-institutional agreement requires all legislation to be checked in order to identify matters that no longer are appropriate for Community action. Moreover, the Commission has to include a subsidiarity justification in all draft legislation, and to produce an annual report on compliance with subsidiarity.

Despite these elaborations, the principle of subsidiarity remains to some degree vague, and it seems likely that the Court of Justice will be required to make judgements in key test cases on subsidiarity issues, though the principle is presently seen as political rather than judicial. (See also, COR, Intergovernmentalism, Federalism, Proportionality).

SUPRANATIONALISM, see **INTERGOVERMENTALISM**

SYSMIN. A complementary scheme introduced by the 1979 Lomé Convention aiming at maintaining the export capacity of mineral products of ACP countries, rather than stabilising export revenues in the way STABEX does for the primary agricultural products. The main products covered are copper, phosphorates, manganese, tin, bauxite, iron ore, aluminium, uranium and cobalt. A fall in the capacity of mineral exports of at least 10 per cent would ensure that the state concerned would receive aid, in order to prevent any capital equipment or distribution facilities, linked to the extraction process, being downgraded. Most of Sysmin aid originates from the European Investment Bank (EIB), the International Bank for Reconstruction and Development (IBRD) and the African Development Bank. (See also, EIB, Lomé Convention).

SYSTRAN. Systran is the mechanical system used by the European Commission to translate documents into the official languages of the Union. Nevertheless, more than one third of the Community's officials are employed in connection with translation and interpretation, as the eleven official languages among them give rise to some 110 combinations.

The European Commission's translation centre, based at Luxembourg, has an annual output of 1 million pages. The Centre translates for all Community institutions except for the European Monetary Institute (EMI). With the enlargement of the Community the situation is bound to get more complex, reviving the debate for a more rigid distinction between working and official languages. (See also, Language).

T

TARGET (TRANS-EUROPEAN AUTOMATED REAL-TIME GROSS SETTLEMENT EXPRESS TRANSFER SYSTEM). This is a system for processing large, cross-border Euro payments. Primarily used for monetary policy purposes and wholesale transactions, Target is a real-time system, that is payments reach their destination within a few minutes. The speed of the transactions and volume capacity should make log-jams unlikely. The system has been developed by the European Central Bank (ECB) and the national banks of the member states, and it is based in Frankfurt. The ECB has granted access to TARGET to the national central banks outside the 11 Economic and Monetary Union (EMU) participants, provided they have real-time gross settlement systems operating in Euro. (See also, ECB, EMU).

TARGET PRICE, see **CAP**

TARIFFS. A tariff or duty is a tax levied on a commodity traded across the borders of a country or of a group of countries, which have formed a customs union. In the context of intra-community trade, abolition of internal tariffs was one of the principal goals of the Treaty of Rome, establishing a customs union among the Six. Originally, the abolition of tariffs was planned to be completed in 1969, but in fact it was realized a year earlier, bringing with it an annual increase of 28.4 per cent in intra-Community trade during the first ten years. By contrast, the average increase of imports from third countries was as low as 10 per cent. New member states were given a transitional period in which to remove their tariffs.

As tariffs were removed in intra-European trade, a common external tariff system was established with the purpose of protecting the internal market from low-price imports. This has been the cause of a long-standing dispute between the European Community and the signatories of the General Agreement on Tariffs and Trade (GATT), especially the USA. Tariffs were constantly removed as a result of the various talks within the GATT framework; the dispute was largely resolved during the Uruguay Round. (See also, CAP, GATT, Trade, VIES).

TAXATION. Being the main source of government revenues, taxation has generally been regarded as the responsibility of national governments. However, the Treaty of Rome stipulated that the harmonization of legislation concerning turnover taxes, excise duties and other forms of indirect taxation is a principal objective of the Community. Two main objectives can be discerned from the interpretation of the Treaty. Tax law should, a) be harmonized to the extent required for the functioning of the common market, rather than to the extent necessary for a perfect fiscal system, and b) contribute to the acceleration of the process of integration.

Consequently, the European Community has intervened considerably in matters relating to indirect taxation, which has come to represent the largest source of Community revenue. The Neumark Committee, appointed by the Commission to study the fiscal systems of member states and to propose ways of harmonising them, recommended the introduction of a Value-added Tax (VAT). The Community accepted the proposals and following a number of Directives, VAT was introduced as the main form of indirect taxation.

In addition, a number of excise duties, that is specific duties on the consumption of certain goods, were introduced. Excise duties constitute a substantial source of state revenue; they are sometimes imposed to discourage the harmful use of tobacco and alcohol, or are applied to curtail the use of mineral oils for saving energy and reducing energy dependence. Member states in the past displayed a large diversity in the imposition of excise duties. Broadly speaking, most of the northern Community countries have imposed heavy duties on tobacco and alcohol, turning them into significant source of revenue, while southern Community countries, in order to protect major home industries, impose no significant duties and therefore derive little revenue from them. Denmark, Ireland and the UK impose the highest rates of tax on these products, while Greece and Italy impose no tax at all on wine, for example. Following a number of proposals by the Commission, member states finally agreed to a minimum rate of excise duty for tobacco, cigarettes, alcohol and mineral oil.

Taxation was one of the major challenges of 1992. The removal of border controls had created a serious problem in the collection of taxes, since taxes continued to be paid in the country of destination, contrary to the principle agreed as early as 1963, that taxes be paid in the country of origin. The 1991 Council Directive established a transitional period, lasting from 1 January 1993 to 31 December 1996. During this period individuals travelling from one member state to another paid VAT in the country of purchasing. If, however, they exceeded the tax exemption limit of 800 cigarettes, 10 litters of spirits and 110 litters of alcoholic beverages, then they would be subject to the same regulations as companies. In the case of companies, VAT was paid by the importers in the country of destination, but from 1

January 1997 a definitive taxation system based on the principle of taxation in the country of origin was to be implemented. Since no definitive taxation system was concluded, the existing transitional system was extended automatically.

A definitive system of excise duties was implemented in accordance with the 1992 Community Directive. Excise duties are paid in the country of actual consumption for goods imported by companies. Individuals, however, purchasing goods for their own consumption in another member state, pay the duty in the country of purchase. In a borderless Community 'duty free' sales have no place, nevertheless they will continue to exist until 1999 under special arrangements. However, there is a tax free limit of ECUs 90 for intra-Community travellers, while for travellers arriving from third countries this limit goes up to ECUs 175.

Direct taxation affects the functioning of the common market and the process of further integration less than indirect taxation. Little progress has therefore been observed in the harmonization of direct taxation, except in the spheres of corporation tax and tax on savings which can affect fair competition in business. To this purpose, the Council of Ministers adopted three Directives in 1990, which provided for a common system of taxation applicable to mergers and subsidiaries or associated companies based in different member states. Consequently, companies view their investment in any member state as investment in a domestic market. (See also, Harmonization, Internal Market, SEM, VAT).

TECHNICAL ASSISTANCE TO THE COMMONWEALTH OF INDEPENDENT STATES (TACIS). This is a programme providing Technical Assistance to the Commonwealth of Independent States (CIS), as well as to Mongolia, Azerbaijan and Georgia during their transition to a market economy and democratic government. The decision to introduce the programme was taken by the European Council meeting in Rome in December 1990. TACIS became operational in 1991 and is administered by the European Commission. The programme gives priority to training, energy (most importantly nuclear safety), transport, support for industrial and commercial enterprises, food production and distribution. In 1994, it amounted to ECUs 510 million. (See also, Agenda 2000, PHARE).

TELECOMMUNICATIONS POLICY. One of the most important Trans-European Networks (TENs), it aims to promote European wide band networks (information highways) and to harmonize and liberalize the telecommunications industry. In 1988 a directive was issued which called for the liberalization of telecommunications equipment; two years later, another directive called for the liberalization of telecommunication services. Further recommendations are included in the Bangemann's report of 1994. Market harmonization is also promoted by means of standardization through further cooperation between the Committee for European Normalization (CEN), the European Committee of Electrotechnical Standardization (CELENEC), the European Conference of Postal and Telecommunications Administrations (CEPT) and the European Telecommunications Standard Institute (ETSI).

The convergence of telecommunications and information technologies is being promoted through a pan-European: land-based public mobile communications, an Integrated Services Digital Network (ISDN)[21], a land-based paging system, standard emergency numbers, a common international dialling code and cross-border electronic clearing systems for banks and credit card transactions. Two major programmes, Research and Development in Advanced Communications Programme for Europe (RACE) and Information Market Policy Actions (IMPACT), have contributed greatly to developments in the field of telecommunications. RACE is concerned with research and development in advanced communication technologies, while IMPACT deals with the establishment of an internal market in information services.

However, the European Commission, because of the rapid technological innovations in this field, has been struggling to keep pace with developments. In addition, it has to deal with difficulties arising from, to a certain extent, conflicting aims, a) full liberalization of frameworks and suppliers of telecommunications in all member states, planned to be completed by 2003, b) provision of a minimum service of a defined quality at an affordable price, known as a universal service, and c) a degree of harmonization of interconnected networks and inter-operability of services. (See also, CEN, STAR, TENs).

THRESHOLD PRICE, see **CAP**

TINDERMANS REPORT. Named after Leo Tindermans, the Prime Minister of Belgium, the Report was a study on a broad range of issues. It proposed a Common Foreign and Security Policy (CFSP),

---

[21] ISDN: Provision of a broad range of voice data and image transmission services

collaboration in the field of defence, the creation of an Economic and Monetary Union (EMU), the development of regional and social policy, a common industrial policy, and a number of institutional reforms. It also developed the notion of a two-speed Europe, as the most acceptable way of achieving the goals of the European Community. Though a point of reference up to 1978, the Report was never discussed in the Council of Ministers, but undoubtedly served as a basis for a number of changes introduced in subsequent years. (See also, CFSP, EMU, Two-speed Europe).

TOTAL ALLOWANCE CATCHES (TACS). A central element of the Common Fisheries Policy (CFP) related to the conservation and management of the fish stocks. Overall quotas for all kinds of fish, which are threatened by overfishing, are fixed by the Council of Ministers annually; accordingly, every state is allocated its own quota.

The implementation of this policy is the responsibility of each member state individually, but the scheme is supervised by a team of inspectors directly accountable to the European Commission. The European Commission has the authority to impose penalties in the event of shared quotas not being respected by member states. (See also, CFP).

TRADE. Increase in trade has been one of the main considerations of the Community ever since its creation. To this end the formation of a customs union between the Six, entailing the abolition of internal barriers to trade and a common trade policy towards third countries, was introduced. In the context of the Common Commercial Policy (CCP) the Community has signed a number of agreements.

As a result, the Community has developed into the world's largest trading unit and has the world's largest market. In 1995, it accounted for about two-fifths of world trade and about a quarter of the world GDP. It is also the world's largest importer of agricultural products, textiles and clothing. However, the Community faces a number of challenges, mainly as a result of structural changes taking place in the global economy. A constant effort therefore has to be made to improve the Union's competitiveness in international markets, given that 12 million jobs depend on the export sector.

European Community trade is divided into trade between Community countries, namely intra-Community trade, and trade between Community countries and the outside world, namely extra-Community trade. Intra-community trade is around 60 per cent of the total Community trade, being mainly intra-industry trade (countries trading the same products) rather than specialized (some countries trading capital goods, while others trade consumer goods).

As for extra-Community trade, the Community's single most important trading partner is the USA, despite all disagreements regarding tariffs, subsidies, etc. The Community's trade with the USA is broadly balanced, in contrast to the substantial trade deficit with its other significant trading partner, Japan; almost all imports from Japan are manufactured goods. On the other hand, the Community has a trade surplus with many developing countries and with many Eastern European partners. The Community exports to Eastern Europe and developing countries consist mainly of manufactured goods, while its imports consist of raw materials and agricultural products. (See also, CCP, Customs Union, Internal Market, SEM; Appendix 24).

TRADE-MARK REGISTRATION. Trade marks are important in specifying the origin and the quality of goods. Currently, national trade marks stand alongside European Community ones. The office for the registration of European Community trade-marks (and designs) is based in Alicante, Spain. Not to be confused with the Munich based office of the European Patent Convention. (See also, Office for Harmonization in the Internal Market)

TRANS-EUROPEAN NETWORKS (TENS). The term refers to programmes in the field of transport, energy, telecommunications and environment infrastructure, which aim to create integrated Community-wide networks. This implies linking together national networks and opening access to them. Community actions in this field seek to promote the interconnection and interoperability of national networks within the frontier-free area.

The Treaty of Rome provided for the establishment and development of European networks, and the Maastricht Treaty further acknowledged their importance in the process of integration and economic growth of the Community. The TENs programmes are intended to reinforce the Community's regional policy by enabling remote regions to develop closer links to the centre, as well as to other remote regions. In addition, the creation of TENs is meant to help economic and social cohesion by enabling citizens, business and local communities to derive full benefits from the establishment of the single market.

To achieve these goals the Community established several guidelines in order to identify projects of common interest and priorities, as well as to harmonize technical standards. The 1993

European Council in Brussels established two working groups: one responsible for transport and energy headed by European Commissioner Henning Cristopherson, and the other responsible for telecommunications headed by European Commissioner Martin Bangemann. In the 1994 European Council summit at Corfu, the responsibility of the first group was extended to environmental infrastructure, and over forty projects were decided upon, while the networks were extended to central and eastern Europe.

In the transport field, TENs include the high-speed railway network (Channel Tunnel) connecting London, Paris, Brussels, Cologne and Amsterdam; the improvement of railway-ferry links between the UK and Ireland. In the energy area there are significant projects connecting the electricity grids of Greece and Italy, and those of Ireland and the UK. In the field of telecommunications, electronic clearing for banks and credit operation and mobile telecommunication networks have been introduced.

The Community's role in the TENs programmes is primarily that of a coordinator. The bulk of funds to TENs is borne primarily by national budgets and private investors, rather than by the Community Budget. The Community finance ministers have suggested that funding of the Community to TENs should not exceed 10 per cent of the total cost. Decisions referring to the TENs are mainly concerned with the identification of projects of common interest, and these are taken under the co-decision procedure. (See also, Energy Policy, Environment Policy, Regional Policy, Telecommunications Policy, CTP).

TRANSNATIONAL FEDERATIONS. Grouped around general principles, transnational federations exist for the purpose of coordinating, propagating and serving electoral needs. They developed in the mid-1970s in an atmosphere of anticipation of the first direct elections for the European Parliament (EP). In fact, the formation of transnational federations was a development of the already existing, but very weak and unofficial cooperation between various political organizations.

However, federations have not succeeded in fulfilling expectations, such as providing leadership, vision and coordination at European level; nor have they done very much for tasks such as long-term policy planning and the harmonization of national party differences.

There are three main federations: the European People's Party (EPP), composed mainly of Christian Democratic Parties and their descendants; the Party of European Socialists (PES), consisting of parties with socialist ideological orientation; and the European Liberal,

Democrat and Reform Party (ELDR), consisting of parties with liberal ideas. In addition to these three main federations, there is a number of other loosely organized groupings, including Communist, Green, Regional and Extreme Right federations. (See also, Political Groups, EP).

TRANSPORT POLICY, see COMMON TRANSPORT POLICY

TREATY OF BRUSSELS. Signed in March 1948 by the UK, France and the Benelux countries, the Treaty provided for military assistance and economic cooperation among the signatory states. It aimed at providing protection to the signatory states in the event of a renewed German aggression, or the Soviet threat. The Treaty provided the basis for both the North Atlantic Treaty Organization (NATO) and the Western European Union (WEU). (See also, NATO, WEU).

TREATY OF DUNKIRK. Signed in 1947 between France and the UK, the Treaty called for bilateral economic assistance and cooperation. However, being the first post-war security pact, its purpose was primarily military, as it guaranteed mutual aid in the event of any future German aggression. The Treaty of Dunkirk served as the precursor of the Treaty of Brussels signed one year later. (See also, Treaty of Brussels).

TREATY OF LUXEMBOURG. This Treaty was signed by the member states of the European Community in 1970 with the primary objective of incorporating the new budgetary system of 'own resources' into the Community structure. The Treaty of Luxembourg constituted an amendment of the Treaty of Rome. (See also, Own Resources).

TREATY OF PARIS. Signed on 18 April 1951 by France, Germany, Italy, Belgium, The Netherlands and Luxembourg, the Treaty established the European Coal and Steel Community (ECSC). The first of the three Communities to be established, the ECSC aimed at creating a common market in the coal and steel sectors. Coal and steel were essential to post-war reconstruction and posed immediate problems as coal was in short supply and steel in excess. They were also considered critical for waging war and their integration was perceived as the means of preventing such an eventuality. The political nature of the Treaty was reinforced further with the provisions made with regard to the institutional structures establishing the first supranational bodies.

In spite of its complexity, consisting of 100 articles and a considerable number of annexes, the Treaty received a rather wide support. Following ratification by the member states, the Treaty came into force on 23 July 1952 for 50 years. Its expressed goals were clearly economic, but having initiated the debate on European cooperation and unity soon after the war, it undoubtedly contributed to the establishment of the European Economic Community (EEC) and European Atomic Energy Community (EURATOM) in 1957. (See also, ECSC).

TREATY OF ROME. The Treaty of Rome was signed for an unlimited duration on 25 March 1957, by France, Germany, Italy, Belgium, The Netherlands and Luxembourg, the same countries that had signed the Treaty of Paris six years earlier. It came into force on 1 January 1958. The Treaty of Rome consists of two separate documents establishing two entities: a) the European Economic Community (EEC), which created a common market among the six signatory states; b) the European Atomic Energy Community (EURATOM) with the purpose of developing peaceful application of atomic energy.

The Treaties followed the failed attempts for European integration launched by the European Defence Community (EDC) and the European Political Community in the early 1950s. The debate was resumed at the Messina Conference in June 1955, where Paul-Henri Spaak presented a memorandum on behalf of the Benelux countries suggesting the formation of an atomic energy community and a common market. These proposals were presented at a meeting of foreign ministers in Venice in 1956, where a protracted process of intergovernmental negotiations for the establishment of the two Communities was inaugurated. The outcome of the negotiations, which came to an end in February 1957, was the signing of the two Treaties.

The Treaty of Rome, which established the EEC went beyond the approach of sectorial integration and promoted political and economic goals; as such proved to be the most important of these two Treaties. Walter Hallstein, the German representative at Messina and the first President of the European Commission, stressed that 'We are not integrating economies, we are integrating politics, ... We are jointly building a new and bigger house'. Moreover, the Treaty clearly referred to the goal of 'an ever closer union of the European Peoples'.

The document establishing the EEC consisted of 248 articles, 4 annexes, 13 protocols, 4 conventions and 9 declarations. Its primary objective was to establish a common market, based on a customs union, which abolished restrictive trade practices among the six signatories, and introduced a common external tariff regime to trade with non-member states. In addition to the free movement of goods, indispensable component of a customs union, the common market also introduced free movement of services, capital and labour.

Common European policies were also established in various sectors, including: a Common Agricultural Policy (CAP) in 1962 consisting of a system of common guaranteed prices assisted by protection against agricultural imports from lower-cost markets outside the EEC; a Common Transport Policy; a system that ensured that competition was not distorted in the common market; procedures for the coordination of common economic policies of member states and the remedy of disequalibria in the balance of payments. In addition, the European Social Fund (ESF) was created in order to improve possibilities of employment for workers and improve standards of living. It provided for the establishment of the European Investment Bank (EIB) which aimed at facilitating economic development in the community, and promoting cooperation with the overseas countries and territories (OCTs) with a view to increasing trade.

The Treaty was to be administered by four main institutions that had to enforce common regulations for the entire community area. The European Commission and the Council of Ministers served the EEC only, while the Common Assembly and the Court of Justice served all the three Communities, namely the European Coal and Steel Community (ECSC), the EEC and EURATOM.

The Treaty of Rome underwent significant amendments by the Single European Act (SEA) of 1986 and the Maastricht Treaty of 1992. In fact, the latter has subsumed the previous Treaties. Yet, the Treaty of Rome constitutes part of the *Acquis Communautaire*, and the three Communities continue to be separate entities within the European Union (EU). On the whole, the Treaty of Rome proved to be a landmark in the history of European integration. Although it left too many issues to be decided by national governments or expressed political goals in economic terms, its importance is not diminished. (See also, CAP, CTP, Customs Union, EDC, EDF, EEC, ESF, European Communities, European Political Community, Merger Treaty, Messina Conference).

TWO-SPEED EUROPE. The idea of a two-speed Europe was first mentioned in the Tindenmans Report of 1975, as the best way for the achievement of Community integration. The prospect was not widely welcomed, but this did not prevent it from developing further. In 1994 Alain Lamassoure, France's European Affairs minister, proposed a 'hard core' of European Community members, consisting of countries implementing all Community policies provided for in the Treaties. In the same year, a similar proposal was put forward in Germany by Karl Lamers in a policy report for the Christian Democratic Union. Both proposals suggested that the 'hard core' would initially consist of the founding members, Germany, France, Italy and the Benelux countries, but would be open to new members. This plan met with opposition, especially from those which would find themselves in the second rank of membership.

Independently of the wishes and the degree of approval of such proposals, Community integration is already proceeding in a rather multi-speed, piecemeal way. Perhaps this is more the outcome of the heterogeneous nature of the Union's membership, than part of a grand design.

The Maastricht Treaty accommodated this multi-speed approach in various ways, the UK was granted an opt-out from social policy and certain aspects of the Economic and Monetary Union (EMU); the Common Foreign and Security Policy (CFSP) and Justice and Home Affairs (JHA) provided for member states to opt out from joint actions; some member states participate in the Eurocorps and the Western European Union (WEU), while others do not; and, more importantly, the single currency project, which commenced on 1 January 1999, proceeded with the participation of only 11 members.

Undoubtedly a multi-speed Europe involves a number of problems, not least the danger that some member states never reach the 'hard core' group, and as a result a two-tier or even a multi-tier Europe is brought about. However, had it not been for this flexibility provided by the Treaties, neither the integration of the Community would have proceeded to this point, nor its enlargement, with the expected accession, would have been possible. (See also, Maastricht Treaty, Tindenmans Report, Wider v. Deeper Integration).

U

UNION OF INDUSTRIAL AND EMPLOYERS CONFEDERATION OF EUROPE (UNICE). A cross-national federation of employers' associations, having as a primary objective the stimulation and elaboration of an industrial policy in a European context. It has acted as a pressure group on the European Community institutions, seeking the introduction of measures favourable to its members. In general, the effectiveness of the group is limited, as there are fundamental differences of interest between its economic and national components. (See also, Industrial Policy).

UNIT FOR THE COORDINATION OF FRAUD PREVENTION (UCLAF), see **FRAUD**

UNITED NATIONS (UN). An international and multipurpose organization with world-wide scope and membership, founded in 1945, as the successor to the League of Nations. According to its Charter, its primary objective is to maintain international peace and security, but also to promote human rights, social progress and better standards of living, and to serve as a centre where nations can coordinate their actions to these ends. It is located in New York, but also has offices in Geneva and Vienna.

The principal organs of the UN are the General Assembly, consisting of representatives of all member states; the Security Council, consisting of five permanent members (USA, UK, France, Russia and China) and ten non-permanent members, mainly concerned with the maintenance of international security; the Economic and Social Council mainly concerned with the management of the UN's social, economic, cultural and humanitarian activities; the International Court of Justice, the judicial body of the UN also known as the World Court, based in the Hague; and the Secretariat, the administrative department of the UN, headed by the secretary-general. The post of secretary-general, appointed for a five-year term by the General Assembly and the Security Council, carries significant political weight.

In addition, the UN supervises a number of other programmes and organizations, including the International Bank for Reconstruction and Development (IBRD); the International Monetary Fund (IMF); the International Labour Organization (ILO); the Food and Agriculture Organization (FAO); the World Health Organization (WHO); the UN's Educational, Scientific and Cultural Organization (UNESCO); and the UNs Children's Fund (UNICEF). Two of these organizations, UNICEF and ILO, were awarded the Nobel Peace Prize in 1965 and 1969, respectively. The UN's peacekeeping forces were also awarded the Nobel Peace Prize in 1988.

The European Community as a separate entity is not represented in the UN, but member states have tried to present a common front within the organisation. The president of the Council of Ministers addresses the General Assembly of the UN every year. Furthermore, the UK and France, being the only member states of the European Community with permanent membership in the Security Council, have been charged by the Maastricht Treaty with the obligation of keeping other members fully informed of developments in the UN and of defending the position of the European Community in the Security Council. (See also, Human Rights, IBRD, IMF, League of Nations).

VALUE-ADDED TAX (VAT). This is a sales tax applied within member states, though with considerable differences in what each country taxed, by how much and in what way. The Community has constantly tried to harmonize these differences so that they no longer influence free movement of goods and services and factors of production.

The European Commission, based on the recommendations of the Neumark Committee for the introduction of a value-added-tax paid in the country of origin, published the first Directive concerning VAT in 1967. It required member states to introduce a system of VAT as the main form of indirect taxation by 1970, and VAT became part of the *Acquis Communautaire*. However, VAT continued to be paid in the country of destination. Harmonization focused on the adoption of a uniform structure, namely the introduction of a number of common taxable activities, a common lower limit for exempted transactions, and a common threshold for taxing. The imposition of VAT common rates was little discussed at the time.

The Single European Act (SEA), which abolished internal frontiers and ensured free movement of goods, persons, services and capital, made the abolition of fiscal barriers to trade paramount. In 1985, the Commission adopted the Cockfield White Paper which approximated remarkably differing VAT standards, ranging from a 30 to a zero per cent rate. However, little progress was made until 1989, when the Commission in order to meet member states' objections offered a compromise. This included a minimum standard VAT rate of 15 per cent; member states were given the freedom to impose higher rates if they wished; a reduced band of no less than 5 per cent was retained, while some items could be zero rated; VAT continued to be paid in the country of destination, but without border controls, the terms 'importation' and 'export' were replaced by 'acquisition' and 'despatch', respectively.

At the Ecofin Council of 1992, an agreement was reached on the Commission's proposals, and a transitional system was established from 1 January 1993. Moreover, the Council decided on a definitive system for the taxation of trade between member states, which required VAT to be paid in the country of origin. Until this definitive system came into effect, the transitional system would automatically be extended. In 1996, the Commission issued the Green Paper, *A Common System of VAT*, which still remains under discussion.

Although no complete harmonization has been achieved, VAT constitutes by far the most important part of Community revenue, amounting to about 40 per cent of the 1997 Budget. From 1986, the contributions of each member state to the Community Budget increased from 1 to 1.4 per cent of the agreed harmonized basis, and not of the actual national VAT base and revenue. This was to be reduced to 1 per cent for the period 1995-99. This was a major shift, for VAT was transformed into an important source of community revenue, but also indirect taxation, once the exclusive control of national governments, was partly brought under European control. (See also, Acquis Commun., Budget, Harmonization, SEM, Taxation, VIES).

VAN GEND & LOOS, see p. 55, n. 6

VEDEL REPORT. Published in 1972 by a working-party, chaired by Georges Vedel, on the request of the Commission, the Report dealt with the enhancement of the powers of the European Parliament (EP). More specifically, it proposed that the powers of the EP should be increased so as to enable it to participate in the appointment of the President of the Commission, and to be granted the right of co-decision in almost all fields of Community legislation.

The Vedel Report was an ambitious reform programme, since at the time of its publication the EP was not even an elected body. It is not surprising, therefore, that some of the proposed reforms, such as the introduction of the co-decision procedure, and the involvement of the EP in the appointment of the President of the Commission, were only put into practice as late as 1992 by the Maastricht Treaty, while others have not yet been introduced. (See also, Maastricht Treaty).

VETO. In the context of the European Community, veto refers to the right of each member state to block a decision in the Council of Ministers. Introduced by the Treaty of Rome, it is exercised by member states in cases which require unanimity in the Council of Ministers.

The use of veto declined, as the Single European Act (SEA), and later the Maastricht Treaty, provided for a large number of issues to be decided by qualified majority rather than unanimity. However, member states have retained the right to veto a number of crucial matters, which still require unanimity. These are, the 'own resources', free movement of persons, amendment to the Treaties and accession of new members, as well as the two intergovernmental pillars, the Common Foreign and Security Policy (CFSP) and Justice and Home Affairs (JHA). The veto mechanism is also applicable in some cases, such as the appointment of the Commission, where the Treaties provide for decisions to be made by representatives of governments of member states acting by common accord.

Outside the Treaty framework, the right of veto was provided by the 1966 Luxembourg compromise, which had no legal force and was seldom used. Nevertheless, it was used as a means of delaying or even blocking certain decisions in the Council of Ministers.

The right of veto has been a very contentious issue, as indeed have all voting methods in the Council of Ministers. Arguably it allows for a small minority to frustrate the will of the majority, or works as a safeguard to the further erosion of national sovereignty. (See also, CFSP, Council of the EU, JHA, Luxembourg Compromise, Majority Voting).

VIES. This is the name of a computerised information exchange system on Value-added Tax (VAT) and excise duties, set up by the Commission. The system provides the fiscal authorities of member states with information on intra-Community trade. (See also, Taxation, VAT).

VISEGRAD GROUP (V4). A group of states consisting of Hungary, Poland, the Czech Republic and Slovakia, which has agreed to a mutual reduction of tariffs by the end of the century, and has formed the Central European Free Trade Area (CEFTA). In spite of their close links, these countries have reorientated themselves towards the European Community. All, including Bulgaria and Romania, which joined the V4 later, have signed agreements with the Community, while Hungary, Poland and the Czech Republic are expected to join the Union by 2002. (See also, Europe Agreements).

W

WARSAW PACT. A mutual defence organization set up by the Warsaw Treaty, signed on 14 May 1955, the same month in which the North Atlantic Treaty Organization (NATO) admitted the Federal Republic of Germany to the organisation. The Warsaw Pact consisted of the Soviet Union, Poland, Hungary, Romania, the German Democratic Republic (East Germany), Albania, Bulgaria and Czechoslovakia[22]. By provisions of the Treaty, Soviet troops were stationed in all the countries of central and eastern Europe; signatory countries were required to assist each other in case of aggression by the western block and provided for joint command of their armed forces.

After the sweeping events of 1989-90 in Eastern Europe, the Warsaw Pact was formally declared defunct on 1 July 1991. Since December 1991, the former Warsaw Pact members and the successor states of the USSR are members of the North Atlantic Cooperation Council (NACC) and are expected gradually to become members of NATO. (See also, NACC, NATO).

WERNER REPORT. Published in 1970 by a Committee headed by Pierre Werner, the Report was a blueprint for an Economic and Monetary Union (EMU). It followed the decision of The Hague summit of 1969, which had called for a full EMU to be achieved by 1980. The Report emphasised that coordination of economic policies, narrowing of exchange-rate margins, integration of capital markets, the establishment of a common currency and a European Central Bank have to be promoted simultaneously in all member states. In addition, the Report recommended that the EMU must be completed in stages.

The Council of Ministers adopted a modified option of the report in 1971 and, after omitting the suggested institutional reforms, set January 1974 as the completion time for the first stage of the EMU. Moreover, member states, in order to limit currency fluctuations, accepted from the outset of the first stage to participate in an exchange rate mechanism, known as Snake. The failure of Snake resulted in the abandonment of the Werner Report, and the EMU project. It was not until 1988 that the question of the EMU was raised again. (See also, EMU, Snake).

---

[22] East Germany entered the Warsaw Pact in 1956, and Albania withdrew in 1968.

WESTERN EUROPEAN UNION (WEU). The WEU was formally established in May 1955 mainly to accommodate the wishes of those who preferred a Western European alliance to the North Atlantic Treaty Organization (NATO). It stemmed from the 1948 Treaty of Brussels which, modified by the Paris agreements of October 1954, enabled West Germany and Italy to become members of the WEU in 1955. By the same criteria West Germany was permitted to join NATO in that same year. The Paris agreements referred to the promotion of European integration as a WEU goal. Following its contribution to the integration of West Germany into NATO and the rebuilding of the Franco-German relations after the war, WEU's role became increasingly important in the 1980s as a variety of proposals regarding further progress in European integration were re-launched.

In 1987, the WEU Council of Ministers re-defined the future of the organization giving European integration a security dimension, as well as reinforcing its role as the European pillar of the Atlantic alliance. Furthermore, in 1992 the Council of foreign and defence ministers issued the Petersburg Declaration, which provided a framework for common conflict prevention and peacekeeping actions in cooperation with the Organization for Security and Cooperation in Europe (OSCE) and the Security Council of the UN. The new role of the WEU as an integral part of the developments of the Union and the expected implications on security and defence matters have been annexed to the Maastricht Treaty in the form of a declaration.

Currently, the WEU consists of ten nations, the seven founding nations of Belgium, France, Luxembourg, The Netherlands, the UK, West Germany and Italy; Portugal and Spain which joined in 1988; and Greece which joined in 1992. There are also five members holding observer status, Ireland, Denmark, Austria, Finland and Sweden; three Associate members, Turkey, Norway and Iceland; and nine associate partners, Hungary, the Czech Republic, Slovakia, Poland, Bulgaria, Romania, Lithuania, Latvia and Estonia. Neither the UK nor Denmark participate in the Common Foreign and Security Policy (CFSP), yet they are members of the WEU. On the other hand, the neutrality status of Ireland, Denmark, Austria, Finland and Sweden does prevent them from being full members of the WEU.

The WEU is administered by a Council consisting of Ministers of Foreign Affairs and of Defence from the member states and a Permanent Council. The Council of Foreign Affairs and Defence Ministers is responsible for policy formation and meets twice a year in the capital of the country which holds the presidency; while the Permanent Council, chaired by the WEU Secretary General and supported by around 100 staff, is responsible for day-to-day management. The WEU was originally based in London, but moved to Brussels in January 1993. (See also, CFSP, NATO, OSCE, Treaty of Brussels; Appendix 17).

WIDER VERSUS DEEPER INTEGRATION. The phrase is used to denote two options for Community integration. A deeper integration implies the further extension of Community activities, as well as the strengthening of Community institutions in terms of composition and decision-making processes. Wider integration refers to the enlargement of the Community with the accession of new members. The former option has been instrumental to the completion of certain principal objectives of the Community, such as the common market, the establishment of common policies, the initiation of political cooperation. Once these fundamental goals were achieved, the way to further enlargement was facilitated.

The debate over the character of Community integration was initiated especially during the period preceding its first enlargement in 1973. It was in The Hague summit of December 1969 that President Pompidou of France lifted the French veto on British accession to the Community. He also emphasised the need for strengthening the existing Community before any steps for further enlargement were taken. The same argument is reiterated in any debate on future enlargement.

The two options used to be seen as opposites. The advocates of a wider integration argued that a further deepening would undermine their prospects, since new members are required to adopt the *acquis communautaire*. On the other hand, wider enlargement would reinforce the heterogeneous character of the Community and in turn would undermine the process of integration. However, the 1992 Lisbon European Council meeting, where the guidelines for the enlargement of the Community were agreed, reached an understanding whereby deeper integration is indispensable to wider integration. The Council acknowledged that enlargement is bound to increase Community diversity, but the challenges of an enlarged Community are to be met successfully only with the simultaneous progress of the deepening process. (See also, Enlargement, Intergovernmentalism, Sovereignty).

WOMEN'S RIGHTS. The Treaty of Rome provided for equal treatment between men and women by ensuring that equal pay is received for equal work. These provisions have been reinforced by various judgements of the Court of Justice and by a number of directives on equal pay, equal treatment and the elimination of discrimination in occupational pension schemes. In addition, the Commission operates a number of equal opportunity action programmes (the fourth began in 1996), and has under its supervision several organizations concerned with equality. Member states have been required to amend their laws and exclude any discriminatory provisions, but the degree of compliance is not satisfactory. On average, women earn 20 per cent less than men employed in equivalent posts.

A number of specialist bodies exist within the European Community. The Women's Employment and Equality Office, part of the Directorate-General V, is responsible for developing and implementing Community policies regarding women's rights, as well as ensuring that gender equality is taken into account in other policy areas. The Advisory Committee on Equal Opportunities represents the statutory bodies promoting equality in member states. The Women's Information Service issues a multi-lingual newsletter with the aim of disseminating information on employment policies. The Committee on Women's Rights, set up by the European Parliament (EP), promotes progress in the field of equal opportunities.

WORKERS' RIGHTS. The Treaty of Rome provided for workers' rights, and member states were required to improve living and working conditions for workers as well as strengthen employee participation and consultation procedures on matters of employment. To this purpose several agencies, including the European Foundation for the Improvement of Living and Working Conditions, were established. However, little progress was made in the 1970s and 1980s mainly because Commission proposals were not adopted by the Council of Ministers, or were blocked by member states.

The Single European Act (SEA), however, provided for the promotion of dialogue between management and labour; and in 1994 the European Works Council Directive on workers consultation in Community-wide companies was accepted by all member states with the exception of the UK. According to this directive, member states were obliged to pass legislation by July 1996, providing for the creation of work councils in multinational companies, with 150 or more employees. In June 1997 a further consultation document extended the implementation of consultation and information committees to companies with more than 50 employees. (See also, Social Charter, Social Policy).

WORLD TRADE ORGANIZATION (WTO). Established by the Final Act of the Uruguay Round in April 1994 in Marrakesh, the WTO replaced the General Agreement on Tariffs and Trade (GATT). In common with the GATT, the WTO encourages member states to reach multilateral agreements, reduce quotas and tariffs and abolish preferential trade agreements as had taken place in the Uruguay Round. The WTO also aims to provide a forum for the negotiation and administration of rules and procedures in the settlement of trade disputes. (See also, GATT).

Y

YAOUNDE CONVENTION. Signed in 1963 at Yaounde, the capital of Cameroon, and renegotiated in 1969, the Convention established relations between the European Economic Community (EEC) and 18 former colonial possessions, known collectively as the Associated African States and Madagascar (AASM). The Convention provided for duty-free access to the Community for almost all AASM products on a non-reciprocal basis. In addition, the AASM countries benefited from grants through the European Development Fund (EDF) and the European Investment Bank (EIB). The Yaounde Convention was superseded by the Lomé Convention of 1970. (See also, EDF, EIB).

YOUTH FOR EUROPE. A Community scheme that provides financial assistance from the Budget to be spent on a broad number of projects relating to young people. The current programme started in 1995 and ends in 1999.

YOUTH TRAINING. In 1983 the Council of Ministers made the training of young people a priority. Those with reduced employment possibilities, because of lack or inadequate of their education and vocational training, were to be of primary concern. Training projects and employment for the under 25s are funded mainly through the European Social Fund (ESF). (See also, ESF).

1. Principal European Community Institutions

Institution	Main Functions
European Commission (appointed)	policy initiation, supervision and implementation, guardian of the Treaties, drafting of the Budget, external relations
European Council (heads of government of member states)	general direction responsible for the two inter-governmental pillars of the Union
Council of the European Union (ministers of member states) (main intergovernmental body)	principal legislative and decision-making body
European Parliament (directly elected	supervisory, budgetary and limited legislative powers
Court of Justice of the European Communities (appointed)	judicial interpretation and enforcement of Community law

2. Other Institutions Constituting an Integral Part in the Functioning of the European Community.

Institution	Main Functions
Economic and Social Committee (appointed)	advise
Committee of the regions (appointed)	advise
Court of Auditors (appointed)	financial auditing
Court of First Instance (appointed)	deals with various disputes except preliminary rulings
European Investment Bank (appointed)	financing Community development projects.

3. Other EU Institutions and specialized Agencies

Institution - Location	Functions
European Agency for Safety and Health at work Bilbao	to collect and disseminate information on health and safety at work
European Centre for the Development of Vocational Training Thessaloniki	to assist the Commission in encouraging the promotion of vocational training
European Foundation for the Improvement of Leaving and Working Conditions Dublin	to gather and disseminate information and formulate policy proposals on the living and working conditions of EU citizens
European Medicine Evaluation Agency London	to provide scientific advice to Community institutions on medicinal products for human and veterinary use
The European Environment Agency Copenhagen	to assist the Commission in drawing and implementing community policy on environmental protection and improvement
The European Foundation for Training Turin	to contribute to the development of vocational training systems of designated central and eastern european countries
The European Monetary Institute Frankfurt	to strengthen the co-operation between central banks and coordination of monetary policies, to monitor the functioning of the EMS, and in general to facilitate the transition to Stage III of the EMU

European Monitoring Centre for Drugs and Drug Addiction Lisbon	to provide information on Drugs and Drug addiction with the purpose of assisting in combating the problem
The European Ombudsman (in the EP) Strasbourg	to deal with maladministration in the activities of the community institutions and bodies
The European Police Office (Europol) The Hague	to enable national authorities to exchange information on interactional crime, drugs and terrorism
The Office for the Harmonization in the Internal Market Alicante	to implement community law in relation to trade marks, designs and models.
The Translation Centre of the Commission Luxembourg	to meet the translation needs of the EU institutions

4. European Commission Directorates- General

DG I	External Economic Relations
DG IA	External Political Relations
DG II	Economic and Financial Affairs
DG III	Industry
DG IV	Competition
DG V	Employment, Industrial Relations and Social Affairs
DG VI	Agriculture
DG VII	Transport
DG VIII	Development
DG IX	Personnel and Administration
DG X	Information, Communication, Culture, Audiovisual
DG XI	Environment, Nuclear Safety and Civil Protection
DG XII	Science, Research and Development Joint Research Centre
DG XIII	Telecommunications, Information Market and Exploitation of Research
DG XIV	Fisheries
DG XV	Internal Market and Financial Services
DG XVI	Regional Policies
DG XVII	Energy
DG XVIII	Credit and Investments
DG XIX	Budgets
DG XX	Financial Control
DG XXI	Customs and Indirect Taxation
DG XXII	Education, Training and Youth
DG XXIII	Enterprise Policy, Distributive Trades, Tourism and Cooperatives
DG XXIV	Consumer Policy and Health Protection

5. Presidents of the European Commission

President	Period of Office	Country of Origin
W. Hallstein	1958-67	W. Germany
J. Rey	1967-70	Belgium
F. M. Malfatti	1970-72	Italy
S. Mansholt	1972-73	Netherlands
F. X. Ortoli	1973-77	France
R. Jenkins	1977-81	UK
G. Thorn	1981-85	Luxembourg
J. Delors	1985-95	France
J. Santers	1995-	Luxembourg

6. Commissioners and their portfolios, 1995-2000

Name - Nationality	Title - Portfolios
Jacques Santer Luxembourg	President, common foreign and security policy (Hans Van den Broek), monetary affairs (Yves-Thibault de Silguy), institutional questions (with Mr Oreja);
Leon Brittan UK	multilateral trade, external relations with China, S.Korea, Hong Kong, Macao, Taiwan, the OECD and WTO
Neil Kinnock UK	transport
Édith Cresson France	science, RTD, human resources, education, training, youth
Yves-Thibault de Silguy France	economic and financial affairs, monetary affairs (with the President)
Monika Wulf-Mathies Germany	regional policies, cohesion fund (with Mr. Kinnock and Mrs Bjerregaard)
Martin Bangemann Germany	industry, information technology, telecommunications
Mario Monti Italy	internal market, financial services, taxation
Emma Bonino Italy	consumer affairs, EC Humanitarian Office, fisheries
Marcelino Oreja Spain	institutional affairs, culture, media
Manuel Marin Spain	external relations with Latin America, Mediterranean, Middle and Near East, Asia (with the exemption of Japan, China, S. Korea, Hong Kong, Macao, Taiwan)
João de Deus Pinheiro Portugal	relations with Africa, Caribbean, Portugal Pacific countries, the Lomé Convention

Karel Van Miert Belgium	competition
Hans Van den Broek The Netherlands	central and eastern Europe, Turkey, Cyprus, Malta, other European countries, Common Foreign and Security Policy (with the President)
Ritt Bjerregaard Denmark	environment, nuclear safety
Pádraig Flynn Ireland	employment, social policy
Christos Papoutsis Greece	SMEs, energy, tourism
Erkki Liikanen Finland	Budget, personnel, translation
Franz Fischler Austria	agriculture and rural development
Anita Gradin Sweden	immigration, home and judicial affairs, relations with the Ombudsman, financial control, anti-fraud measures

7. Political Groups in the European Parliament

PES	Group of the Party of European Socialists	214 members
EPP	European People's Party (Christian Democrats)	181 members
UE	Union for Europe Group	55 members
ELDR	Group of the European Liberal, Democratic and Reformist Party	41 members
GUE	Confederal Group of United Left - Nordic Green Left	33 members
GRN	Green Group in the European Parliament	28 members
ERA	Group of the European Radical Alliance	20 members
EN	Europe of Nations Group	18 members
IND	Non-attached members	36 members

8. List of European Parliament Presidents since 1979

1979-82	Simone Veil (France)
1982-84	Pieter Dankert (Netherlands)
1984-87	Pierre Pflimlin (France)
1987-89	Lord Henry Plumb (UK)
1989-92	Enrique Baron Crespo (Spain)
1992-94	Egon Klepsch (Germany)
1994-97	Klaus Hansch (Germany)
1997-	Jóse-Maria Gil-Robles (Spain)

9. Parliamentary Committees

Agriculture, Fisheries and Rural Development
Budgets
Budgetary Control
Civil Liberties and Internal Affairs
Development and Cooperation
Economic and Monetary Affairs and Industrial Policy (subcommittee on monetary affairs)
Energy, Research and Technology
Environment, Public Health and Consumer Protection
External Economic Relations
Fisheries
Foreign Affairs and Security (2 subcommittee, one on security and disarmament, one on human rights)
Institutional Affairs
Legal Affairs and Citizens's Rights
Petitions
Regional Policy, Regional Planning and Relations with Regional and Local Authorities
Rules of Procedure, the Verification of Credentials and Immunities
Social Affairs Employment and the Working Environment
Transport and Tourism
Unemployment (Temporary Committee)
Women's Rights
Youth, Culture, Education and Media

10. Electoral systems used in European Parliament elections

Proportional representation, national lists
Denmark
France
Germany
Greece
Luxembourg
Netherlands
Portugal
Spain

Proportional representation, regional lists
Belgium
Italy

Constituency based
Ireland (Multi-member list)
UK (Single-member list)

11. Representation of Member States in the Main Community Institutions

	Comm.	EP	VC	ESC	COR
Austria	1	21	4	12	12
Belgium	1	25	5	12	12
Denmark	1	16	3	9	9
Finland	1	16	3	9	9
France	2	87	10	24	24
Germany	2	99	10	24	24
Greece	1	25	5	12	12
Ireland	1	15	3	9	9
Italy	2	87	10	24	24
Luxembourg	1	6	2	6	6
Netherlands	1	31	5	12	12
Portugal	1	25	5	12	12
Spain	2	64	8	21	21
Sweden	1	22	4	12	12
UK	2	87	10	24	24
Total	20	626	87	222	222

Comm. = European Commission
EP = European Parliament
VC = Votes in the Council of the EU
ESC = European Social Committee
COR = Committee of the Regions

12. European Community Budget 85, 90, 96, 97

Revenues	1985	1990	1996	1997
Customs duties	31.9	27.6	18.7	16.5
Agricultural levies	8.3	1.8	0.1	0.9
VAT	59.8	69.9	52.8	42.3
GNP based resources	-	0.7	28.4	40.3
Expenditure				
CAP-Guarantee	70.2	57.7	50.5	47.0
Structural operations	14.4	23.9	31.8	36.3
Internal policies	2.5	4.8	5.8	5.8
External policies	3.9	2.8	6.0	6.5
Administration	4.6	5.3	4.8	3.1
Miscellaneous	4.4	5.5	1.1	1.3

Source: Commission 1996,Bulletin of the European Union

13. Member states performance in relation to convergence

Country	Inflation Jan. '98	Deficit (% of GDP) 1997	Debt (% of GDP) 1997	Long-term interest rates Jan. '98**
Austria	1.1	2.5	66.1	5.6
Belgium	1.4	2.1	122.2	5.7
Denmark	1.9	-0.7	65.1	6.2
Finland	1.3	0.9	55.8	5.9
France	1.2	3.0	58.0	5.5
Germany	1.4	2.7	61.3	5.6
Greece	5.2	4.0	108.7	9.8
Italy	1.8	2.7	121.6	6.7
Ireland	1.2	-0.9	66.3	6.2
Luxembourg	1.4	-1.7	6.7	5.6
Netherlands	1.8	1.4	72.1	5.5
Portugal	1.8	2.5	62.0	6.2
Spain	1.8	2.6	68.8	6.3
Sweden	1.9	0.8	76.6	6.5
UK	1.8	1.9	53.4	7.0
EU	1.6	2.4	72.1	6.1

*A negative sign for the deficit index indicates a surplus
** Long-term interest rates refer to loans with an average maturity of 10 years.

Source: Commission

14. The seven Titles of the Maastricht Treaty

Title I: Articles A-F. Common Provisions. Proclaiming the formation of the European Union, setting out its tasks and objectives, defining the powers of the major European Union institutions, requiring the respect by the Union of the national identities of member states.

Title II: Articles G-G86. Provisions amending to the Treaty of Rome, with a view to replacing the term European Economic Community with the term European Community. This Title is extensive and includes a number of provisions on the powers of the Community institutions, Union citizenship and the responsibilities of the Community in the various policy areas, including the economic and monetary policies.

Title III: Articles H-H21. Provisions amending the Treaty of Paris establishing the ECSC.

Title IV: Articles I-I29. Provisions amending the Treaty of Rome, more specifically the part of it establishing the European Atomic Energy Community.

Title V: Articles J-J11. Provisions on the Common Foreign and Security Policy.

Title VI: Articles K-K9. Provisions on Cooperation in the fields of Justice and Home Affairs.

Title VII: Articles L-S. Provision on various institutional issues, enlargement of the Union and ratification of the Treaty.

15. Types of Government of the Member States of the EU

Austria	Republic (federal)
Belgium	Constitutional Monarchy (King Albert II), (federal)
Denmark	Constitutional Monarchy (Queen Margaret II)
Finland	Republic
France	Republic
Germany	Republic (federal)
Greece	Republic
Ireland	Republic
Italy	Republic
Luxembourg	Constitutional Monarchy (King Jean)
Netherlands	Constitutional Monarchy (Queen Beatrice)
Portugal	Republic
Spain	Constitutional Monarchy (King Juan Carlos I)
Sweden	Constitutional Monarchy (King Carl XVI Gustav)
UK	Constitutional Monarchy (Elizabeth II)

16. Prime Ministers of the EU Member States

Austria	Victor Klima (federal chancellor)
Belgium	Jean-Luc Dehaene
Denmark	Poul Nyrup Rasmussen
Finland	Paavo Lipponen
France	Lionel Jospen
Germany	Gerhard Schröder (federal chancellor)
Greece	Konstantinos Simitis
Ireland	Bertie Ahern
Italy	Massimo D'alemma
Luxembourg	Jean-Claude Juncker
Netherlands	Wim Kok
Portugal	António Guterres
Spain	Jóse Maria Aznar López
Sweden	Göran Persson
UK	Tony Blair

17. Security Organizations — Membership

Categories	NATO	NACC	PFP	WEU	OSCE	CE
European Community						
Belgium	x	x	x	x	x	x
France	x	x	x	x	x	x
Denmark	x	x	x	o	x	x
Germany	x	x	x	x	x	x
Greece	x	x	x	x	x	x
Ireland	-	o	-	o	x	x
Italy	x	x	x	x	x	x
Luxembourg	x	x	x	x	x	x
Netherlands	x	x	x	x	x	x
Portugal	x	x	x	x	x	x
Spain	x	x	x	x	x	x
UK	x	x	x	x	x	x
Austria	-	o	x	o	x	x
Finland	-	o	x	o	x	x
Sweden	-	o	x	o	x	x
EFTA						
Iceland	x	x	x	am	x	x
Liechtenstein	-	-	-	-	x	x
Norway	x	x	x	am	x	x
Switzerland	-	-	-	-	x	x
Non-EU Mediterranean States						
Cyprus	-	-	-	-	x	x
Malta	-	-	x	-	x	x
Turkey	x	x	x	am	x	x
Central/Eastern European & ex-USSR Countries						
Albania	-	x	x	-	x	x
Armenia	-	x	x	-	x	-
Azerbaijan	-	x	x	-	x	-
Belorus	-	x	x	-	x	-
Bosnia	-	-	-	-	x	-
Bulgaria	-	x	x	ap	x	x

Cont.

Categories	NATO	NACC	PFP	WEU	OSCE	CE
Croatia	-	-	-	-	x	-
Czech Republic	-	x	x	ap	x	x
Estonia	-	x	x	ap	x	x
Georgia	-	x	x	-	x	-
Hungary	-	x	x	ap	x	x
Kazakhstan	-	x	x	-	x	-
Kyrgyzstan	-	x	x	-	x	-
Latvia	-	x	x	ap	x	x
Lithuania	-	x	x	ap	x	x
FYROM	-	-	x	-	x	x
Moldova	-	x	x	-	x	x
Poland	-	x	x	ap	x	x
Romania	-	x	x	ap	x	x
Russia	-	x	x	-	x	x
Slovakia	-	x	x	ap	x	x
Slovenia	-	o	x	-	x	x
Tajikistan	-	x	-	-	x	-
Turkmenistan	-	x	x	-	x	-
Ukraine	-	x	x	-	x	-
Uzbekistan	-	x	x	-	x	-
Former-Yugoslavia-	-	-	-		s	-
North America						
USA	x	x	x	-	x	-
Canada	x	x	x	-	x	-

x = full member, - = non-member, o = observer status,
am = associate member, ap = associate partner, s = suspended

18. ACP Countries

Angola, Antigua and Barbuda, Bahamas, Barbados, Belize, Benin, Botswana, Burkina Faso, Burundi, Cameroon, Cape Verde, Central African Republic, Chad, Comoros, Congo, Congo (ex-Zaire), Ivory Coast, Djibouti, Dominica, Dominican Republic, Equatorial Guinea, Eritrea, Ethiopia, Fiji, Gabon, Gambia, Ghana, Grenada, Guinea, Guinea Bissau, Guyana, Haiti, Jamaica, Kenya, Kiribati, Lesotho, Liberia, Madagascar, Malawi, Mali, Mauritania, Mauritius, Mozambique, Namibia, Niger, Nigeria, Papua New Guinea, Rwanda, St. Kitts and Nevis, St.Lucia, St.Vincent and the Grenadines, Samoa, Sao Tomé and Principe, Senegal, Seychelles, Sierra Leone, Solomon Islands, Somalia, South Africa, Sudan, Suriname, Swaziland, Tanzania, Togo, Tonga, Trinidad and Tobago, Tuvalu, Uganda, Vanuatu, Zambia, Zimbabwe.

19. List of OCTs

British Octs: Anguilla, Antigua, the British Virginia Islands, the Cayman Islands, Montserrat, the Turks and Caicos Islands, the Falkland Islands, Saint Helena and its dependencies, South Georgia and South Sandwich Islands, Pitcairn, British Antarctic Territory, British Indian Ocean Territory.

Danish Octs: Greenland (In 1973, Greenland as an integral part of Denmark joined the European Community. In 1982, as a result of a considerable degree of home rule granted to it, Greenland held a referendum on whether to remain in the Community. The vote was in favour of withdrawal).

Dutch Octs: Aruba, The Netherlands Antilles (Bonaire, Curacao, St.Martin, Saba, St. Eustache)

French Octs: French Polynesia, New Caledonia and its dependencies, Wallis and Futuna Islands, French Southern and Antarctic Territories. Also the 'territorial collectivities' of Mayotte off the cost of Madagascar and St.Pierre and Miquelon.

20. The Size of the European Community in 1996

Countries	Area (1000 km^2)	Population (millions)	Density (inh./km^2)
Austria	83.9	8.0	95
Belgium	30.5	10.2	334
Denmark	43.1	5.2	121
Finland	338.3	5.1	15
France	551.5	58.4	106
Germany	357.0	81.8	229
Greece	132.0	10.5	79
Ireland	70.2	3.6	51
Italy	301.3	57.4	190
Luxembourg	2.6	0.4	154
Netherlands	41.5	15.5	373
Portugal	92.1	9.9	107
Spain	504.7	39.3	78
Sweden	450.0	8.9	20
UK	244.1	58.7	240
EU 15	3244.1	372.9	115

Source: Commission (1996)

21. The European Community: GDP, GDP per inhabitant, unemployment (1997)

Countries	GDP (Mrd ECU)	GDP per capita (ECU per inhabitant)	Unemployment
Austria	182.01	22,516	4.4
Belgium	213.70	20,998	9.2
Denmark	140.05	26,537	5.5
Finland	104.68	20,368	13.1
France	1,223.15	20,869	12.4
Germany	1,853.34	22,585	10.0
Greece	105.71	10,051	9.6
Ireland	66.62	18,169	10.1
Italy	1,011.86	17,276	12.1
Luxembourg	13.91	33,035	2.6
Netherlands	318.30	20,392	5.2
Portugal	88.63	8,919	6.8
Spain	472.04	11,887	20.8
Sweden	202.01	22,803	9.9
UK	1,134.03	19,234	7.0
EU 15	7,130.04	18,983	10.7

Source: New Cronos Database

22. Employment by sector, %, 1995

Country	Agriculture	Industry	Services
Austria	7.1	35.6	57.3
Belgium	2.9	30.9	66.2
Denmark	5.1	27.4	67.4
Finland	8.6	27.8	63.6
France	5.9	29.6	64.5
Germany	3.7	39.1	57.2
Greece	21.9	25.4	52.7
Italy	7.9	33.2	58.9
Ireland	13.8	28.9	57.3
Luxembourg	3.1	29.6	67.3
Netherlands	3.9	25.2	70.9
Portugal	11.5	32.6	55.9
Spain	10.1	32.7	57.2
Sweden	3.2	26.6	70.2
UK	2.2	30.2	67.6
EU	5.8	32.6	61.6

Source: Commission (1996)

23. Gross value added by sector, 1995

Country	Agriculture	Industry	Services
Austria	3.4	43.9	52.7
Belgium	1.8	31.4	66.8
Denmark	3.6	27.2	69.2
Finland	6.7	38.0	55.3
France	3.1	30.9	66.0
Germany	1.2	39.4	59.4
Greece	17.0	27.3	55.7
Italy	3.3	33.5	63.2
Ireland	7.6	38.0	54.4
Luxembourg	1.7	35.8	62.5
Netherlands	4.0	30.9	65.1
Portugal	6.3	39.0	54.7
Spain	3.8	34.0	62.2
Sweden	3.1	40.4	56.2
UK	1.5	34.5	64.0

Source: Commission (1996)

24. Share of intra-European trade, %, 1996

Country	Imports	Exports
Austria	75	66
Belgium/Luxembourg	73	77
Denmark	70	67
Finland	65	55
France	68	62
Germany	59	56
Greece	63	50
Ireland	66	71
Italy	61	55
Netherlands	64	81
Portugal	75	80
Spain	68	67
Sweden	69	57
UK	55	58
EU	64	63

Source: Bulletin of the EU, 4, 1997

25. Foreign trade, % GDP, 1995

Country	Imports	Exports
Austria	38.6	37.6
Belgium	68.5	74.2
Denmark	29.6	33.7
Finland	30.0	37.6
France	21.1	23.5
Germany	22.0	23.0
Greece	26.9	16.5
Ireland	61.9	76.3
Italy	23.4	27.6
Luxembourg	81.4	91.4
Netherlands	46.7	52.5
Portugal	37.7	29.6
Spain	23.6	23.7
Sweden	34.5	40.8
UK	29.0	28.0
EU	27.4	29.2

Figures represent intra-European and extra-European trade
Source: Commission (1996)

PART III: QUESTIONS

1. HISTORY OF THE EUROPEAN COMMUNITY

1. The Treaty of Paris was signed on:
   a. 9 May 1950
   b. 18 April 1951
   c. 1 January 1958
   d. 23 July 1952

2. The Schuman Plan aimed at reconstructing the:
   a. French economy
   b. German economy
   c. European economy
   d. world economy

3. Jean Monnet was:
   a. French Prime Minister
   b. Chairman of the High Authority of ECSC
   c. President of the European Parliament
   d. President of the Commission

4. The Treaty of Paris:
   a. expires in 2002
   b. remains in force indefinitely
   c. expires in 2020
   d. is valid for 100 years

5. The Treaty of Rome was signed on:
   a. 25 March 1957
   b. 1 February 1958
   c. 9 May 1950
   d. 1 January 1958

6. The Treaty of Rome stipulated the formation of:

    a. the ECSC

    b. the ECSC and EURATOM

    c. EURATOM and the EEC

    d. EURATOM

7. The Treaty of Rome, which established the EEC, does not stipulate:

    a. trade liberalisation

    b. free movement of capital

    c. common defence policy

    d. harmonization of indirect taxes

8. EURATOM's expressed purpose was the:

    a. promotion of the development of nuclear industries

    b. speedy development of nuclear weapons

    c. protection of the environment from nuclear waste

    d. reduction of oil prices

9. The European Defence Community was established in:

    a. 1950

    b. 1951

    c. 1956

    d. None of the above is true

10. The Merger Treaty came into force in:

    a. 1965

    b. 1967

    c. 1968

    d. 1964

11. The fusion of the Communities in 1967 did not result in the:

    a. creation of one Commission

    b. establishment of one budget

    c. creation of one judicial body

    d. creation of one Council

12. The Single European Act came into force in:

    a. February 1986
    b. July 1987
    c. December 1987
    d. February 1988

13. The Single European Act officially recognized one of the following bodies the:

    a. European Council
    b. Committee of the Regions
    c. European Monetary Institute
    d. European Bank for Reconstruction and Development

14. The Single European Act was subject to a referendum in:

    a. Greece
    b. Italy
    c. Ireland
    d. UK

15. The Single European Act:

    a. was the first thorough amendment of the founding Treaties
    b. established the European Monetary System
    c. established the single currency
    d. established the principle of subsidiarity

16. The Single Market has had no immediate consequences on:

    a. further liberalization of movement of people
    b. VAT paid in the country of origin
    c. removal of technical barriers to trade
    d. freedom of capital movement

17. From 1.1.93 any European citizen can:

    a. travel to another Community country without going through any border formalities
    b. buy as much tobacco or as many cigars as he/she likes
    c. buy as much alcohol as he/she likes
    d. None of the above is true

18. Initially, the European Community consisted of 6 member states. Since then, it has undergone enlargement in:
    a. 2 stages
    b. 4 stages
    c. 3 stages
    d. 6 stages

19. The 'Luxembourg Compromise' of 1966:
    a. slowed down the decision-making in the Council of Ministers
    b. dealt with the decision-making of the Commission
    c. encouraged a further liberalization of trade
    d. addressed the inefficiencies of the Schengen Agreement

20. In accordance with the 1993 decision of the Council of Ministers, one of the following member states has been allocated more than one European organisation:
    a. Spain
    b. Belgium
    c. Greece
    d. France

21. German reunification took place on:
    a. 9 November 1989
    b. 9 November 1990
    c. 3 October 1990
    d. 10 May 1991

22. One of the following organizations has not been established or fully recognized by the Maastricht Treaty:
    a. the Committee of the Regions
    b. the Europol
    c. the European Bank for Reconstruction and Development
    d. the Court of Auditors

23. The Maastricht Treaty:

   a. abolished the Treaty of Paris
   b. amended the Treaty of Rome only
   c. amended the Single European Act
   d. re-named the European Economic Community to European Community

24. The Stresa Conference was concerned with the:

   a. reunification of Germany
   b. establishment of the CAP
   c. cessation of the war in Yugoslavia
   d. dissolution of the Warsaw Pact

25. In 1996 the European Community consisted of:

   a. 12 members
   b. 15 members
   c. 13 members
   d. 10 members

26. In 1997 the cultural month took place in:

   a. London
   b. St. Petersburg
   c. Ljubljana
   d. Barcelona

27. The Maastricht Treaty was signed on:

   a. 7 February 1992
   b. 1 November 1993
   c. 1 January 1994
   d. 1 January 1995

28. Messina II dealt with the:

   a. reform of the CAP
   b. investigation on the feasibility of a common market
   c. preparation of the 1996 IGC
   d. preparation of the Amsterdam summit of the European Council

29. The *Ode to Joy* was adopted by the Council of Europe as the European anthem in:
    a. 1972
    b. 1957
    c. 1986
    d. 1965

30. The European flag was adopted as the flag of the European Community in:
    a. 1993
    b. 1985
    c. 1951
    d. 1957

31. The European flag depicts a circle of:
    a. 12 stars
    b. 15 stars
    c. 10 stars
    d. 13 stars

32. The European Political Cooperation was given legal status by the:
    a. Treaty of Rome
    b. Single European Act
    c. Helsinki Final Act
    d. Maastricht Treaty

33. One of the following members rejected proposals for a common defence policy at Maastricht:
    a. the UK
    b. Germany
    c. Luxembourg
    d. Denmark

34. The Amsterdam Treaty was signed on:
    a. 18 June 1997
    b. 2 October 1997
    c. 2 January 1998
    d. none of the above is true

35. By February 1990, one of the following member states had not ratified the Amsterdam Treaty:

    a. Germany
    b. Sweden
    c. Austria
    d. France

2. INSTITUTIONS OF THE EU
2.1. European Parliament

36. In 1998, the number of MEPs was:

    a. 567
    b. 626
    c. 610
    d. 627

37. In 1998, the President of the European Parliament was:

    a. Lord Henry Plumb
    b. Jóse-Maria Gill-Robles
    c. Egon Klepsch
    d. Klaus Hansch

38. The European Parliament holds its plenary sessions in:

    a. Strasbourg
    b. Brussels
    c. Luxembourg
    d. Bonn

39. The first direct elections for the European Parliament were held in:

    a. 1979
    b. 1976
    c. 1980
    d. 1973

40. The Single European Act empowered the European Parliament with:

    a. the cooperation procedure
    b. the consultation procedure
    c. the co-decision procedure
    d. none of the above is true

41. Direct elections for the European Parliament are held:

    a. every 4 years by proportional representation
    b. every 5 years in the electoral system of each individual country
    c. every 5 years in a uniform electoral system introduced by the European Parliament
    d. None of the above is true

42. The term of office for the president of the European Parliament is:

    a. 5 years
    b. 4 years
    c. 2 and a half years
    d. 3 years

43. One of the following combinations regarding the number of EMPs is false:

    a. Germany 99 - Luxembourg 6
    b. Britain 87- Ireland 15
    c. France 87- Belgium 25
    d. Italy 87 - Greece 19

44. How many women have served as presidents of the European Parliament:

    a. 0
    b. 2
    c. 1
    d. 3

45. The European Parliament may dismiss the Commission:

    a. by qualified majority

    b. by a two-thirds majority of the votes cast

    c. by unanimity

    d. It has no such a right

46. The Secretariat of the European Parliament is based in:

    a. Luxembourg

    b. Brussels

    c. Strasbourg

    d. Paris

47. Political groups in the European Parliament are constituted according to :

    a. ideological and political affiliation

    b. common interest in a particular subject

    c. economic interests for the groups themselves

    d. None of the above is true

48. The Bureau of the European Parliament consists of:

    a. the president of the European Parliament and the chairmen of the political groups

    b. the president and the vice-presidents of the European Parliament

    c. the president of the European Parliament and the College of Quaestors

    d. the presidents of the European Parliament and the representatives of the Commission and the Council of Ministers

49. EMPs vote:

    a. in person

    b. by proxy

    c. en block

    d. by post

50. One of the following is false: The Maastricht Treaty empowered the European Parliament with:
    a. the co-decision procedure
    b. an extension of the assent procedure
    c. a decisive say in the appointment of the Commission
    d. the cooperation procedure

51. The next elections for the European Parliament will be held in:
    a. June 1999
    b. September 1999
    c. February 1999
    d. June 2000

52. The European Parliament is empowered to:
    a. modify the Council of Ministers' proposals on compulsory expenditure
    b. amend the Council of Ministers' proposals on compulsory expenditure
    c. reject the Council of Ministers' proposals on compulsory expenditure
    d. None of the above is true

2.2. European Commission

53. Currently, the Commission consists of:
    a. 17 members
    b. 15 members
    c. 20 members
    d. 12 members

54. The Commission is:
    a. elected by national parliaments
    b. appointed by member states after consultation with the European Parliament
    c. appointed by a decision of the European Parliament and the Council of Ministers
    d. elected by national parliaments and approved by the European Parliament

55. In accordance with the 1977 resolution of the European
Parliament, the European Commission is obliged to publish
every year a:

    a. report on competition
    b. general report
    c. report on the progress of integration
    d. report on the activities of the Court of Justice

56. The Commission's term of office is:

    a. 3 years
    b. 4 years
    c. 6 years
    d. 5 years

57. The longest serving President of the European Commission
is:

    a. W. Hallstein
    b. J. Delors
    c. R. Jenkins
    d. G. Thorn

58. One of the following statements is false: The Commission
is empowered to:

    a. initiate policy
    b. manage and execute Community policies and international
       trade relations
    c. watch the implementation of the Treaties
    d. legislate

59. Individual commissioners may be dismissed by the:

    a. Court of Justice
    b. European Parliament
    c. Council of Ministers
    d. Court of Justice in consultation with the EP

60. One of the following countries has two commissioners:

    a. Denmark
    b. The Netherlands
    c. Sweden
    d. Spain

61. One of the following pairs never held the presidency of the Commission:
    a. Portugal - Greece
    b. Belgium - France
    c. Germany - UK
    d. Italy - Luxembourg

62. The Commission decides by:
    a. qualified majority
    b. unanimity
    c. simple majority
    d. absolute majority

63. One of the following statements is false: The Commission is obliged to:
    a. serve Community interests
    b. serve national interests
    c. ensure that competition in the internal market is not distorted
    d. ensure the application of the Treaties

64. The Commission has two delegations in:
    a. Australia
    b. the USA
    c. Russia
    d. New Zealand

65. In accordance with the Amsterdam Treaty, despite enlargement, the number of the commissioners will not exceed:
    a. 25
    b. 26
    c. 23
    d. 20

66. The Commission is accountable to the:
    a. European Parliament
    b. Court of Justice
    c. European Parliament and the Court of Justice
    d. European Council

67. In an average year the Commission sends to the Council of Ministers between:

   a. 1000-1200 proposals and recommendations
   b. 5000-6000 proposals and recommendations
   c. 200-300 proposals and recommendations
   d. 600-800 proposals and recommendations

2.3. The Council of European Union

68. The Council of Ministers is the European Community's:

   a. executive body
   b. main legislative body
   c. consultative body
   d. None of the above

69. The Council of Ministers consists of:

   a. Heads of Governments
   b. ministers with responsibility for the area under discussion
   c. ministers and members of the Economic and Social Committee
   d. representatives of the national banks and European Central Bank

70. The presidency of the Council of Ministers is arranged:

   a. in alphabetical order, based on the name of each member state in their native language
   b. by a decision of the Council of Ministers itself
   c. according to a combination of population size and order of accession to the Community
   d. None of the above is true

71. The presidency of the Council of Ministers rotates between member states every:

   a. six months
   b. one year
   c. five years
   d. two and a half years

72. In accordance with the Ioannina Compromise, the blocking minority in the Council of Ministers is:
    a. 21 votes
    b. 27 votes
    c. 26 votes
    d. 31 votes

73. One of the following combinations is true. In case of qualified majority voting in the Council of Ministers member states carry the following weightings:
    a. Germany, Spain 10 each
    b. France, Spain 8 votes each
    c. Belgium, Greece 5 votes each
    d. Austria, Sweden 3 votes each

74. COREPER is a Committee consisting of representatives of:
    a. the European Parliament to the meetings of the Council of Ministers
    b. permanent ambassadors of member states to the European Community
    c. temporary ambassadors of member states to the European Community
    d. ambassadors of member states in Belgium

75. In the Council of Ministers unanimity is required for:
    a. social security
    b. EMU
    c. European Social Funds
    d. transport policy

76. The presidency of the Council of Ministers for the first six months of 1998 was held by:
    a. Netherlands
    b. Ireland
    c. UK
    d. Luxembourg

2.4. The Court of Justice of the European Communities - The Court of First Instance

77. The Court of Justice consists of:
   a. 9 judges and 15 advocates general
   b. 15 judges and 15 advocates general
   c. 15 judges and 9 advocates general
   d. 15 judges and 12 advocates general

78. The Court of First Instance consists of:
   a. 15 judges
   b. 12 judges
   c. 9 judges
   d. 10 judges

79. The Court of Justice sits in:
   a. Brussels
   b. Luxembourg
   c. Strasbourg
   d. Hague

80. Members of both the Court of First Instance and the Court of Justice are appointed by a:
   a. common accord of member states
   b. decision of the Council of Ministers
   c. decision of the Council of Ministers after consultation with the European Parliament
   d. None of the above is true

81. The term of office for the members of the Court of Justice is:
   a. 3 years
   b. 5 years
   c. 6 years
   d. 4 years

82. One of the following statements is false. The role of the Court is to ensure that Community law is :
   a. interpreted in line with the Treaties
   b. implemented in accordance with the Treaties
   c. generally observed in all activities of the Community
   d. extended to criminal matters

83. One of the following is false. Decisions of the Court of Justice:
   a. may override national legislation
   b. cover all judicial matters
   c. are binding on all courts and individuals in member states
   d. may overrule national court verdicts

84. Appeal to the decisions of the Court of Justice may be made to the:
   a. European Council
   b. International Court of Justice
   c. Council of Ministers
   d. None of the above is true

85. The Court of Justice has jurisdiction over:
   a. the European Council
   b. the Common Foreign and Security Policy
   c. the Justice and Home Affairs (JHA)
   d. aspects of JHA related to the interpretation of conventions

86. Appeal against the decisions of the Court of First Instance may be made to the:
   a. European Council
   b. Court of Justice
   c. Council of Ministers
   d. None of the above is true

2.5. Court of Auditors

87. The Court of Auditors consists of, and is based at:
    a. 15 members - Luxembourg
    b. 15 member - Brussels
    c. 12 members - Luxembourg
    d. 9 members - Luxembourg

88. The members of the Court of Auditors are:
    a. appointed by the member states
    b. appointed by a unanimous decision of the Council of Ministers after consultation with the European Parliament
    c. appointed by the Commission
    d. elected by the European Parliament

89. The term of office for the members of the Court is:
    a. 6 years
    b. 3 years
    c. 5 years
    d. 4 years

90. One of the following statements is false. The aim of the Court of Auditors is to check that:
    a. revenues have been collected
    b. expenditure has occurred in a lawful manner
    c. the Communities' financial affairs are properly managed
    d. None of the above is true

91. The Court of Auditors adopts its decisions by a:
    a. majority vote
    b. unanimous vote
    c. qualified majority vote depending on the subject under discussion
    d. a three-fifths majority of its present members

2.6. Economic and Social Committee

92. The Economic and Social Committee consists of:
   a. representatives of the Commission, the Council of Ministers and the European Parliament
   b. representatives of the Council of Ministers and the European Parliament
   c. a broad cross-section of the Union's economic and social interests
   d. members of national parliaments and the European Parliament

93. The Economic and Social Committee consists of, and serves for the duration of:
   a. 222 members and a four year term
   b. 222 members and a five year term
   c. 222 members and a three year term
   d. 225 members and a four year term

94. The members of the Economic and Social Committee are:
   a. nominated by member states
   b. nominated by member states but formally appointed by the Council of Ministers
   c. appointed by the Council of Ministers after consultation with the European Parliament
   d. appointed by common accord of the Council of Ministers, the Commission and the European Parliament

95. The Economic and Social Committee meets monthly in:
   a. Strasbourg
   b. Brussels
   c. Luxembourg
   d. Frankfurt

96. The President of the Economic and Social Committee is:
   a. C. Ferres
   b. N. Kinnock
   c. T. Jenkins
   d. J. Priestley

2.7. Committee of the Regions

97. The Committee of the Regions consists of, and serves for a duration of:

   a. 222 members and a four year term
   b. 222 members and a five year term
   c. 222 members and a three year term
   d. 225 members and a four year term

98. The Committee of the Regions consists of representatives of:

   a. the European Parliament and the Council of Ministers
   b. local and regional authorities
   c. regional authorities
   d. industrial interests and regional authorities

99. The Committee of the Regions is located in, and holds:

   a. Brussels - five plenaries per year
   b. Brussels - one plenary monthly
   c. Luxembourg - five plenaries per year
   d. None of the above is true

100. The Committee of the Regions was established by the:

   a. Single European Act and is a decision making body
   b. Maastricht Treaty and is a decision making body
   c. Maastricht Treaty and is a consultative body
   d. Maastricht Treaty and it is not committed to the subsidiarity principle

101. The Committee of the Regions is not consulted in the domain of:

   a. regional interest
   b. education
   c. culture
   d. social policy

2.8. Other European Institutions

102. The European Monetary Institute is based at:
    a. Berlin
    b. Frankfurt
    c. Brussels
    d. London

103. The European Foundation for the Improvement of Living and Working Conditions is based in:
    a. Barcelona
    b. Dublin
    c. Thessaloniki
    d. Florence

104. The participants in the European System of Central Banks are:
    a. governors of the national banks appointed by the member states
    b. representatives of the European Monetary Institute
    c. representatives of the Commission, the Council of Ministers and the European Parliament
    d. governors of the national banks and the European Central Bank

105. CEN is a:
    a. Committee for European normalization of standards of manufactured goods
    b. Committee for Nuclear Energy
    c. Committee of European Navy
    d. Committee for European normalization of standards of manufactured goods except electrical

106. The Office for the registration of European Community trade-marks is based in:
    a. in Munich
    b. Alicante
    c. Bilbao
    d. Dublin

107. COPA is the name given to the:
  a. transnational federation of national farming unions and associations
  b. transnational federation of trade unions
  c. transnational federation of the Christian Democratic Parties
  d. transnational institution carrying out research in nuclear energy and physics

108. CENELEC is a:
  a. Committee for European normalization of manufactured standards of electrical goods
  b. Committee for Nuclear Energy
  c. Committee for harmonization of European Navy standards
  d. Committee for the study of harmonization of excise duties

109. The European Space Agency is:
  a. based in London
  b. a European Union organisation
  c. not a European Union organisation
  d. based in Geneva

110. The Centre for research in nuclear fusion (JET) is based in:
  a. Culham
  b. Cadarace
  c. Ispra
  d. Petten

3. POLICIES OF THE EUROPEAN COMMUNITY

111. The Manshlot Plan was concerned with the:
  a. restructuring of agriculture
  b. grants to the coal industry
  c. creation of the ECU
  d. criteria for stage III of the Economic and Monetary Union

112. ECHO is:

    a. a European Community action scheme for the mobility of university students

    b. a humanitarian organization of the Community

    c. an International Centre for science and technology

    d. the title of an official Community publication

113. One of the following is not a programme aimed at helping declining industries:

    a. RECHAR

    b. KONVER

    c. RESIDER

    d. YOUTHSTART

114. The EAGGF is a Community fund for:

    a. agriculture

    b. handicapped people

    c. industrial development

    d. technological development

115. One of the main principles of CAP is:

    a. Community preference

    b. preference of agricultural products of Lomé signatories

    c. promotion of organic farming

    d. promotion of national markets

116. Delors Package I introduced:

    a. the fourth resource of revenue

    b. an increase in the CAP expenditure

    c. an increase in the Community budget by almost 2/3

    d. Trans-European networks as a new area of Community competence

117. Over the period 1994-99 the European Regional Development Fund amounts approximately to:

    a. 74 per cent of the structural funds

    b. less than 50 per cent of the structural funds

    c. for more than 90 per cent of the structural funds

    d. None of the above is true

118. The Erasmus programme was concerned with:
    a. illiteracy in Europe
    b. cooperation in education
    c. vocational training
    d. improvement of the welfare state for aged people

119. HELIOS is a programme assisting:
    a. solar power research
    b. handicapped people in Europe
    c. nuclear research
    d. clean environment techniques

120. MEDA is a Community programme assisting:
    a. certain Lomé countries
    b. Hungary and Poland
    c. certain countries of the Commonwealth of Independent States
    d. Mediterranean countries

121. Objective 6 of the Structural Funds assists:
    a. regions affected by decline of traditional industry
    b. workers to adapt to technological change
    c. structural reform in agriculture and rural areas
    d. Arctic regions

122. STABEX is a:
    a. programme used by Eurostat
    b. stabilization scheme of export revenue earnings of ACP countries
    c. stabilization scheme of export revenue earnings of ASEAN countries
    d. a special aid programme directed to emergency assistance

123. The European Social Fund aims at:
    a. combating long term unemployment
    b. assisting people over 50 years of age to integrate into the labour market
    c. assisting less developed regions of the Community
    d. assisting Arctic regions

124. The Davignon Plan was concerned with:
    a. the crisis in steel industry
    b. the crisis in nuclear industry after the Chernobil disaster
    c. the development of a common foreign policy
    d. cooperation in justice and home affairs

125. The Cohesion Fund finances programmes in member states:
    a. with a GDP of less than 90 per cent of the Community average
    b. which have been part of the Community for no more than 5 years
    c. with declining traditional industry
    d. with high foreign deficit

126. Within the framework of CAP fixed prices for agricultural products must be achieved primarily through:
    a. intervention buying
    b. subsidisation
    c. direct income support
    d. free competition

127. The green rates are:
    a. special exchange rates aiming at the uniform and stable prices for agricultural products
    b. fines imposed on those polluting the environment
    c. a new form of taxation to be imposed on those whose consumption of fuel exceeds a certain level
    d. None of the above is true

128. One of the following is false. The revised in 1983 Common Fisheries Policy was a response to the:
    a. diminishing fish stocks
    b. loss of traditional fishing grounds for Community fishermen
    c. increasing number of member states interested in the area
    d. implementation of high subsidies

129. The Common Fisheries Policies involves:

   a. high subsidies
   b. implementation of overall quotas for all kinds of fish
   c. extension of 3 mile coastal exclusion zone to 6 miles
   d. increase from 7 to 15 per cent in the joint share of member states in world catches

130. One of the following is false. In regard to the CFSP the:

   a. European Parliament has limited powers
   b. Council of Ministers decides with unanimity
   c. Commission does not have the exclusive right to initiate policy
   d. European Parliament has the right to veto the Council's decision

131. The industrial policy of the Community was introduced by the:

   a. Treaty of Rome
   b. Single European Act
   c. Maastricht Treaty
   d. Amsterdam Treaty

132. The industrial policy of the Community focuses on assistance to:

   a. large multinational companies
   b. state owned enterprises
   c. traditional industries only
   d. small and medium enterprises

133. The Common Transport Policy has implemented:

   a. a restrictive system of quotas for lorries reaching other member states
   b. a system of Community licences regulating commercial road transport
   c. a firm protectionist system in air transport
   d. None of the above is true

134. Euros is the name given to:
    a. the single currency
    b. a licence allowing hauliers to pick or deliver goods anywhere in the Community
    c. a registration system for ships
    d. a pilot programme for transport

135. One of the following is false. The Commission's Transport Action programme for 1995-2000 aims at:
    a. improving the quality of transport systems
    b. removing any remaining restrictions in the single market
    c. developing transport links with the countries of Eastern Europe
    d. lifting any restrictions to air transport

136. The Competition policy was introduced by the:
    a. Treaty of Paris
    b. Treaty of Rome
    c. Single European Act
    d. Maastricht Treaty

137. One of the following areas is largely exempted from the Competition Policy rules:
    a. CAP
    b. Common Commercial Policy
    c. consumer policy
    d. industrial policy

138. One of the following is false. The Common Commercial Policy entails:
    a. a common tariff regime
    b. common trade agreements with third countries
    c. the establishment of a free trade area
    d. uniform application of trade policy

139. The Commission has stated that state aid is justifiable:
    a. under any circumstances
    b. as part of a restructuring programme
    c. if leading to an expansion of capacity
    d. if under ECU 50.000 per year

140. The Commission may:

  a. prevent cross-border mergers resulting to dominant position
  b. impose fines of 50 per cent of the annual sales on mergers taking place without clearance
  c. intervene in mergers with a world wide turnover of under ECUs 5 billion
  d. None of the above is true

141. The cultural policy contributes to the:

  a. development of the theatre
  b. development of film and television industry
  c. preservation of the traditional ways of living
  d. restoration of historical monuments

142. The education policy was addressed specifically in the:

  a. Treaty of Rome
  b. Single European Act
  c. Maastricht Treaty
  d. None of the above is true

143. Community aid to the developing countries is granted through:

  a. the European Development Fund (EDF)
  b. the EDF and the Budget
  c. individual member state contributions only
  d. None of the above is true

144. In the context of development policy the European Community is entirely responsible for:

  a. humanitarian aid
  b. trade aspects
  c. formulating the policy on behalf of member states
  d. managing the total amount of aid directed to the developing world

145. JOULE promotes research in:

  a. energy efficiency
  b. non-nuclear technology
  c. nuclear energy technology
  d. renewable energy sources

146. The foremost producer of nuclear energy in the European
     Community is:
     a. Germany
     b. Luxembourg
     c. France
     d. Belgium

147. The European Environment Agency:
     a. publishes a report on the state of the environment every
        three years
     b. collects the fines imposed on those found guilty of
        polluting the environment
     c. aims at implementing the energy tax
     d. None of the above is true

148. Support to European industry is provided mainly through
     the:
     a. structural funds and the European Investment Bank
     b. cohesion fund
     c. European Development Fund
     d. None of the above is true

149. The 1989 'Television Without Frontiers' programme
     calls member states to ensure that:
     a. at least 60 per cent of air time is devoted to programmes
        of EU origin
     b. at least 10 per cent of air time is devoted to programmes
        of EU origin
     c. they take advantage from the funding of the EU to film
        industry
     d. None of the above is true

150. The most representative example of regional disparities
     within a member state is found in:
     a. Germany
     b. France
     c. Finland
     d. The Netherlands

151. In the 1992 Earth Summit, the Community agreed:

   a. to an increase of no more than 5 per cent in carbon dioxide emissions
   b. to stabilize by the year 2000 emissions of carbon dioxide at the 1990 level
   c. not to participate
   d. None of the above is true

152. CORDIS is a:

   a. centralized information service on Community RTD
   b. major research project in RTD
   c. programme aiming at transferring RTD research from national to European level
   d. programme dealing with environmental issues in a global scale

153. The social dimension to the Community was:

   a. added by President Delors in 1989
   b. thoroughly implemented since the foundation of the Community
   c. initiated by the Maastricht Treaty
   d. related only to employment issues

154. Article K4 of the Maastricht Treaty provides for a Committee to assist the Council' s work in regard to :

   a. JHA
   b. CFSP
   c. external trade
   d. None of the above is correct

155. TENs enjoy:

   a. EU support of around 50 per cent of the total cost
   b. no EU funding at all
   c. EU support of approximately 10 per cent of the total cost
   d. the support of the private sector only

4. ECONOMY

156. In 1998 the average inflation rate of the Community was approximately:
    a. 1.5%
    b. 2%
    c. 3%
    d. 5%

157. In 1997, the second largest contributor to the Community budget was:
    a. U.K
    b. Italy
    c. Spain
    d. France

158. The 1997 Community budget amounted to around:
    a. 86 billion ECUs
    b. 50 billion ECUs
    c. 95 billion ECUs
    d. 65 billion ECUs

159. The official budgetary authority of the Community is the:
    a. European Parliament and the Council of Ministers
    b. European Parliament and the Commission
    c. European Parliament
    d. Commission

160. The ECU was the name given to:
    a. the European currency
    b. a basket of currencies consisting of specific amounts of national currencies
    c. a basket of currencies consisting of equal amounts of national currencies
    d. None of the above is true

161. The highest number of people in the Community is engaged in the:

    a. agricultural sector

    b. industrial sector

    c. textile industry

    d. services

162. In 1995, the percentage of the Community's active population employed in agriculture was approximately:

    a. 12%

    b. 6%

    c. 10%

    d. 20%

163. In 1997, the country with the highest debt as percentage of the GDP was:

    a. Belgium

    b. Italy

    c. Greece

    d. Sweden

164. As a proportion of the GNP, the most substantial donor of development aid to the developing world is:

    a. the European Community

    b. Japan

    c. USA

    d. Australia

165. The Community's most densely populated member state is:

    a. Belgium

    b. Netherlands

    c. Germany

    d. The UK

166. The largest source of Community revenues is:

    a. the VAT

    b. agricultural levies

    c. member states contributions

    d. customs duties

167. One of the following is not part of the structural funds:

    a. ERDF
    b. EAGGF
    c. EDF
    d. FIFG

168. The population of the 15 states consisting the European Community is approximately:

    a. 370 million inhabitants
    b. 260 million inhabitants
    c. 550 million inhabitants
    d. 410 million inhabitants

169. One of the following statements is false. The European Monetary System:

    a. intends to create a zone of monetary stability within Europe
    b. intends to strengthen cooperation between member states in the field of monetary policy
    c. requires its participants to join the Exchange Rate Mechanism
    d. came into force in 1979

170. One of the following members does not participate in Stage III of the Economic and Monetary Union:

    a. The UK
    b. Portugal
    c. France
    d. Italy

171. One of the following member states joined the Exchange Rate Mechanism in 1998:

    a. Greece
    b. Portugal
    c. Germany
    d. Spain

172. Member states eligible for entry to Stage III of the Economic and Monetary Union are required to have a budget deficit below:

    a. 3 per cent of the GDP
    b. 1.5 per cent of the GDP
    c. 1 per cent of the GDP
    d. 5 per cent of the GDP

173. In 1997, one of the following member states did not have a budget deficit:

    a. Sweden
    b. Finland
    c. Netherlands
    d. Luxembourg

174. Member states eligible for entry to Stage III of the Economic and Monetary Union are required not to have devalued their currency in the last:

    a. 1 year
    b. 5 years
    c. 2 years
    d. 6 years

175. The highest expenditure of the Community budget is for:

    a. structural funds
    b. industrial policy
    c. agriculture
    d. development

176. One of the following is false. The term 'dumping' denotes:

    a. sale of products at prices lower than the domestic sale price
    b. buying of products at an intervention price
    c. sale of products at prices lower than the production cost
    d. sale of products at prices lower than the highest export price to any third country

177. One of the following is false. The European Monetary Institute aims at:

    a. preparing member states for stage III of the Economic and Monetary Union

    b. monitoring the functioning of the European Monetary System

    c. facilitating the use of ECU

    d. fixing exchange rates irrevocably

178. One of the following national currencies is the milestone of the Economic and Monetary Union:

    a. Deutsch Mark

    b. Escudo

    c. French Franc

    d. Pound sterling

179. One of the following Community 'own resources' came into effect in 1988:

    a. VAT

    b. levies on agricultural products either imported or in surplus within the Community

    c. customs duties

    d. contributions of member states

180. Eurocheques are not valid in:

    a. USA

    b. Morocco

    c. Egypt

    d. Malta

181. In 1997 unemployment in the European Community accounted for:

    a. 11 per cent

    b. 9 per cent

    c. 13 per cent

    d. 16 per cent

182. One of the following countries benefits mostly from the Cohesion fund over the period 1993 - 1999:
    a. Spain
    b. Greece
    c. Ireland
    d. Austria

183. Since 1993, VAT:
    a. is paid in the country of origin
    b. is paid in the country of destination
    c. is arranged at a standard rate of 14 per cent
    d. None of the above is true

184. Agenda 2000 concerns:
    a. pre-accession assistance to central and eastern European countries
    b. aid to developing countries
    c. assistance to the peripheral member states
    d. the financial framework for the period 2000-2004

185. One of the following types of Committees can block a Commission's proposal:
    a. advisory
    b. regulatory
    c. management
    d. None of the above is true

186. Troika is the name given to meetings of:
    a. the presidents of the European Parliament, the Council of Ministers and the Commission
    b. the present and the future president of the Council of Ministers
    c. Commissioners and the president of the Council of Ministers
    d. the present, the last and future president of the Council of Ministers

187. In 1996 which of the following member states had the highest percentage of imports in intra-European trade:
    a. Ireland
    b. Italy
    c. Belgium
    d. Austria

188. In 1995 which of the following member states had the highest percentage of exports in foreign trade:
    a. The Netherlands
    b. Ireland
    c. Luxembourg
    d. Sweden

189. The exclusive right to authorise the issue of Euro banknotes and coins is given to the:
    a. European Central Bank
    b. European Monetary Institute
    c. Council of Ministers
    d. European Investment Bank

190. The Euro banknotes and coins will start to circulate along with national currencies:
    a. at the beginning of Stage III of the Economic and Monetary Union
    b. in 2002
    c. in 2000
    d. None of the above is true

191. One of the following is false. From 1 January 1999, starting date of the EMU, the Euro:
    a. became the monetary policy currency of the participant member states
    b. is used by private agents
    c. became the basis on which conversion rates are to be conducted
    d. provides the basis for irrevocable fixing of conversion rates among currencies of members states

192. One of the following is false. The European System of Central Banks's main objectives are to:

a. maintain price stability
b. define and implement the monetary policy of the Community
c. hold and manage the official reserves of the member states
d. issue the single currency

193. The Exchange Rate Mechanism aimed at:

a. minimising currency fluctuations
b. issuing the single currency
c. maintaining a tight monetary policy
d. None of the above is true

194. Participation to Stage III of the Economic and Monetary Union amounts to:

a. 11 member states
b. 15 member states
c. 10 member states
d. 14 member states

5. THE EU AND THE REST OF THE WORLD

195. One of the following is part of the EU:

a. Monaco
b. Guadelupe
c. Andorra
d. Mount Athos

196. The International Court of Justice is based in:

a. Geneva
b. The Hague
c. London
d. New York

197. The Channel Islands are:
    a. not part of the UK and therefore no part of the EU
    b. part of the UK, but not of the EU
    c. not exempted from the Community competition rules
    d. subject to Community VAT rules

198. The 'partnership for peace' is nominated by:
    a. NATO
    b. The UN
    c. The WEA
    d. The EU

199. The Charter of Paris was signed in:
    a. 1990, and introduced a permanent character to the Conference on Security and Cooperation in Europe
    b. 1975 with the objective to reduce tensions between the Warsaw Pact and the western world
    c. 1995, and renamed the Organization for Security and Cooperation in Europe
    d. None of the above is true

200. One of the following is not a full member of the Council of Europe:
    a. Bosnia
    b. the Former Yugoslav Republic of Macedonia
    c. Albania
    d. Moldova

201. CERN is a:
    a. European Nuclear Research Organisation
    b. USA Nuclear Research Agency
    c. European Telecommunications Agency
    d. Commission Committee planning nuclear research

202. Aid to ACP countries derives mainly from the:
    a. European Development Fund
    b. European Monetary Institute
    c. EU budget
    d. European Bank for Reconstruction and Development

203. In 1982, Greenland decided to:
   a. withdraw its membership from the Community, but to remain part of Denmark
   b. remain a member of the Community
   c. withdraw its membership from the Community
   d. None of the above is true

204. On behalf of the EU international agreements are negotiated by:
   a. the Commission
   b. representatives of the Council of Ministers and the European Parliament
   c. a committee of representatives of the member states
   d. the Committee of the Regions

205. The ACP consists of:
   a. African, Caribbean and Pacific states
   b. America, Canada and Pacific states
   c. Australia, Canada and Philippines
   d. Australia, Caribbean and Philippines

206. The Uruguay Round concerned the:
   a. GATT
   b. World Bank
   c. UNICEF
   d. IMF

207. In 1994 GATT was replaced by the:
   a. World Trade Organisation
   b. World Free Trade Association
   c. Organization for Trade Liberalisation
   d. None of the above is true

208. One of the following acted as the European Community mediator in the Yugoslav conflict:
   a. Carl Bildt
   b. Roy Jenkins
   c. Helmut Smith
   d. François Mitterrand

209. The PFP initiative launched in 1994 by President Clinton involved:

    a. participation of Eastern European countries in the political and military bodies at NATO headquarters

    b. participation of Hungary, Poland and the Czech Republic in non-military activities of NATO

    c. the establishment of a framework for further cooperation between NATO and WEU

    d. None of the above is true

210. One of the following countries is not a member of the European Economic Area:

    a. Liechtenstein

    b. Switzerland

    c. Norway

    d. Denmark

211. One of the following countries is not a full member of the Western European Union:

    a. Denmark

    b. UK

    c. Greece

    d. Italy

212. The total population of the planet is approximately:

    a. 5 billion

    b. 4 billion

    c. 3 billion

    d. 8 billion

213. The International Atomic Energy Agency is based at:

    a. Brussels

    b. Vienna

    c. New York

    d. Frankfurt

214. NAFTA denotes the:
   a. custom union among the USA, Canada, Mexico
   b. free trade zone of commerce among the USA, Canada and Mexico
   c. confederation among the USA, Canada and Mexico
   d. monetary union between the countries of Central America and the USA

215. In the GATT negotiations the Community was represented by:
   a. a Committee consisting of European Parliament and Council of Ministers' representatives
   b. the Commission
   c. a committee consisting of representatives appointed by the member states directly
   d. the Council of Ministers

216. TACIS is a programme assisting:
   a. certain Lomé countries
   b. the Commonwealth of Independent States, Mongolia, Azerbaijan and Georgia
   c. members of the Mercosur
   d. the Mediterranean countries

217. The Conflict between the EU and Canada in March 1995 regarded:
   a. fishing arrangements
   b. environmental issues
   c. export regulations
   d. spatial research programmes

218. The capital of Slovenia is:
   a. Cracow
   b. Ljubljana
   c. Budapest
   d. Bratislava

219. The College of Europe is based:

a. in Florence
b. in Bruges
c. in Geneva
d. partly in Florence and partly in Bruges

220. The Prime Minister of Sweden is currently:

a. Paavo Lipponen
b. Wim Kok
c. Poul Nyrup Rasmussen
d. Göran Persson

221. By 1998 the Lomé Convention was signed by:

a. 18 members
b. 71 members
c. 40 members
d. 68 members

222. Currently the full members of the Western European Union are:

a. all member states of the Community
b. ten Community states
c. all member states of the Community and Russia
d. all member states of the Community, the USA, Canada

223. One of the following is not a permanent member of the UN's Security Council:

a. France
b. UK
c. Germany
d. USA

224. One of the following countries is not a member of the Organization of Petroleum Exporting Countries:

a. Jordan
b. Nigeria
c. Venezuela
d. Saudi Arabia

225. One of the following is not an ASEAN member:

    a. Indonesia
    b. Cambodia
    c. Thailand
    d. Brunei

226. One of the following is not a European Union institution:

    a. the Council of Europe
    b. the European Coal and Steel Community consultative
       committee
    c. the Committee of the Regions
    d. the Court of Auditors

227. One of the following institutions was not established by
    the Conventions of Human Rights and Fundamental
    Freedoms:

    a. the European Commission of Human Rights
    b. the International Court of Justice
    c. the Committee of Ministers
    d. the European Court for Human Rights

228. COST is a scheme providing:

    a. European cooperation in the field of scientific and
       technical research
    b. cooperation in the field of nuclear research
    c. cooperation in the field of renewable energy resources
    d. None of the above is true

229. European citizenship provides for the right:

    a. of voting in national elections in the country of residence
    b. to reside in any country of the European Community
    c. to serve in the national army in the country of residence
    d. None of the above is true

230. The European Bank for Reconstruction and Development
    is based in:

    a. Athens
    b. Frankfurt
    c. Paris
    d. London

231. The European Bank for Reconstruction and Development provides assistance mainly to:
    a. less developed European Union member-states
    b. to Eastern Europe
    c. to ASEAN countries
    d. to European companies investing in Eastern Europe

232. One of the following combinations is not true:
    a. Sweden - Helsinki
    b. Greece - Athens
    c. Slovakia - Bratislava
    d. Ukraine - Kiev

6. GENERAL QUESTIONS ON THE EUROPEAN COMMUNITY

233. The word Europa, found in ancient Greek mythology, was assigned to:
    a. a geographical entity and a person
    b. a geographical entity
    c. a person
    d. a holy mountain

234. 'Assizes' is the name given to the meetings of:
    a. members of the national parliaments and the Commission
    b. members of national parliaments and the European Parliament
    c. members of the European Parliament and Economic and Social Committee
    d. None of the above is true

235. The term European Union came into being by the:
    a. Maastricht Treaty replacing the term European Communities
    b. Maastricht Treaty, though the European Communities remain separate entities
    c. Single European Act
    d. None of the above is true

236. One of the following is the main intergovernmental institution of the European Community:

    a. European Commission
    b. European Parliament
    c. Court of Justice
    d. Council of Ministers

237. The principle of subsidiarity refers to the:

    a. devolution of power to the political unit closest to citizens
    b. subsidies going to the Mediterranean countries
    c. limitation of the power of the national parliaments
    d. principle of the qualified majority voting

238. Accession treaties is the name given to treaties signed between:

    a. the European Union and the Lomé countries
    b. the European Union and the eastern and central European countries
    c. the European Union and candidate states
    d. None of the above is true

239. Acquis Communautaire is an expression used to describe collectively:

    a. all primary and secondary legislation of the Community
    b. all primary and secondary legislation of the Community and the judgements of the Court of Justice of the European Communities
    c. all primary legislation of the Community
    d. all secondary legislation of the Community

240. Direct effect is the principle according to which:

    a. national courts have to recognize and enforce Community law
    b. national courts have to recognize and enforce Community law only in the event of conflict
    c. certain provisions of the Common Foreign and Security Policy are directly applicable on member states
    d. Community law applies to all judicial matters

241. The Blair House Accord was concerned with:
    a. agricultural subsidies
    b. the reduction of tariffs in industrial goods
    c. the audiovisual sector
    d. intellectual property

242. Intergovernmental conferences consist of:
    a. representatives of governments of members states
    b. representatives of national and European parliaments
    c. experts on institutional matters
    d. None of the above is true

243. The British Budget crisis was concerned with:
    a. German demands for a higher contribution of the UK to the Community budget
    b. British demands for the reduction of UK contributions to the Community budget
    c. British demands for further reductions of agricultural subsidies
    d. None of the above is true

244. The Co-decision procedure empowers the European Parliament with the right to:
    a. veto by an absolute majority a legislative measure upon which agreement cannot be reached with the Council of Ministers
    b. veto any decision of the Council
    c. veto by a qualified majority a legislative measure upon which agreement cannot be reached with the Council of Ministers
    d. be consulted three times before a legislative measure is enacted

245. The consultation procedure empowers the European Parliament:
    a. simply to give an opinion
    b. to give an opinion which the Council of Ministers has to adopt
    c. to consult with any Community institutions
    d. None of the above is true

246. The Cooperation Procedure empowers the European Parliament with the right to:

    a. be consulted twice before a legislative measure is enacted

    b. amend the common position of the Council of Ministers by qualified majority

    c. reject the common position of the Council of Ministers by qualified majority

    d. None of the above is true

247. The term common position is used to describe:

    a. the agreement of the Council of Ministers to the European Parliament's amendments at its first reading

    b. the stance taken by member states individually in the framework of Common Foreign and Security Policy

    c. the stance taken by member states individually in the framework of Justice and Home Affairs

    d. the agreement of the Commission to the European Parliament's amendments

248. The Ombudsman is empowered to receive complaints concerning maladministration in the activities of:

    a. all Community institutions, with the exception of the Court of Justice and the Court of First Instance

    b. all European institutions and bodies

    c. the European Parliament only

    d. the European Commission only

249. The Cohesion Fund seeks to:

    a. reduce disparities between member states

    b. reduce regional disparities within member states

    c. combat long-term unemployment

    d. contribute to the transformation of central and eastern Europe into a market economy

250. Asylum seekers may seek asylum in:

    a. the member state which first receives them

    b. the member state of their choice

    c. no more that three member states

    d. None of the above is true

251. One of the following is false. Committees are formed with the objective of:

   a. supervising the implementation of Community law deriving from the European Commission's powers of decision as a right

   b. supervising the implementation of Community law deriving from the European Commission's powers of decision conferred upon it by the Council of Ministers

   c. supervising the activities of the European Parliament

   d. studying a variety of issues, mostly of technical nature.

252. In the Community context the term democratic deficit refers specifically to:

   a. the powers transferred from national to European level and the degree to which these remain subject to democratic control existing at national level

   b. centralization of decision making in the Council of Ministers

   c. the extensive powers of the Court of Justice

   d. None of the above is true

253. Additionality is the principle according to which:

   a. decisions have to be taken at the level closest to the citizens

   b. action to achieve an objective should be in proportion to the objectives to be achieved

   c. agricultural levies have to be additional to member states' contributions to the Community budget

   d. sums from the Community budget allocated to member states have to be additional to the relevant funding provided by national governments

254. TAC is an abbreviation used in relation to:

   a. fishing

   b. border policing

   c. agriculture

   d. technological development

255. One of the following countries does not participate in the EUROCORPS:

a. France
b. Germany
c. Belgium
d. Italy

256. The *Official Journal of the European Communities* is published in:

a. 11 languages
b. 9 languages
c. 8 languages
d. 13 languages

257. One of the following countries is expected to become member of the European Community by 2002:

a. Bulgaria
b. Slovakia
c. Malta
d. Slovenia

258. Occasionally the G7 is called G8 depending on the participation in the summits of:

a. Russia
b. Germany
c. Australia
d. Japan

259. The Cecchini Report and the Cockfield White Paper were fundamental to the establishment of the:

a. Single European Market
b. enhancement of the European Parliament powers
c. European Defence Community
d. None of the above is true

260. The 2000 Olympic games will take place in:

a. Atlanta
b. Athens
c. Sidney
d. Barcelona

261. The Airbus is the outcome of collaboration among:
    a. France, Germany, UK, Spain
    b. France, Germany, UK, Italy
    c. France, Germany, Belgium, The Netherlands
    d. France, Germany, Spain, Italy

262. Currently one of the following countries does not participate in the Eurofighter project:
    a. Britain
    b. France
    c. Germany
    d. Spain

263. ANSA is based in:
    a. Rome
    b. London
    c. Frankfurt
    d. Paris

264. The Schengen Agreement refers to:
    a. free movement of goods
    b. free movement of people
    c. free movement of people among the Benelux countries
    d. the European regional policy

265. The Conciliation Committee:
    a. has the final saying in the event of disagreement between the European Parliament and the Council of Ministers
    b. consists of equal number of representatives of the Council of Ministers and the European Parliament
    c. must be consulted in all legislative procedures
    d. None of the above is true

266. In 1991, the number of official languages of the European Community was:
    a. 7
    b. 5
    c. 9
    d. 10

267. One of the following countries has neutral status:

    a. UK
    b. Italy
    c. Sweden
    d. Netherlands

268. One of the following is an organization of the UN:

    a. WHO
    b. NATO
    c. OECD
    d. WEU

269. In one of the following countries voting for the European Parliament elections is compulsory:

    a. Italy
    b. Denmark
    c. Spain
    d. Sweden

270. One of the following treaties established the conditions of visa policy:

    a. the Single European Act
    b. the Schengen Agreement
    c. the Maastricht Treaty with Article 100c
    d. the Maastricht Treaty in the context of Justice and Home Affairs

271. The Council of Ministers decides on matters related to visa policy by:

    a. qualified majority
    b. unanimity
    c. simple majority
    d. None of the above is true

272. The European Court of Human Rights is based in:

    a. Strasbourg
    b. The Hague
    c. London
    d. Geneva

273. SYSTRAN is:
    a. a system of transmitting documents
    b. an electronic way of translating documents
    c. the name of the European launcher
    d. an automated system of counting votes in the European Parliament

274. In 1977 the European Culture City was:
    a. Thessaloniki
    b. Weimar
    c. London
    d. Copenhagen

275. One of the following judicial acts does not have to be published in the *Official Journal of the European Communities* :
    a. a regulation
    b. an opinion
    c. a decision
    d. a directive addressing all member states

276. The accession of a candidate state to the Community is decided by:
    a. the Council of Ministers and the European Parliament
    b. the Council of Ministers and the Commission
    c. the Commission
    d. the Court of Justice and the Council of Ministers

277. The European passport:
    a. must have a uniform format
    b. is not valid outside the European Community
    c. is issued by a European Community authority
    d. should be of navy blue colour

278. One of the following countries does not have borders with another European Community member:
    a. Portugal
    b. Ireland
    c. Greece
    d. Italy

279. SIGMA is :

    a. an international programme for science and development

    b. a publication of the statistical office of the EU

    c. a financial instrument for the environment

    d. a plan for the conversion of armament industry

280. A free trade association like the EFTA aims at:

    a. concluding common trade agreements with third countries

    b. abolishing duties and tariffs on trade among signatories

    c. aligning VAT rates

    d. None of the above is true

281. In 1996, the European Community institutions employed permanently approximately the following number of staff:

    a. 26000

    b. 40000

    c. 45000

    d. 30000

282. In accordance with the Maastricht Treaty Community citizens, in their country of residence, have the right to vote for:

    a. national elections

    b. elections for the European Parliament

    c. national and European Parliament elections

    d. local and national elections

283. 'Cassis de Dijon' case concerned:

    a. the liberalization of the movement of people

    b. mutual recognition of product standards

    c. the imposition of limits on tobacco

    d. reforms in the procedure of decision making of the Court of Justice

284. EURONEWS is a:

    a. European news agency

    b. European publishing house

    c. newspaper concerned mainly with European news

    d. European TV channel

285. One of the following member states did not initially accept the Social Charter of 1989:

a. Italy
b. UK
c. Luxembourg
d. Greece

286. In federal states one of the following policies is not the responsibility of the central government:

a. fiscal
b. defence
c. foreign
d. social

287. Discharge to the European Commission is granted by the:

a. Council of Ministers
b. European Parliament acting under the recommendation of the Council of Ministers and the Court of Auditors
c. European Parliament
d. Council of Ministers under the recommendations of the Court of Auditors

288. The term 'non-tariff barriers to trade' refers to:

a. quotas and tariffs
b. levies
c. different products specifications
d. None of the above is true

289. In the literature of the Community 'cabotage' refers to:

a. reservation of the internal land, sea or air traffic of a member state to its carriers
b. reservation of the fishing grounds of a member state to its fishing fleets
c. the opening of member states' markets to intra-Community competition
d. None of the above is true

7. GENERAL KNOWLEDGE

290. Kosovo is:

   a. an autonomous province of Serbia inhabited by a majority of Albanian origin
   b. part of Albania
   c. recently annexed by the Newly Formed Republic of Macedonia
   d. None of the above is true

291. The International Women's Day is on:

   a. the 8th of May
   b. the 8th of March
   c. the first Sunday of May
   d. the second Sunday of May

292. One of the following is not a Monarchy:

   a. Spain
   b. Portugal
   c. Belgium
   d. Luxembourg

293. In 1991 Aung San Suu Kyi got the Nobel Prize for:

   a. economics
   b. literature
   c. physics
   d. peace

294. One of the languages spoken by the largest number of people is:

   a. Spanish
   b. English
   c. Portuguese
   d. German

295. The Shining Path is:

   a. illegal army in Romania
   b. a left wing movement in Peru
   c. a Basque separatist movement
   d. a Community programme for the environment

296. The work *A Treatise of Human Nature* was written by:
    a. Descartes
    b. Berkeley
    c. Locke
    d. Hume

297. The dome of the Florence Cathedral was designed by:
    a. Giotto
    b. Leonardo da Vinci
    c. Brunelleschi
    d. Michelangelo

298. One of the following is not a play of Shakespeare:
    a. Romeo and Juliette
    b. The Merry Wives of Windsor
    c. Venus and Adonis
    d. The Merchant of Venice

299. The Yalta Conference agreed on the incorporation of:
    a. East Prussia into Poland
    b. Moldavia into the Soviet Union
    c. Silesia into Poland
    d. Ruthenia into Romania

300. DNA is a:
    a. double helix
    b. spherical helix
    c. single linear nucleic acid molecule
    d. None of the above is correct

ANSWERS

1. b.	39. a.	77. c.	115. a.	153. a.
2. c.	40. a.	78. a.	116. a.	154. a.
3. b.	41. b.	79. b.	117. a.	155. c.
4. a.	42. c.	80. a.	118. b.	156. a.
5. a.	43. d.	81. c.	119. b.	157. d.
6. c.	44. a.	82. d.	120. d.	158. a.
7. c.	45. b.	83. b.	121. d.	159. a.
8. a.	46. a.	84. d.	122. b.	160. b.
9. d.	47. a.	85. d.	123. a.	161. d.
10. b.	48. b.	86. b.	124. a.	162. b.
11. c.	49. a.	87. a.	125. a.	163. a.
12. b.	50. d.	88. b.	126. a.	164. a.
13. a.	51. a.	89. a.	127. a.	165. b.
14. c.	52. a.	90. d.	128. d.	166. a.
15. a.	53. c.	91. a.	129. b.	167. c.
16. b.	54. b.	92. c.	130. d.	168. a.
17. a.	55. a.	93. a.	131. c.	169. c.
18. b.	56. d.	94. a.	132. d.	170. a.
19. a.	57. b.	95. b.	133. b.	171. a.
20. a.	58. d.	96. c.	134. c.	172. a.
21. c.	59. a.	97. a.	135. d.	173. d.
22. c.	60. d.	98. b.	136. b.	174. c.
23. d.	61. a.	99. a.	137. a.	175. c.
24. b.	62. c.	100. c.	138. c.	176. b.
25. b.	63. b.	101. d.	139. b.	177. d.
26. c.	64. b.	102. b.	140. a.	178. a.
27. a.	65. d.	103. b.	141. b.	179. d.
28. c.	66. c.	104. d.	142. c.	180. a.
29. a.	67. d.	105. d.	143. b.	181. a.
30. b.	68. b.	106. b.	144. b.	182. a.
31. a.	69. b.	107. a.	145. b.	183. b.
32. b.	70. a.	108. a.	146. d.	184. a.
33. d.	71. a.	109. c.	147. a.	185. c.
34. b.	72. c.	110. a.	148. a.	186. d.
35. d.	73. c.	111. a.	149. a.	187. d.
36. b.	74. b.	112. b.	150. a.	188. c.
37. b.	75. a.	113. d.	151. b.	189. a.
38. a.	76. c.	114. a.	152. a.	190. b.

191. b.	217. a.	243. b.	269. c.	295. b.
192. d.	218. b.	244. a.	270. c.	296. d.
193. a.	219. b.	245. a.	271. a.	297. c.
194. a.	220. d.	246. a.	272. a.	298. c.
195. b.	221. b.	247. a.	273. b.	299. a.
196. b.	222. b.	248. a.	274. a.	300. a.
197. a.	223. c.	249. a.	275. b.	
198. a.	224. a.	250. a.	276. a.	
199. a.	225. b.	251. c.	277. a.	
200. a.	226. a.	252. a.	278. c.	
201. a.	227. b.	253. d.	279. b.	
202. a.	228. a.	254. a.	280. b.	
203. c.	229. b.	255. d.	281. a.	
204. a.	230. d.	256. a.	282. b.	
205. a.	231. b.	257. d.	283. b.	
206. a.	232. a.	258. a.	284. d.	
207. a.	233. a.	259. a.	285. b.	
208. a.	234. b.	260. c.	286. d.	
209. a.	235. b.	261. a.	287. b.	
210. b.	236. d.	262. b.	288. c.	
211. a.	237. a.	263. a.	289. c.	
212. a.	238. c.	264. b.	290. a.	
213. b.	239. b.	265. b.	291. b.	
214. b.	240. a.	266. c.	292. b.	
215. b.	241. a.	267. c.	293. d.	
216. b.	242. a.	268. a.	294. a.	

BIBLIOGRAPHY

Anderson, K. and Blackhurst, R. eds, *Regional Integration and the Global Trading System* (Hemel Hempstead, 1993).

Archer, C. and Butler, F. *The European Community: Structure and Process* (Pinter Publishers, 1992).

Armstrong, H. and Taylor J. *Regional Economics and Policy* (Hemel Hempstead, 1993).

Arter, D. *The Politics of European Integration in the Twentieth Century* (Aldershot, 1993).

Artis, M. & Lee, N. eds, *The Economics of the European Union: Policy and Analysis* (Oxford, 1994).

Aylott, N., 'The European Union: Widening, Deepening and the Interests of a Small Member State', *Manchester Papers in Politics*, EPRU Paper No. 3/95 (University of Manchester, 1995).

Bainbridge, T. and Teasdale, A. *The Penguin Companion to the European Union* (Penguin, 1998).

Baldwin, R. E. *Towards an Integrated Europe*, Centre for Economic Policy Research, (London, 1994).

Blacksell, M. and Williams, A. M. eds, The European Challenge (Oxford, 1994).

Bloed, A. & Wessel, R. A. eds *The Changing Functions of the Western European Union* (London, 1994).

Borner, S. and Grubel, H. *The European Community after 1992*, (London, 1992).

Brown, L. N. *The Court of Justice of the European Communities*, 3rd ed., (London, 1989).

Bulmer, S. and Scott, A. eds *Economic and Political Integration in Europe* (Oxford, 1994).

Bulmer, S. and Wessels, W. *The European Council* (London, 1987).

Burgess, M. *Federalism and European Union* (London, 1989).

Cecchini, P. *The European Challenge: 1992 The Benefits of a Single Market* (Aldershot, 1988).

Church, C. H. and Phinnemore, D. *European Union and European Community: A Handbook and Commentary on the Post-Maastricht Treaty* (Hemel Hempstead, 1994).

Close, P. *Citizenship, Europe and Change* (London, 1995).

Cockfield, Lord *The European Union: Creating a Single Market*, (London, 1994).

Cram, L. *Policy Making in the EU* (London, 1997).

Dinan, D. *Ever Closer Union? An Introduction to European Community* (London, 1994).

Duff, A. *Subsidiarity within the EC*, Federal Trust for Education and Research, Britain (1993).

Duff, A., Pinder J. & Pryce R. *Maastricht and Beyond: Building the European Union* (London, 1994).

Duchêne, F. *Jean Monnet: The First Statesman of Independence* (New York-London, 1994).

Dyker, D. *The National Economies of Europe* (Harlow, 1995).

Edwards, J. and Spence, D. eds *The European Commission*, Longman Current Affairs (1995).

El-Agraa, A. M., Ali Mohammed *The Economics of the European Community* (Hemel Hempstead, 1994).

El-Agraa, A. M., Ali Mohammed *The European Union, history, institutions, economics and policies*, Prentice Hall Europe, (London, 1998).

European Commission *Industrial Policy in the Community: Memorandum from the Commission to the Council* (Brussels, 1970).

European Commission *Memorandum on the Technological and Industrial Policy Progress* (Brussels, 1973).

European Commission 'European Union' [the Tindemans Report], *Bulletin EC*, supplement (1976).

European Commission *Completing the Internal Market* (Brussels, (1985).

European Commission 'Social Dimension of the Internal Market', *Social Europe'*, special edition (1988).

European Commission *Eighteen Report on Competition Policy*, Luxembourg (1989).

European Commission *Environmental Policy in the European Community*, Office for Official Publications, Luxembourg (1990).

European Commission *Europe's Industrial Policy in the 1990s*, supplement 3/91 (1990).

European Commission *Political Union: the structure of the Draft Treaty. Contribution by the European Commission to the Intergovernmental Conference*, Brussels (1991).

European Commission *The Development and Future of the CAP* (Brussels, 1991).

European Commission *The regions in the 1990s*, Fourth Periodic report on the Social and Economic Situation and Development of the regions of the Community, Office for the Official Publications of the European Communities (Luxembourg, 1991).

European Commission 'Growth, Competitiveness, Employment: the challenges and way forward into the 21st century', White Paper, *Bulletin of the European Communities*, supplement 6/93 (1993).

European Commission, The Group of Personal Representatives of the Heads of State or Government Report (1993).

EC *Industrial Policy in a Open and Competitive Environment* (Luxembourg, 1990).

Featherstone, K. and Ginsberd, R.H. *The United States and the European Union in the 1990s* (London, 1996).

Fennell, R. *The Common Agricultural Policy* (Oxford, 1997).

García, S. ed., *European Identity and Search for Legitimacy* (London-New York, 1993).

Gardner, N. *A Guide to United Kingdom and European Union Competition Policy* (London, 1996).

George, S. *Politics and Policies in the European Community* (Oxford, 1985).

Gold, M. ed., *The Social Dimension: Employment Policy in the European Community* (London, 1993).

Grilli, E. *The European Community and the Developing Countries* (Cambridge, 1993).

Hantrais, L. *Social Policy in the European Union* (London, 1995).

Hartley, T. C. *The Foundations of European Community Law*, 3rd ed., (Oxford, 1994).

Hayes, J. *Making Trade Policy in the European Community* (London, 1993).

Hill, B. *The European Union* (London, 1994).

Hill, C. *The Actors in Europe's Foreign Policy* (London, 1996).

Hinsley, F. H. *Sovereignty* (Cambridge, 1986).

Hitiris, T. *European Union Economics* (Prentice Hall Europe, 1998).

Holden, M. *The Common Fisheries Policy: Origin, Evaluation and Future* (Oxford, 1994).

Holland, M. *European Integration: from Community to Union* (London, 1995).

Jacobs, F. and Corbett, R. *The European Parliament*, 3rd ed. (London, 1995).

Jones, R. *The Politics and Economics of the European Union* (Cheltenham, 1996).

Johnson, S.P. and Corcelle, G. *The Environmental Policies of the European Communities* (London, 1995).

Kirchner, E. *Decision-making in the European Community* (Manchester, 1992).

Kiriazidis, T. *European Transport: Problems and Policies* (Aldershot, 1994).

Laffan, B. *Integration and Cooperation in Europe* (London, 1992).

Lifferink, J.D., Lowe, P.D. and Mol, A.P.J. *European Integration and Environmental Policy* (London, 1993).

Lippert, B. & Schneider, H. eds *Monitoring Association and Beyond: The European Union and the Visegrad States* (Bonn, 1995).

Lister, M. *European Union Development Policy* (London, 1998).

Lodge, J. *The European Community and the Challenge of the Future* (London, 1993).

Maravegias, N. and Tsinisizelis, M. *The Integration of the European Union* (Athens, 1995).

Martin Martinez, M. M. *National Sovereignty and International Organisations* (The Hague, 1996).

McCormick, J. *The European Union* (London, 1996).

Mazey, S. and Richardson, J. *Lobbying in the European Community* (Oxford, 1993).

Meehan, E. *Citizenship and the European Community* (London, 1993).

Meyrs, J., 'The Western European Union: Pillar of NATO or Defence Arm of the EC?' (The Centre for Defence Studies, 1993).

Moussis, N. *Access to the European Union*, 4th rev. ed. (EDIT-EUR, 1994).

Nugent, N. *The Government and Politics of the European Union* (London, 1994).

Pinder, J. *The European Community and Eastern Europe* (London, 1991).

Pinder, J. *The European Community: building of a Union* (Oxford, 1991).

Redmond, J. ed., *Prospective Europeans, New Members for the European Union* (New York-London, 1994).

Roney, A. *EC/EU Fact Book* (London, 1998).

Ross, G. *Jaques Delors and European Integration*, Cambridge (1995).

Rummel R. ed., *Towards Political Union- Planning of Common Foreign and Security Policy* (Oxford, 1992).

Springer, B. *The European Union and its Citizens: The Social Agenda* (London, 1994).

Tansey, P. 'The Economic Consequences of Maastricht', Occasional Papers, No 2 (Institute of European Affairs, 1993).

Tsoukalis, L. *The New European Economy: The Politics and Economics of Integration* (Oxford, 1992).

Turner, C. *Trans-European Networks: The challenges for industrial policy* (London, 1997).

Weatherill, S. and Beaumont, P. *EC Law: The Essential Guide to legal Workings of the European Community* (Penguin, 1992).

Welsh, M. *Europe United?* (London, 1996).

Westlake, M. *A Modern Guide to the European Parliament* (London, 1994).

Westlake, M. *The Commission and the Parliament, partners and rivals in the European policy-making process* (London, 1994).

Wistrich, E. *The United States of Europe* (London, 1994).

Treaties

Treaty Establishing the European Coal and Steel Community, in *European Law*, by R.M. MacLean (London, 1995).

Treaty Establishing the European Economic Community, in *European Law*, by R.M. MacLean (London, 1995).

Treaty Establishing a Single Council and a Single Commission of the European Communities, in *European Law*, by R.M. MacLean (London, 1995).

Single European Act, in *The European Union: The Lawyers's Guide*, by P. Duffy and J. Yves de Cara (London, 1992).

Treaty on the European Union, in *The European Union: The Lawyers's Guide*, by P. Duffy and J. Yves de Cara (London, 1992).

Amsterdam Treaty http://ue.eu.int/Amsterdam/en/amsteroc/en/treaty/htm.

SELECT INDEX

Only terms and names which have no main entry but occur in the Dictionary, and which might be useful to the reader, have been listed here

Adonnino committee 87
Agence France-Presse 144
Agenzia Nazionale Stampa Associata .... viii, 144
Äland Islands 32
Andorra 39, 167, 168, 261
Associated Press 144
Attali, Jacques 73
Bangemann, Martin 182, 185, 207
Bildt, Carl 67, 263
Blocking minority 42, 120, 238
Bosnia-Herzegovina 67
Briand, Aristide 100
Bussingen 32
Cabotage 30, 31, 278
Channel Islands 32, 167, 168, 262
Children's Fund 190
Combined Joint Task Forces (CJTFS) 147
Conflict Prevention Centre 16
Consumer Policy Service 37, 56
Consumer's Consultative Council 37
Coudenhove-Kalergi 100
Croatia 39, 67, 218
Cultural months 48
Cyprus 9, 25, 32, 39, 139, 140, 167, 168, 208, 217
Czech Republic 39, 63, 67, 71, 147, 153, 194, 196, 218, 264
de Gaulle, Charles 106, 118, 132
Declaration on democracy, transparency and subsidiarity 43
Deeper integration 53, 174, 189, 197
Delegations 28, 78, 92, 236
Deutsche-Presse Agentur 144
Earth Summit 66, 253
Energy tax 66, 252
Europa 71, 100, 268
European Culture City 48, 276
European People's Party (EPP) 185
European-Mediterranean Partnership 140

EUROS 31, 250
Excise duties 164, 165, 179-181, 194, 245
Export levies 22
Export refunds 22, 72
Faroe Islands 32
Food and Agriculture Organization 190
French Overseas Departments 32, 150
French Overseas Territories 32
General Affairs Council 28, 40
Georgia 67, 85, 181, 218, 219, 265
German Reunification 102, 228
Gibraltar 102, 167, 168
Greenland 219, 263
Guadeloupe 32, 150
Guiana 32, 150
Hallstein, Walter 187, 206, 235
Helgoland 32
High Commissioner on National Minorities 16
International Labour Organization (ILO) 190
Jenkins, Tim 61, 206, 235, 242, 263
Joint Declaration on Fundamental Rights 114
Kosovo 67, 279
Lamassoure, Alain 188
Lamers, Karl 189
Lamfalussy, Alexander 89
Liechtenstein 39, 82, 86, 95, 167, 168, 217, 264
Livigno-Campione 32
Malta   9, 25, 39, 64, 139, 140, 144, 149, 167, 168, 208, 217, 258, 273
Martinique 32, 150
Monaco 95, 167, 168, 261
Non-contractual liability 45, 46
Non-Europe 15
Office of Democratic Institutions and Human Rights (ODIHR) . . . 16
Owen, David 67
Partnership for Peace (PFP) 146
Party of European Socialists 185, 209
Petersburg Declaration 196
Pre-accession instruments 4
Press Association 144
Public procurement 34
Réunion 32, 150
Ritzaus Bureau 144

San Marino 39, 167, 168
Sectorial integration 96, 142, 187
Slovenia 39, 63, 67, 71, 146, 218, 265, 273
Spaak, Paul-Henri 141, 174, 187
Spinelli, Altiero 47, 57
Trevi process 124
Troika 43, 259
UNESCO .... xii, 190
UNICEF 190, 263
Uruguay Round 11, 15, 24, 109, 179, 199, 263
Vatican City 167, 168
Visa Policy 6, 123, 275
Voluntary Export Restraints 25
World Health Organization 190